Teach Yourself VISUALLY™

MacBook Air®

by Guy Hart-Davis

V isual

A Wiley Brand

Teach Yourself VISUALLY™ MacBook Air®

Published by
John Wiley & Sons, Inc.
10475 Crosspoint Boulevard
Indianapolis, IN 46256

www.wiley.com

Published simultaneously in Canada

Wiley publishes in a variety of print and electronic formats and by print-on-demand. Some material included with standard print versions of this book may not be included in e-books or in print-on-demand. If this book refers to media such as a CD or DVD that is not included in the version you purchased, you may download this material at http://booksupport.wiley.com. For more information about Wiley products, visit www.wiley.com.

Library of Congress Control Number: 2013949524

ISBN: 978-1-118-81628-8

Manufactured in the United States of America

10 9 8 7 6 5 4 3

Trademark Acknowledgments

Contact Us

For general information on our other products and services please contact our Customer Care Department within the U.S. at 877-762-2974, outside the U.S. at 317-572-3993 or fax 317-572-4002.

For technical support please visit www.wiley.com/techsupport.

Sales | Contact Wiley at (877) 762-2974 or fax (317) 572-4002.

Credits

Acquisitions Editor
Aaron Black

Project Editor
Lynn Northrup

Technical Editor
Dennis Cohen

Copy Editor
Lauren Kennedy

Director, Content Development & Assembly
Robyn Siesky

Vice President and Executive Group Publisher
Richard Swadley

About the Author

Guy Hart-Davis is the author of *Teach Yourself VISUALLY MacBook Pro Second Edition, Teach Yourself VISUALLY iMac,* and *iMac Portable Genius Fourth Edition.*

Author's Acknowledgments

My thanks go to the many people who helped create the highly graphical book you are holding. In particular, I thank Aaron Black for asking me to write the book; Lynn Northrup for keeping me on track and guiding the editorial process; Lauren Kennedy for skillfully editing the text; Dennis Cohen for reviewing the book for technical accuracy and contributing helpful suggestions; and TCS/SPS for laying out the book.

How to Use This Book

Who This Book Is For

This book is for the reader who has never used this particular technology or software application. It is also for readers who want to expand their knowledge.

The Conventions in This Book

① Steps

This book uses a step-by-step format to guide you easily through each task. Numbered steps are actions you must do; bulleted steps clarify a point, step, or optional feature; and indented steps give you the result.

② Notes

Notes give additional information — special conditions that may occur during an operation, a situation that you want to avoid, or a cross-reference to a related area of the book.

③ Icons and Buttons

Icons and buttons show you exactly what you need to click to perform a step.

④ Tips

Tips offer additional information, including warnings and shortcuts.

⑤ Bold

Bold type shows command names, options, and text or numbers you must type.

⑥ Italics

Italic type introduces and defines a new term.

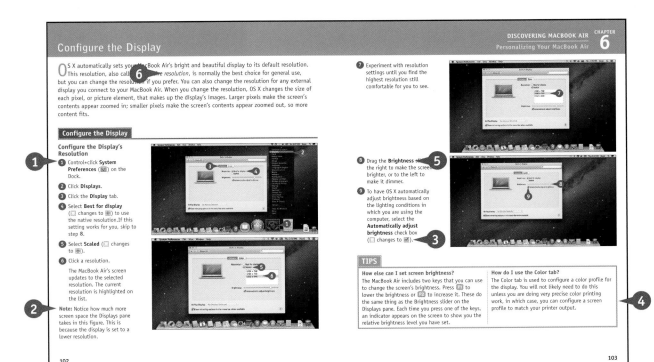

Table of Contents

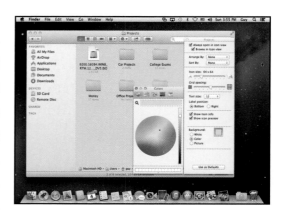

Chapter 3 — Managing the MacBook Air Desktop Workspace

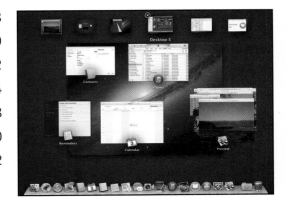

Chapter 4 — Working on the Mac Desktop

Table of Contents

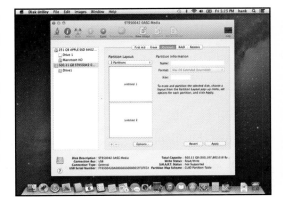

Table of Contents

Chapter 11 | Surfing the Web

Chapter 12 | E-Mailing with Mail

Table of Contents

Part IV Taking MacBook Air Further

Chapter 15 | Managing Contacts

Chapter 16 | Managing Calendars

Table of Contents

| Chapter 19 | Using iPhones, iPods, and iPads with Your MacBook Air |

PART I

Discovering
MacBook Air

The MacBook Air is the best ultra-portable laptop you can get.
Incredibly small and sleekly beautiful, the MacBook Air combines
cutting-edge technology and enough power to sail through everyday
computing tasks wherever you take it. In this part, you learn
fundamentals that will help you get the most out of your MacBook Air.

Tour MacBook Air

The MacBook Air laptops are elegantly designed and incredibly slim and lightweight. But each is also a powerful computer that can handle all your everyday computing tasks with ease. Here you learn about the MacBook Air's major features from the outside, including its controls, ports, and other features that you use to control your MacBook Air and to connect it to other devices. The various models of MacBook Air have slightly different features, such as screen sizes, processors, memory, ports, and storage.

MacBook Air

A Display

The MacBook Air's display provides a sharp, bright, and colorful view into all that you do.

B Camera

The built-in camera enables you to videoconference, take photos, and more.

C Keyboard

Along with the standard letter and number keys, the keyboard provides function keys to control your MacBook Air. The keyboard has a backlight that illuminates automatically when you are using the MacBook Air in dim light, enabling you to see what you are doing.

D Trackpad

The trackpad enables you to manipulate objects on the screen using finger gestures. The entire trackpad is also the button that you click or double-click to give commands.

E Ports

The ports connect your MacBook Air to other devices, such as hard drives, external displays, iPods, and so on.

F Microphones

The microphones enable you to use your MacBook Air for audio and video calls without needing to connect a headset.

G Speakers

The speakers, hidden under the keyboard, enable you to listen to music or other audio.

MacBook Air Keyboard

Ⓐ Brightness

Press **F1** to decrease your screen's brightness or **F2** to increase it.

Ⓑ Mission Control

Press **F3** to open Mission Control so you can quickly move between working spaces.

Ⓒ Launchpad

Press **F4** to open or close the Launchpad.

Ⓓ Keyboard Backlight Brightness

Press **F5** to decrease the brightness of the keyboard backlighting, or press **F6** to increase it.

Ⓔ Previous/Rewind

Press **F7** to move to the previous item or rewind in iTunes and other applications.

Ⓕ Play/Pause

Press **F8** to play or pause iTunes and other applications.

Ⓖ Next/Fast Forward

Press **F9** to move to the next item or fast-forward in iTunes and other applications.

Ⓗ Volume

Press **F10** to mute the MacBook Air, **F11** to turn the volume down, and **F12** to turn it up.

Ⓘ Power Button

Press the Power button to turn MacBook Air on; press and hold it to force MacBook Air to turn off.

Ⓙ Alternate Function Key

Hold down the Alternate Function key while pressing a function key to perform the alternate task.

Ⓚ Modifier Keys

Press the modifier keys to invoke keyboard shortcuts.

Ⓛ Scroll Keys

Press the scroll keys to move around the screen.

continued ▶

Tour MacBook Air

A MacBook Air includes the ports you need to connect to other devices, such as external displays, speakers, iPhones, iPads, iPods, disk drives, and more. The specific port you use for any task depends on the devices to which you are connecting your MacBook Air. And some devices have options; for example, you can use USB or Thunderbolt depending on the kind of drive you are connecting.

The 11-inch and 13-inch MacBook Air have slightly different types and numbers of ports, but you can easily identify the ports on either type using the illustrations in this section.

Ports on the 11-Inch MacBook Air

Ⓐ Thunderbolt Port

Use this high-speed port to connect external displays and Thunderbolt hard drives to your MacBook Air.

Ⓑ USB Ports

Use these ports to connect USB devices, such as iPods, iPhones, iPads, and disk drives to your MacBook Air. The ports support USB 1.1, 2, and 3 versions. You can connect USB devices directly or connect a USB hub that provides extra ports, enabling you to connect many more devices.

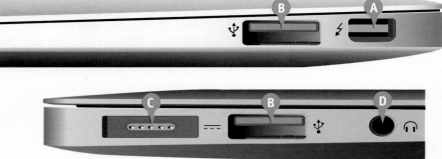

Ⓒ MagSafe 2 Port

Connect the MacBook Air power adapter to this port. The MagSafe 2 connector attaches magnetically, providing a secure connection but detaching easily if force is applied — for example, if someone's foot snags the power cord.

Ⓓ Analog/Digital Audio In/Out

Connect headphones or analog speakers or use a TOSLINK adapter to connect digital audio equipment, such as surround-sound speakers. Connect a microphone or other sound input device to use the audio it provides.

Ports on the 13-Inch MacBook Air

Ⓐ Thunderbolt Port

Use this high-speed port to connect external displays and Thunderbolt hard drives to your MacBook Air.

Ⓑ USB Ports

Use these ports to connect USB devices, such as iPods, iPhones, iPads, and disk drives to your MacBook Air. The ports support USB 1.1, 2, and 3 versions. You can connect USB devices directly or connect a USB hub that provides extra ports, enabling you to connect many more devices.

Ⓒ SDXC Card

You can insert SDXC and other types of SD cards here so you can store files. SDXC is the abbreviation for Secure Digital eXtended Capacity.

Ⓓ MagSafe 2 Port

Connect the MacBook Air power adapter to this port. The MagSafe 2 connector attaches magnetically, providing a secure connection but detaching easily if force is applied — for example, if someone trips over the power cord.

Ⓔ Analog/Digital Audio In/Out

Connect headphones or analog speakers or use a TOSLINK adapter to connect digital audio equipment, such as surround-sound speakers. Connect a microphone or other sound input device to use the audio it provides.

Start Up and Log In

To start your MacBook Air, you simply press the power button and wait a few seconds while OS X loads. You then may need to log in to your user account. OS X enables a Mac to have multiple user accounts, so each person who uses the MacBook Air can have his own files and folders. You created your user account when you first set up your MacBook Air. The automatic login feature bypasses the login process. If it is not turned on, you need to know a username and password to be able to log in to a user account.

Start Up and Log In

Start Up

1. Open MacBook Air by lifting its lid.

2. Press the **Power** button.

   When the startup process is complete, you see the Login window if automatic login is turned off or the OS X desktop if automatic login is turned on.

Log In with the User List

1. Start up the MacBook Air.

   The Login window appears, showing a list of user accounts on the MacBook Air.

2. Slide your finger across the trackpad until the pointer is over the appropriate user account.

3. Press the trackpad.

Note: To click the trackpad button, just press down once on the trackpad; the whole trackpad is a button.

8

The Password field appears.

4 Type the password for the user account.

Note: Passwords are case sensitive, so you must type them with exactly the correct capitalization.

5 Click ➡ or press **Return**.

OS X logs you in to the user account.

The OS X desktop appears.

Log In with a Username

1 Start up the MacBook Air.

The Login window appears, showing the Name and Password fields.

2 Type the name of the user account in the Name field.

3 Type the password for the account in the Password field.

4 Press **Return**.

OS X logs you in to the user account.

The OS X desktop appears.

TIP

What if I forget my password?

If you enter a password incorrectly, the Login screen shudders when you try to log in. This lets you know that the password you provided does not work. Make sure Caps Lock is off — a green light appears on the button if it is on — and try entering the password again. If that does not help, click the **Password Hint** icon (🔲) and a password hint appears on the screen if a hint was configured for your account. If you still cannot log in, try a different user account or ask an administrator for help.

Explore the OS X Desktop

Your MacBook Air runs the OS X operating system, which is currently in version 10.9, called Mavericks. The Macintosh operating system has long been known for being very intuitive and is also pleasing to look at. It was the first major system interface to focus on graphical elements, such as icons. The OS X desktop is the overall window through which you view all that happens on MacBook Air, such as looking at the contents of folders, working on documents, and surfing the web.

OS X Desktop

Ⓐ Menu Bar

A menu bar usually appears at the top of the screen so that you can access the commands it contains. OS X hides the menu bar in certain situations. The menu bar shows the menus for the active application.

Ⓑ Drives

The MacBook Air stores its data, including the software it needs to work, on an internal drive. This drive is a solid-state device, or SSD, rather than a hard drive with moving platters, but it is often referred to as a hard drive. You can also connect external drives for extra storage.

Ⓒ SuperDrive

You can connect an external SuperDrive or other compatible optical drive to read from and write to CDs and DVDs.

Ⓓ Folders

Folders are containers that you use to organize files and other folders stored on your MacBook Air.

Ⓔ Files

Files include documents, applications, or other sources of data. There are various kinds of documents, such as text, graphics, songs, or movies.

Ⓕ Finder Windows

You view the contents of drives, folders, and other objects in Finder windows.

Ⓖ Application and Document Windows

When you use applications, you use the windows that those applications display, for documents, web pages, games, and so on.

10

Finder Menu Bar and Menus

Ⓐ Apple Menu

This menu is always visible so that you can access special commands, such as Shut Down and Log Out.

Ⓑ Finder Menu

This menu enables you to control the Finder application itself. For example, you can display information about the Finder or set preferences to control how it behaves.

Ⓒ File Menu

This menu contains commands you can use to work with files and Finder windows.

Ⓓ Edit Menu

This menu is not as useful in the Finder as it is in other applications, but here you can undo what you have done or copy and paste information.

Ⓔ View Menu

This menu enables you to determine how you view the desktop; it is especially useful for choosing Finder window views.

Ⓕ Go Menu

This menu takes you to various places, such as specific folders.

Ⓖ Window Menu

This menu enables you to work with open Finder windows.

Ⓗ Help Menu

This menu provides help with OS X or the other applications.

Ⓘ Configurable Menus

You can configure the menu bar to include specific menus, such as Screen Mirroring, Volume, Wi-Fi, Battery, and many more.

Ⓙ Clock

Here you see the current time and day.

Ⓚ Fast User Switching

This feature enables you to change user accounts and open the Login window.

Ⓛ Spotlight Menu

This menu enables you to search for information on your MacBook Air.

continued ▶

The Finder application controls the OS X desktop, and so you see its menu bar whenever you work with this application. When you view the contents of a folder, you do so through a Finder window. There are many ways to view the contents of a Finder window, such as Icon view and List view. The Sidebar enables you to quickly navigate the desktop and to open files and folders with a single click. The Dock and Sidebar on the desktop enable you to access items quickly and easily.

Finder Windows

A Close Button
Click to close a window.

B Minimize Button
Click to shrink a window and move it onto the Dock.

C Zoom Button
Click to expand a Finder window to the maximum size needed or possible; click it again to return to the previous size.

D Window Title
The name of the location whose contents you see in the window.

E Toolbar
Contains tools you use to work with files and folders.

F Search Box
Enables you to find files, folders, and other information.

G Sidebar
Enables you to quickly access devices, folders, files, and tags, as well as searches you have saved.

H Files and Folders
Shows the contents of a location within a window; this example shows the Icon view.

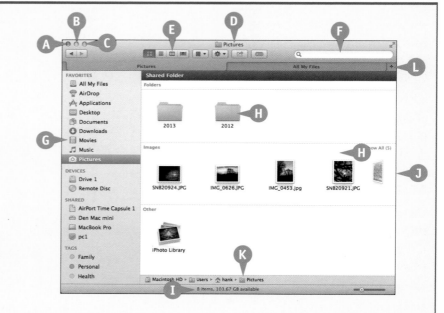

I Status Bar
Shows information about the current location, such as the amount of free space when you are viewing the MacBook Air's drive.

J Window Border
Drag a border or a corner to change the size of a window.

K Path Bar
Shows the path to the location of the folder displayed in the window.

L Tab Bar
Enables you to open multiple tabs containing different Finder locations within the same Finder window and quickly switch among them.

Dock and Sidebar

A **Favorites**

Contains files, folders, searches, and other items that you can open by clicking them.

B **Devices**

Contains your internal drive, any DVD or CD in an external optical drive, external hard drives, and other devices that your MacBook Air can access.

C **Shared**

Displays computers and other resources being shared on a network.

D **Tags**

Shows the list of tags you can apply to files and folders to help you identify and sort them easily.

E **Dock**

Shows applications, files, and folders you can access with a single click, along with applications currently running.

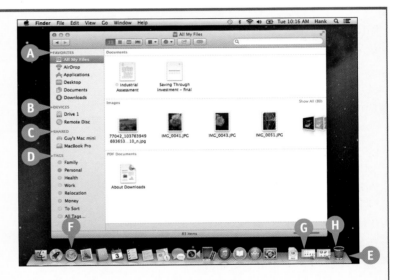

F **Applications**

Icons on the left side of the Dock are for applications; each open application has a glowing dot under its icon unless you turn off this preference.

G **Files, Folders, and Minimized Windows**

Icons on the right side of the Dock are for files, folders, and minimized windows. The default Dock includes the Downloads folder for files you download from the Internet along with your Documents folder.

H **Trash/Eject**

OS X puts items you delete in the Trash; to get rid of them, you empty the Trash. When you select an ejectable device, such as a DVD, the Trash icon changes to the Eject icon.

Point and Click, Double-Click, or Secondary Click

If you logged in using the earlier steps, you know the basics of using the trackpad. To tell the MacBook Air what you want to do, point the on-screen pointer to the object that you want to work with by sliding a finger over the trackpad. After you point to something, you tell the computer what you want to do with it. You do this by pressing the trackpad down to click it. This is referred to as clicking the trackpad. The number of times you click and how you do so determines what happens to the object you point at.

Point and Click, Double-Click, or Secondary Click

Point and Click

1. Slide your finger on the trackpad until the pointer points at an icon.

2. Press the trackpad once to click the trackpad. This is a single click.

   The object is highlighted to indicate that it is now selected.

Double-Click

1. Slide your finger on the trackpad until the pointer points at an icon.

2. Click the trackpad twice.

   Your selection opens.

Point, Click, and Drag

1. Slide your finger on the trackpad until the pointer points at an icon.

2. Press down the trackpad and hold it.

   The object at which you were pointing becomes attached to the arrow and remains so until you release the trackpad.

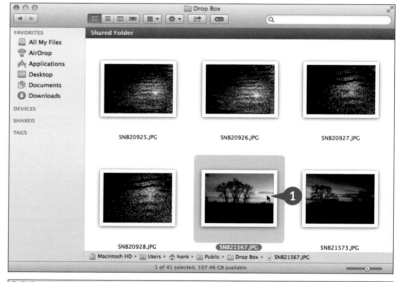

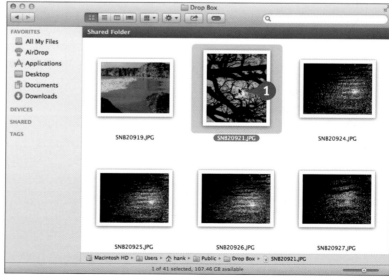

③ Drag your finger on the trackpad to move the object.

④ When you get to the object's new position, release the trackpad.

Note: Dragging something to a different hard drive, flash drive, or disk volume copies it there. Changing its location on the same disk moves it instead.

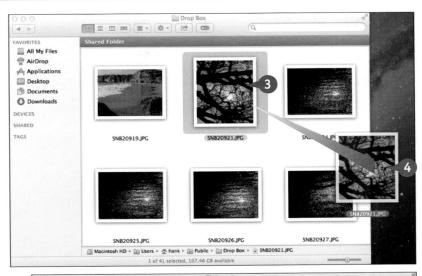

Secondary Click (Control+Click)

① Point to an object on the desktop or even the desktop itself.

Note: To select more than one item at the same time, press and hold ⌘ while you click each item you want to select.

② Press and hold Control.

③ Click the trackpad.

A contextual menu appears.

④ Choose a command on the resulting menu by pointing to it and clicking the trackpad once.

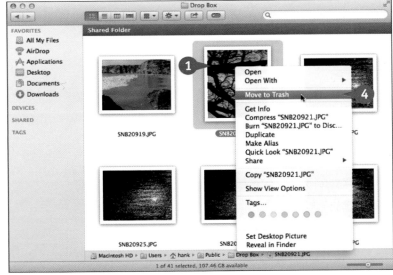

TIP

Why do things I click stick to the arrow?
You can configure the trackpad so you can drag things without having to hold down the trackpad. When this setting is on and you click something, it gets attached to the pointer. When you move the pointer, the object moves too. To configure this setting, see the section "Configure the Trackpad."

Understanding Drives, Volumes, Optical Discs, Folders, and Files

As you use your MacBook Air, you work with data. Underlying all this data is the need to store and organize it. This section describes the major items that OS X uses for storing and organizing data.

These items include drives, volumes, discs, folders, and files. The Finder manages these items, and you access them directly from the desktop or from within applications. You can use different types of devices for different purposes. For example, you can use an external hard drive to back up the data stored on your MacBook Air.

Drive

A drive is one type of physical device that you use to store data. Drives come in different types. The MacBook Air has one internal drive — a solid-state device, or SSD — that contains the software it needs to work, applications you install, and documents you create. You can connect external disk drives to expand the available storage room. OS X uses different icons to represent different kinds of drives. For example, an internal drive such as the SSD appears with a different icon from an external drive.

Volume

A volume is an area of a disk created using software rather than a physical space. A drive can be partitioned into multiple volumes, where each volume acts like a separate drive. A volume performs the same task as a drive, which is to store data. You can access volumes being shared with you over a network. Volumes are used to organize data in different ways and to represent various resources you work with.

Optical Discs

CDs and DVDs serve many purposes. Examples abound, including listening to audio CDs, watching DVD movies and TV shows, and installing applications stored on a CD or DVD. You can also put your own data on CD or DVD, such as burning audio CDs with iTunes and backing up your data on DVD. The MacBook Air does not have a built-in optical drive, but you can easily connect an external SuperDrive or another compatible optical drive via USB.

Folders

Like manila folders in the physical world, folders on a MacBook Air are a means to organize things, such as files and even other folders. OS X includes many folders by default, including Music, Pictures, and Documents. You can create, name, delete, and organize folders in your user account freely; if you have an Administrator account, you can alter some system folders as well, but it is better to leave them alone. You open a folder in a Finder window to view its contents.

Files

A file is a container for data. Files can contain many different kinds of data. For example, some files are documents, such as text documents you create with a word processor. Files can also be images, songs, movies, and other kinds of content. Files also make up the OS X operating system that runs your MacBook Air; you typically do not interact with system files directly. Files have names that include filename extensions, such as .jpg and .doc, and are represented by icons in Finder windows and e-mail attachments. Icons show a preview of what the file contains in their thumbnail image.

Configure the Keyboard

One of the main ways of communicating with your MacBook Air is the keyboard, through which you issue commands, add content to documents, send and receive e-mail, and so on. You can configure the keyboard to work the way you want it to. You use the Keyboard pane of the System Preferences application to configure your keyboard. For example, you can set keyboard shortcuts for commands so you can activate the command by pressing a combination of keys.

Configure the Keyboard

Configure Keyboard Settings

1 Control+click **System Preferences** (⬚).

2 Click **Keyboard**.

3 Click the **Keyboard** tab.

4 Drag the **Key Repeat** slider.

5 Drag the **Delay Until Repeat** slider to set the repeat delay.

6 To use the built-in function keys as normal function keys, select the **Use all F1, F2, etc. keys as standard function keys** check box (☐ changes to ☑).

7 Select the **Adjust keyboard brightness in low light** check box (☐ changes to ☑) to have the backlight dim or brighten automatically.

8 Drag the slider to set the backlight duration.

9 Click **Modifier Keys**.

10 In the Modifier Keys dialog box, select the key presses associated with the various modifier keys.

11 Click **OK**.

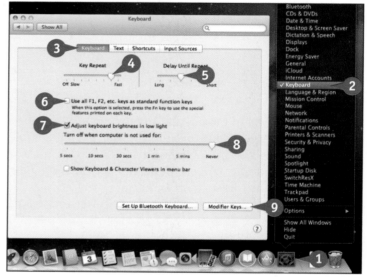

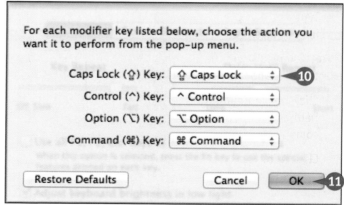

Configure Keyboard Shortcuts

1 Click **Shortcuts**.

The Shortcuts pane appears.

2 Click a category.

3 Deselect a shortcut's check box (☑ changes to ☐) to disable it.

4 To change the keys used for any shortcut, select the current shortcut and then press the new keyboard combination you want to use.

5 To add a new keyboard shortcut, click the **Application Shortcuts** category and then click **Add** (⊞).

The New Shortcut sheet opens.

6 Click the **Application** pop-up menu (▯) and then click the application to which the shortcut applies.

Note: Choose **All Applications** to have the new shortcut affect all of them.

7 Type the name of the command in the Menu Title field.

Note: You must type the name exactly as it appears on the menu.

8 Click in the **Keyboard Shortcut** field and press the key combination you want to use.

9 Click **Add**.

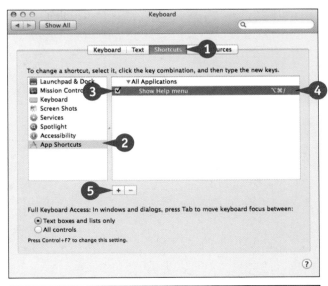

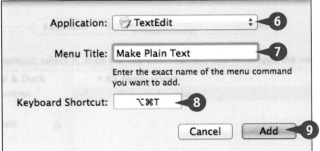

TIP

How do I get back to the original shortcuts?

Display the Shortcuts tab, select any category but Application Shortcuts, and click the **Restore Defaults** button to set all keyboard shortcuts as they were when you first started your MacBook Air. You lose any changes you have made over time, so if you want to reset only a couple of shortcuts, just change those back to what you want them to be.

Configure the Trackpad

The other primary control MacBook Air has is its trackpad. You can use the trackpad to move the pointer on the screen by dragging your finger around the trackpad. You also click the trackpad to perform various actions, such as to select a command on a menu. Beyond these basics, you can perform a wide variety of gestures with the trackpad. You can also configure it so that you can scroll in windows, rotate objects, and much more using up to four fingers.

Configure the Trackpad

1 Click **Apple** (🍎).

The Apple menu opens.

2 Click **System Preferences**.

The System Preferences window opens.

3 Click **Trackpad**.

The Trackpad pane appears.

4 Click **Point & Click**.

The Point & Click pane appears.

Note: You can point to a gesture to play a video explaining the gesture in the Preview pane in the lower-right corner of the Trackpad window.

5 Select a gesture (☐ changes to ☑) to turn it on.

6 If the gesture has a menu, click the menu and choose which option to use.

7 Repeat steps **5** and **6** until you have set up the point and click gestures you want to use.

8 Drag the **Tracking speed** slider to adjust the amount the pointer moves for the same amount of finger movement.

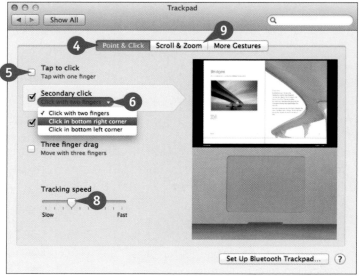

9 Click **Scroll & Zoom**.

The Scroll & Zoom pane appears.

10 Choose which scroll and zoom gestures to use.

Note: OS X is designed to take advantage of gestures on the trackpad so it is worth your time to explore all the options and adjust them over time to make using your MacBook Air even more efficient.

11 Click **More Gestures**.

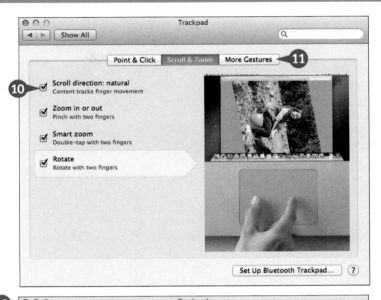

The More Gestures pane appears.

12 Choose which additional gestures you want to use.

13 Click **Close** (⊗).

The System Preferences window closes.

How can I use a mouse with MacBook Air?
You can connect any Mac-compatible USB mouse to your MacBook Air. You can also use a Bluetooth mouse; see Chapter 8 for the steps to configure and use a Bluetooth mouse. When a mouse is connected, use the Mouse pane of the System Preferences application to configure it.

How do I drag things with a gesture on the trackpad?
You can use the method described earlier, but it is even easier to enable the Three finger drag preference on the Point & Click tab. With this enabled, you can touch the trackpad with three fingers while you are pointing to what you want to move. As you move your fingers on the trackpad, the object moves on the screen. When it is in its new position, lift your fingers off the trackpad.

Sleep, Log Out, Restart, or Shut Down

There are several ways to stop using your MacBook Air. Most of the time, you either put it to sleep or log out. During sleep, everything you have open remains open, but the MacBook Air goes into low-power mode; you can wake it up to quickly get back to whatever you were doing. When you log out, all open documents and applications close and you return to the Log In screen. When you want to turn the MacBook Air off, you shut it down. There may also be times when you want to restart the MacBook Air.

Sleep, Log Out, Restart, or Shut Down

Sleep or Log Out

1 Click **Apple** (🍎).

The Apple menu opens.

2 Highlight **Sleep** or **Log Out**.

3 Click the trackpad.

If you selected **Sleep**, most activity on the computer stops.

Note: You can put your MacBook Air to sleep even faster by simply closing its lid.

If you selected **Log Out**, the Log Out confirmation dialog appears.

4 To reopen your applications and documents when you log back in, select the **Reopen windows when logging back in** check box (☐ changes to ☑).

5 Click **Log Out**.

All applications and documents close, and the Log In screen appears.

Note: A faster way to log out is to press Option + ⌘ + Shift + Q.

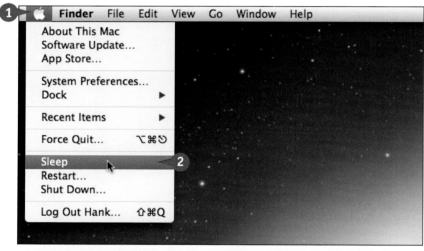

Restart or Shut Down

1 Click **Apple** (🍎).

The Apple menu opens.

2 Drag down the trackpad to highlight **Restart** or **Shut Down**.

3 Click the trackpad.

Depending on which option you chose, the appropriate confirmation dialog appears.

4 If you want all your open documents, Finder windows, and applications to open again when the computer restarts (whether you choose Restart or Shut Down), select the **Reopen windows when logging back in** check box (☐ changes to ☑).

5 To restart your MacBook Air, click **Restart**.

Your MacBook Air shuts down and then starts up again. If you selected the Reopen option, all the windows you had open are restored.

6 To shut down your MacBook Air, click **Shut Down**.

Your MacBook Air turns off.

Note: You can also put your MacBook Air to sleep easily by pressing the **Power** button.

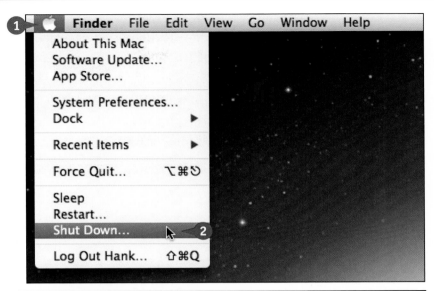

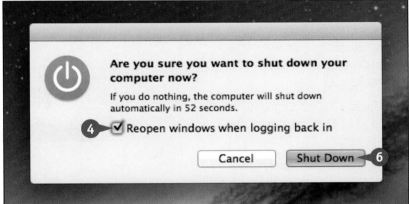

TIP

How often should I turn my MacBook Air off?
Just putting it to sleep is usually better than shutting it down. When you want to use it again, wake it up and it is ready in just a few seconds. If you will not be using the MacBook Air for an extended period of time and it is not connected to the power adapter, shutting it down so the battery does not get completely drained is better.

Understanding Finder, Application, and Document Windows

Like windows in the physical world, windows on your MacBook Air enable to you to view objects on-screen, such as folders, files, applications, and documents. By learning to work with windows efficiently, you can accomplish your tasks more quickly and easily.

In OS X, most windows have common elements no matter what application you are using. In some cases, particularly with games and utilities, you might not see familiar windows when you run those applications. Instead, you see windows that are customized to perform specific functions. Being comfortable with any kind of window you encounter is important.

Finder Windows

Ⓐ Title

Shows the name of the drive, folder, or other location you are currently viewing.

Ⓑ Toolbar

Contains tools to control windows, move among them, change views, and perform actions.

Ⓒ Search Box

Enables you to search for files or folders.

Ⓓ Files and Folders

The contents of the drive, folder, or other location you are viewing appear within the main part of Finder windows.

Ⓔ Sidebar

Contains icons for locations, files, and folders; you can click an icon to view its contents in the Finder window or to open an application or document.

Ⓕ Status Bar

Displays status information for what you are viewing, such as available disk space on the current drive. Click **View** and **Show Status Bar** to display the status bar.

Ⓖ Scroll Bars

When you scroll or hover the pointer over the scroll area, the scroll bars appear to indicate your position in the window.

Ⓗ Border

Drag a window border to change the window's size and shape. Drag a corner to resize the window both horizontally and vertically at the same time.

Ⓘ Size Slider (Icon View Only)

Drag to the left to make icons smaller or to the right to make them larger.

Application Windows

Ⓐ Application Title

The name of the application window.

Ⓑ Window Controls

Enable you to close, minimize, or zoom the window.

Ⓒ Toolbar

Provides buttons and controls for specific actions in the application.

Ⓓ Content

The content appears in the main part of the window.

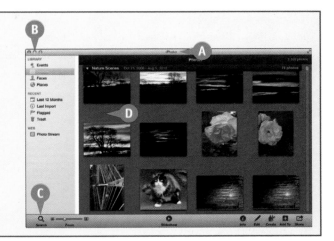

Document Windows

Ⓐ Document Title

The name of the file that appears in the window.

Ⓑ Scroll Bars

Enable you to move up, down, left, or right within a window to see all of its contents and show you your relative position in the document.

Ⓒ Border

Drag a border to resize the window. Drag a corner to resize the window both horizontally and vertically at the same time.

Ⓓ Application-Specific Tools

Most applications provide tools in their windows specific to the application.

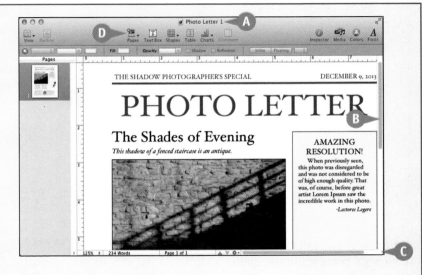

View Finder Windows in Icon View

Icon view represents each file or folder as a graphical icon that indicates the kind of object it represents, such as a file or folder. Icon view can be useful for looking through graphical items, such as images. You can adjust the icon size from tiny to huge to suit your preferences. In Icon view, you can set the window's background color or use an image as the background.

View Finder Windows in Icon View

1 Click a folder in the Sidebar to view its contents.

2 Click **Icon View** (⊞).

3 Drag the slider to change the icon size.

4 Click **Arrange** (▦▾) and select how you want the icons grouped.

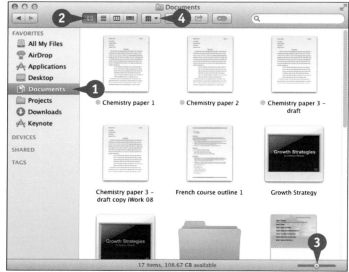

5 Click **View** and select **Show View Options**.

6 Select the **Always open in icon view** check box (☐ changes to ☑) to have the folder always open in Icon view.

7 Select the **Browse in icon view** check box (☐ changes to ☑) if you want folders in the current folder to appear in Icon view.

8 Click the **Arrange By** arrows and select the arrangement to use.

9 Click the **Sort By** arrows and select the sort type.

10 Drag the **Icon size** slider to set the icon size.

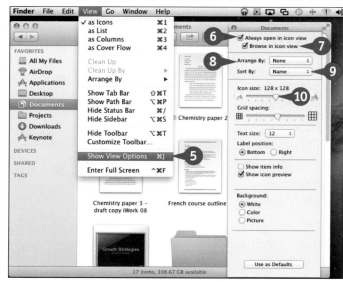

11 Drag the **Grid spacing** slider to set the icon spacing.

12 Click the **Text size** arrows and select the text size.

13 Select a **Label position** option to place text labels on the bottom or on the right.

14 Select the **Show item info** check box (☐ changes to ☑) to show additional information about items.

15 Select the **Show icon preview** check box (☐ changes to ☑) to show a preview if it is available.

16 Select the **Color** option (◯ changes to ◉) to use a background color.

17 Click the color button.

18 In the Colors window, select the color you want for the background.

19 Click **Close** (⊗) to close the Colors window.

Ⓐ To use a picture background, select **Picture** (◯ changes to ◉) and then drag an image file onto the image well.

20 Click **Use as Defaults** to have every window you open in Icon view use the current settings by default.

21 Click **Close** (⊗) to close the View Options dialog.

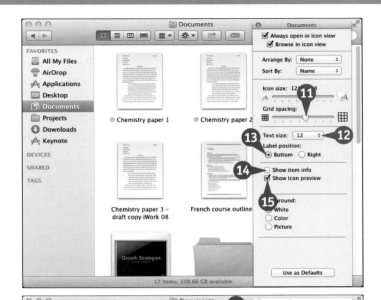

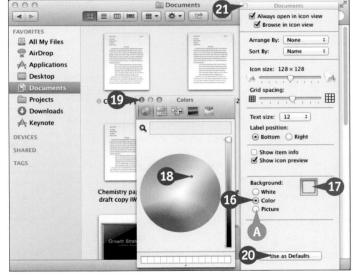

How can I browse items when I have grouped them?

Items you group are placed in categories by the criterion you select, such as Size. If a particular group has more items than can be displayed, the remaining items appear in either a fan or grid on either side of the displayed items. Click the indicator on either side to move through the items.

View Finder Windows in List View

List view may not look as colorful as Icon view, but it provides much more information. You can more easily sort the content in windows so that the items appear in the order you want. You can also select items stored in different folders at the same time.

View Finder Windows in List View

1 Click a folder in the Sidebar.

2 Click **List View** (≣).

3 Click the **View** menu and select **Show View Options**.

4 Select the **Always open in list view** check box (☐ changes to ☑) if you want the folder to always open in List view.

5 Select the **Browse in list view** check box (☐ changes to ☑) to cause all the folders within to display in List view too.

6 Click the **Arrange By** menu and choose the arrangement.

7 Click the **Sort By** menu and choose how to sort items.

8 In the Icon size area, click **small** or **large** (☐ changes to ◉).

9 Click the **Text size** pop-up menu and select the text size.

10 Select the check box options for each column to display.

11 Select the **Use relative dates** check box (☐ changes to ☑) if you want to see relative dates, such as Yesterday or Today.

12 Select the **Calculate all sizes** check box (☐ changes to ☑) to see folder sizes.

13 Select the **Show icon preview** check box (☐ changes to ☑) to see previews.

14 Click **Use as Defaults** to use the current settings by default.

15 Click **Close** (⊗).

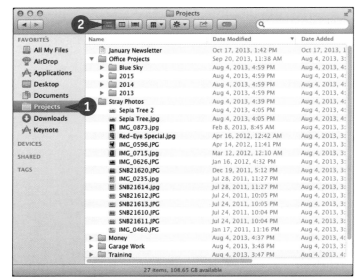

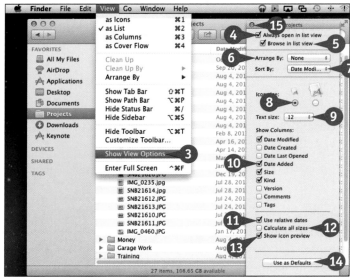

16 Drag a column heading to the left or to the right to change the order in which columns appear in the window.

Note: The Name column always appears on the far left; you cannot move it or move another column ahead of it.

17 Release the trackpad when the column is in its new position.

18 To change the order in which the items are sorted, click the column heading by which you want to sort the items.

19 To reverse the sort order, click ▲.

20 To reveal the contents of a folder, click ▶ or press ⌘ + →.

Ⓐ The folder expands so that you can see the folders and files it contains.

21 Click ▼ to collapse a folder or press ⌘ + ←.

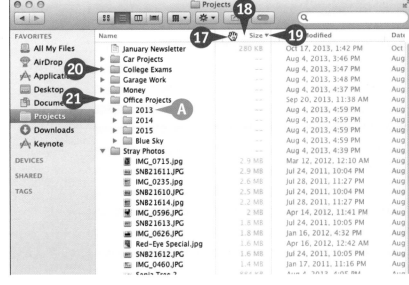

How do I expand all the folders within a window at the same time?
Press and hold Option while you click a folder's ▶. The folder expands, along with all the folders contained within that folder. Press and hold Option and click any folder's ▼ to collapse all the folders in the window again. From the keyboard, you can press Option + ⌘ + → to expand all the folders or Option + ⌘ + ← to collapse them.

How do I tell where a folder is when I view its window?
Click **View** and then click **Show Path Bar**. A bar appears at the bottom of the window that shows you the path from the startup disk to the location of the current folder.

View Finder Windows in Column View

Column view is best for navigating quickly around your MacBook. This view allows you to see the contents of folders along with the locations of those folders. You can click any folder's icon to immediately see the contents of that folder in the same window. This view is the default view for Open dialogs.

View Finder Windows in Column View

1 Click a folder in the Sidebar.

2 Click **Column View** (▥).

3 Click **View** and select **Show View Options**.

4 Select the **Always open in column view** check box (☐ changes to ☑) if you want the folder to always open in Column view.

5 Select the **Browse in column view** check box (☐ changes to ☑) to have subfolders display in Column view too.

6 Select an option on the **Arrange By** pop-up menu to arrange items.

7 Select an option on the **Sort By** pop-up menu to sort items.

8 Open the **Text size** pop-up menu to choose the text size.

9 Select the **Show icons** check box (☐ changes to ☑) display icons.

10 Select the **Show icon preview** check box (☐ changes to ☑) to see icon previews.

11 To show a preview of a file, select the **Show preview column** check box (☑).

12 Click **Close** (⊗).

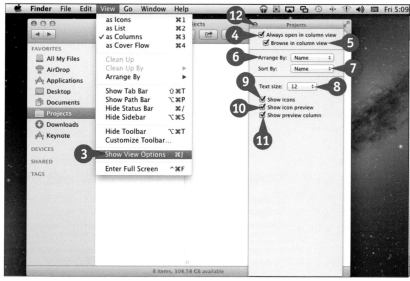

13 Select a location in the Sidebar to view it.

14 Click a folder to see its contents.

A The contents of the folder appear in the column to the right of the one on which you clicked.

Note: As you move through the folder hierarchy, columns shift to the left so that you always see the last column opened toward the right side of the window.

15 Click a file.

B You see information about the file in the far right column, including a preview of the file if that option is enabled. You can page through files such as text documents and PDF files. If the file is dynamic, such as audio or video, you can play its content in the preview.

16 To change the width of a column, drag the handle at the base of its right edge to the left or right.

17 To group items, click **Arrange** (▦▾) and choose how you want the window grouped.

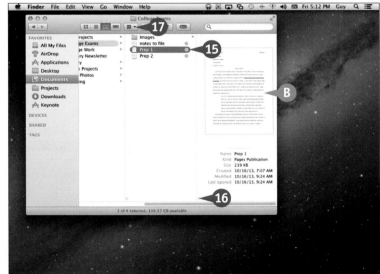

TIPS

How do I resize all the columns at once?
Press and hold **Option** while you drag one column's handle. All the columns are resized at the same time. Double-click a column's handle to resize the column to show the longest file or folder name.

How do I tell the difference between a folder and a file?
In Column view, folders always have a right-facing triangle at the right edge of their column to show that when you select this triangle, the folder's contents appear in a new column to the right. Files do not have this arrow.

View Finder Windows in Cover Flow View

C over Flow view provides a graphical way for you to quickly scan the contents of a Finder window. It displays thumbnail images for items, enabling you to scroll through files and folders with ease. You can flip through the various folders and files to browse them in the Cover Flow viewer, which appears in the top part of the window. In the bottom part of the window, you see the items in the folder you are browsing in List view.

View Finder Windows in Cover Flow View

1 Open a Finder window.

2 Click **Cover Flow View** (▥).

Ⓐ The Cover Flow viewer appears in the upper part of the window.

Ⓑ The items in the folder you are viewing appear in the lower part of the window in List view.

3 To browse the contents of the folder quickly, drag across the "covers" to the left or right.

As you browse, a preview of each item flips by in the Cover Flow viewer in the upper part of the window.

Ⓒ The item currently selected is the one directly facing you and is highlighted on the list in the lower part of the window.

4 To jump to a specific file or folder, click its icon.

5 To make the Cover Flow viewer larger or smaller, drag ▤ up or down.

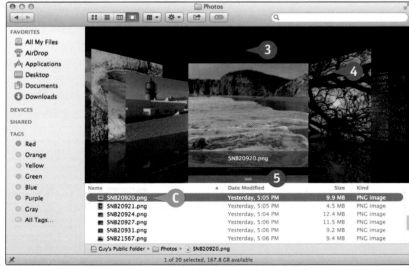

Configure the Sidebar

The Finder's Sidebar enables you to navigate easily among files, folders, and applications. The Sidebar contains several default locations and folders, but you can add and remove items so the Sidebar contains the items you use most frequently. The Sidebar contains four sections. Favorites are your favorite items; a number of defaults are stored here. Devices include hard drives and other devices (such as iPods) connected to your MacBook Air. Shared includes disk drives or computers you are accessing over a network. Tags shows the list of tags you can use for easy reference and access to items.

Configure the Sidebar

1 To remove an item from the Sidebar, Control+click it.

2 Click **Remove from Sidebar**.

The item is removed from the Sidebar but remains on your MacBook Air.

3 To add something to the Sidebar, click its icon, open the **File** menu, and choose **Add to Sidebar**.

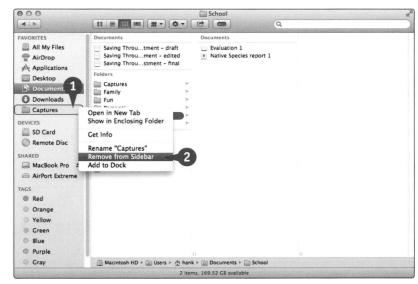

4 To change the order of items in the Sidebar, drag them up or down the list.

5 To collapse a section of the Sidebar, point to that section and click **Hide**.

6 To expand a section of the Sidebar, point to that section's title and click **Show**.

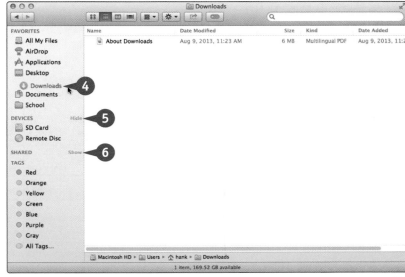

Work with Finder Tabs

When you are managing your files, you will often find you need to work in multiple folders at the same time. Instead of opening multiple Finder windows and arranging them so you can see them all, you can open multiple tabs within the same Finder window and navigate quickly among the tabs by using the tab bar. Finder tabs are especially useful if you switch a Finder window to full-screen mode. You can drag files or folders from one Finder tab to another to copy or move the items.

Work with Finder Tabs

1 Open a Finder window.

2 Click the folder you want to view in the window.

3 Click the button for the view you want. For example, click **Columns** (▥) to switch to Columns view.

4 Press ⌘ + T or click **File** and **New Tab**.

Note: The Finder hides the tab bar by default when only one tab is open. You can display the tab bar by clicking **View** and **Show Tab Bar** or pressing Shift + ⌘ + T.

Ⓐ The tab bar appears.

Ⓑ A new tab opens, showing your default folder or view.

5 Click the folder you want to view.

6 Click the button for the view you want. For example, click **Icon** (▦) to switch to Icon view.

7 Click **New Tab** (➕).

A new tab opens, showing your default folder or view.

Note: You can use a different view in each tab if you like, so you can set up your folders the way you prefer them.

⑧ Drag the tab along the tab bar to where you want it.

Note: You can drag a tab to another Finder window if you want. You can also drag a tab out of a Finder window to turn it into its own window.

⑨ Click **Full Screen** (🖼).

The Finder window appears full screen, giving you more space for working with files, folders, and tabs.

Note: To exit Full Screen view, move the mouse pointer (🖱) to the top of the screen so that the menu bar appears, and then click **Exit Full Screen** (▣). Alternatively, press Esc.

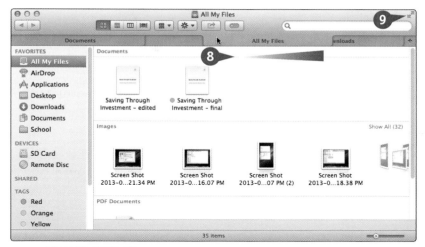

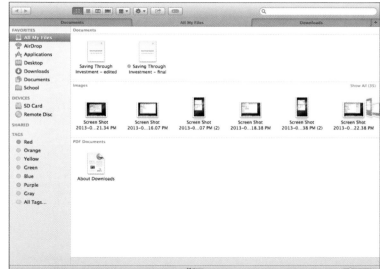

TIPS

How do I close a Finder tab?
Move the mouse 🖱 over the tab, and then click **Close** (▣) when it appears. You can also press ⌘ + W or click **File** and **Close Tab**.

How do I copy or move files using Finder tabs?
Select the files in the source tab, and then drag them to the destination tab on the tab bar. To put the files in the folder open in the destination tab, drop the files on the destination tab in the tab bar. To navigate to a subfolder, hold the mouse 🖱 over the destination tab until its content appears, and then drag the items to the subfolder.

Using the Action Pop-up Menu and Quick Look

The Action pop-up menu is a convenient means for giving commands in Finder windows. This contextual menu contains a list of commands that you can use on the files or folders you have selected. The list is contextual, so it changes depending on what objects you have selected; the Action pop-up menu shows the same commands as the contextual menu you can display by Control+clicking an item. The Finder's Quick Look command enables you to view the contents of a file or group of files without actually opening them. This can save time, especially when you are looking for specific files.

Using the Action Pop-up Menu and Quick Look

Using the Action Pop-up Menu

1 Open a Finder window.

2 Click the file you want to affect.

3 Click the **Action** pop-up menu (⚙▾).

4 Select the command.

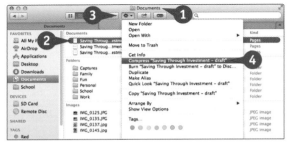

Using Quick Look

1 Open a Finder window containing files.

2 Select the files you want to view.

Note: To select multiple files at the same time, click the first file, and then press and hold ⌘ while you click the other files.

3 Press Spacebar.

The Quick Look window opens and shows the contents of the files you have selected.

4 To move forward and backward through the items you selected, click ➡ or ⬅.

5 To see thumbnails of each item you selected, click **Thumbnails** (🔡).

6 To see Quick Look in full screen, click **Full Screen** (⛶).

7 To open the file in a related application, click the **Open With** button.

8 When you are done with Quick Look, click **Close** (✖).

Configure the Finder Window Toolbar

The toolbar that appears at the top of the Finder window contains buttons that you can use to access commands quickly and easily. For example, the various View buttons appear there along with the Action menu button. Although the Finder toolbar includes a number of buttons by default, you can configure the toolbar so that it contains the buttons you use most frequently.

Configure the Finder Window Toolbar

1 Open a Finder window.

2 Click **View** and select **Customize Toolbar**.

3 To remove a button from the toolbar, drag its icon from the toolbar onto the desktop.

When you release the trackpad, the button disappears in a puff of smoke.

4 To add a button to the toolbar, drag its icon from the sheet and drop it on the toolbar at the location in which you want to place it.

When you release the trackpad, the button is added to the toolbar.

5 To change the location of a button on the toolbar, drag its icon from the current location to where you want it.

6 When you are finished customizing the toolbar, click **Done**.

The Customization sheet closes and you see your customized toolbar.

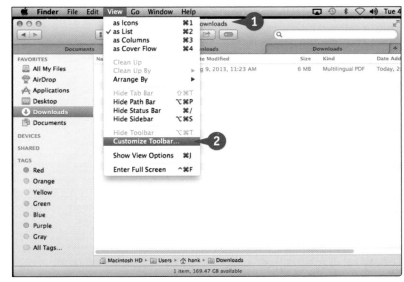

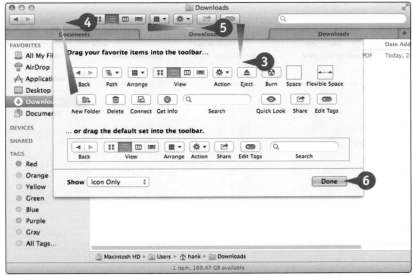

Understanding Desktop Management Tools

Your MacBook Air has a lot going on. You will use multiple applications to work on documents, send e-mails, surf the web, and more. Each task has one or more windows associated with it. This can really clutter up the desktop, making you less efficient and your work less enjoyable. Fortunately, OS X provides powerful tools that enable you to manage your desktop efficiently.

Dock

The Dock provides you with one-click access to applications, folders, and documents. It also holds the Trash icon, which both holds files you no longer want and provides a handy way to eject optical discs and other removable items. OS X installs a number of applications and folders on the Dock by default, but you can easily configure the Dock to contain only the items you find the most useful. You can also configure the Dock's location on the desktop, along with its size and behavior.

Mission Control

Mission Control helps you make even better use of your desktop: With a swipe on the trackpad or the press of a button and a swipe, you can quickly cycle through your Dashboard, desktops and spaces, and applications in Full Screen mode. When you see what you want to work with, you can jump right to it.

Window Control

Mission Control also enables you to quickly arrange open windows on the desktop so that you can more easily move between them. For this purpose, Mission Control has three modes. When you open Mission Control, OS X reduces all the open windows in size and groups them by application. You can click a window to jump to it. It can also shrink all the open windows for an application so you can see them all at the same time; click a window to move to it. In addition, you can use Mission Control to quickly move all open windows off the sides of the screen so you can access the desktop.

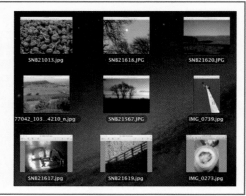

Desktops

Desktops, also called *spaces*, are collections of applications that you can switch between quickly and easily to work with a different space. For

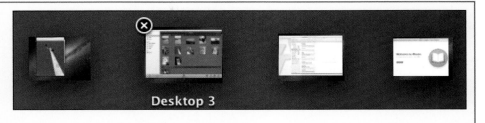

example, you might have one desktop with your communication applications, such as e-mail, chat, and so on. Another desktop might have your work applications, such as Pages and Numbers. Yet another might have entertainment apps in it. With a gesture and a click, you can move from one set to another.

Dashboard

The Dashboard contains "mini applications" called *widgets*. You can quickly pop open the Dashboard, use your widgets, and close the Dashboard again to move it out of the way. The Dashboard contains several widgets by default, but like other desktop management tools, you can customize its contents to suit your needs.

Launchpad

The Launchpad presents icons for all the applications stored in the Applications folder or other system folders on your MacBook Air on multiple screens. The first screen contains OS X's default applications along with other Apple applications, such as the iLife applications. You can drag your fingers across the trackpad to flip through the screens to see the other applications you have. When you see an application, you want to use, click its icon. Because the Launchpad is focused on helping you use applications, its section is in Chapter 5.

Using and Configuring the Dock

The Dock provides single-click access to various items, including applications, documents, and folders. The Dock includes a number of default icons, and you can add as many icons to your Dock as you want. You can also customize the way the Dock looks and works to suit your preferences. Clicking an application's icon in the Dock opens the application — if it is not open already — and makes it active. Clicking the icon for a minimized window restores that window to its previous size.

Using and Configuring the Dock

Use the Dock

1 Point to an icon on the Dock.

The name of the related item appears above the icon.

2 Click an item to take action on it; for example, clicking an application opens it.

3 To open a Dock icon's contextual menu, either Control+click or click and hold on the icon.

4 Choose the command you want to use from the menu.

A You can also display one of the application's open windows by clicking it on the menu.

Note: As more icons appear on the Dock, the Dock expands until it takes up the full width of the screen. After that, OS X makes the icons smaller so that they fit on it.

Configure the Dock

1 Control+click the dashed dividing line just to the right of the last application icon.

The Dock menu appears.

2 Click **Dock Preferences**.

3 Drag the **Size** slider left or right to resize the Dock.

4 To magnify icons when you point to them, select the **Magnification** check box (☐ changes to ☑) and then drag the slider.

5 Position the Dock by clicking **Left**, **Bottom**, or **Right** (◯ changes to ⦿).

6 Click the **Minimize windows using** pop-up menu (⇕) and select the effect you want to use.

7 Select the **Double-click a window's title bar to minimize** check box (☐ changes to ☑) to minimize a window by double-clicking its title bar.

8 Click **Close** (⊗) or press ⌘ + Q to close the System Preferences application.

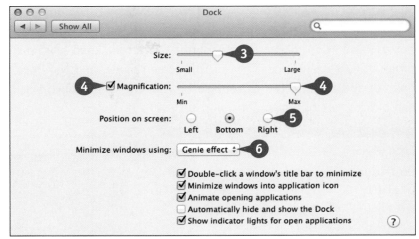

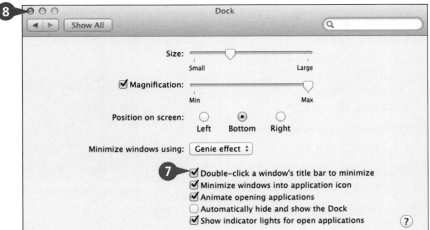

TIP

What are the other options in the Dock pane in System Preferences?
Select the **Minimize windows into application icon** check box (☐ changes to ☑) to minimize a window into its application's icon instead of to an icon on the right side of the Dock. Select the **Animate opening applications** check box (☐ changes to ☑) to have icons bounce while their applications are opening. Select the **Automatically hide and show the Dock** check box (☐ changes to ☑) to automatically hide the Dock when you are not pointing to it. Select the **Show indicator lights for open applications** check box (☐ changes to ☑) to display a blue dot under each open application's icon.

Manage the Desktop with Mission Control

M ission Control is a quick way to get to any open window on your MacBook Air. You can also use it to get to the Dashboard, applications running in Full Screen mode, and your desktops. When you open Mission Control by using gestures on the trackpad, at the top of the screen you see thumbnails of your desktops, applications in Full Screen mode, and the Dashboard. You see thumbnails of the open applications in the current desktop in the center part of the screen, and you see the Dock. You can quickly get to any window you see.

Manage the Desktop with Mission Control

Configure the Mission Control Gesture

① Control+click **System Preferences** ( ) in the Dock.

The contextual menu opens.

② Click **Trackpad**.

Note: If System Preferences ( ) does not appear on the Dock, click **Apple** ( ) and then click **System Preferences**. In the System Preferences window, click **Trackpad**.

The System Preferences application opens, displaying the Trackpad pane.

③ Click **More Gestures**.

The More Gestures pane appears.

④ Select the **Mission Control** check box (changes to).

⑤ Click the menu under Mission Control and select **Swipe up with three fingers** or **Swipe up with four fingers** to suit your preference.

⑥ Click **Close** ( ).

The System Preferences application closes.

42

Use Mission Control

1 Using three or four fingers, swipe up the trackpad toward the screen.

Note: You can also press `F3` or Control+`⬆` on the keyboard to open Mission Control.

Mission Control opens.

Ⓐ At the top of the screen, you see a thumbnail for your current desktop on the far left.

Ⓑ Next at the top of the screen is the thumbnail for the Dashboard.

Ⓒ To the right of the Dashboard, you see a thumbnail for each desktop or full-screen application.

Ⓓ In the center of the screen, you see thumbnails for all the open windows in the current desktop. The windows are grouped by the application with which they are associated.

2 Swipe to the left or right to change the focus to the previous or next desktop.

3 To display an application in Full Screen mode, or the Dashboard, click its thumbnail. To display a specific window within the space in focus, click in it.

Note: When you point to a window, a blue box outlines it, indicating it will be your destination when you click.

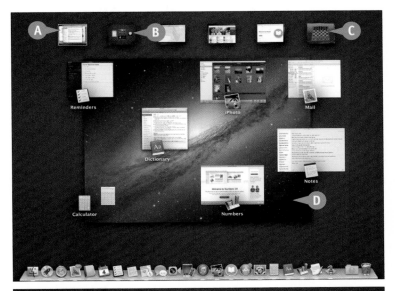

TIP

Can I have a different desktop picture in each desktop?
Yes. Configure System Preferences to be in either no desktop or all of them — you learn how to do this later in this chapter. Move into each desktop and set the background picture for that desktop. When you move into a desktop, its background picture appears.

Configure and Use Mission Control and Desktops

D esktops are collections of applications and documents that you can use to move easily and quickly between sets of windows. When you use desktops, you do not have to bother locating individual windows. Instead, you can see the windows in each desktop and quickly move to the window with which you want to work. For example, if you typically use several Internet applications at the same time, you can create an Internet desktop and add your applications to it. To use the Internet, you just display this desktop, and its open applications are ready to use immediately.

Configure and Use Mission Control and Desktops

Configure Mission Control

1 Control+click **System Preferences** ( ).

2 Click **Mission Control**.

3 Select the **Show Dashboard as a Space** check box (changes to ✓) to include the Dashboard.

4 Select the **Automatically rearrange Spaces based on most recent use** check box (changes to ✓).

5 Select the **When switching to an application, switch to a Space with open windows for the application** check box (changes to ✓).

6 Select the **Group windows by application** check box (changes to ✓) to group windows.

7 Select the **Displays have separate Spaces** check box (changes to ✓).

8 Click these menus and select keyboard shortcuts.

9 Click **Hot Corners** and choose an action for each screen corner.

10 Click **Close** ( ).

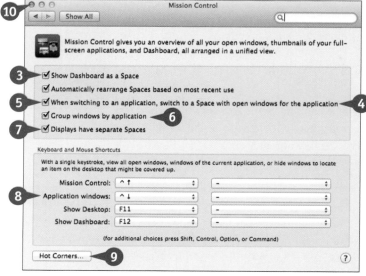

Create Desktops

1 Activate Mission Control. For example, drag four fingers up the trackpad.

The Dashboard, current desktops, and applications in Full Screen mode appear at the top of the screen. The applications and windows open in the current desktop appear in the center of the screen.

2 Point to the upper-right corner of the screen, and click the **Add** button (■) that appears.

Note: If you have positioned the Dock on the right side of the screen, point to the upper-left corner of the screen to display the Add button (■).

A new space called desktop *X*, where *X* is the next unused number, appears and is ready for you to configure.

3 Repeat step **2** until you have created all the desktops you want.

Delete Desktops

1 Activate Mission Control.

2 Point to the desktop you want to delete.

3 Click **Delete** (⊗).

OS X removes the desktop.

TIP

How many desktops should I use?
This depends on how many applications you use, how you use them, and whether you use an external display to extend your MacBook Air's screen. Experiment with three or four desktops to start with. If you need more desktops, you can create them in moments; and if you find you have too many desktops, you can delete surplus ones equally easily.

continued ▶

Desktops are a powerful feature, but they can take a bit of getting used to. It might take some trial and error to configure your desktops in a way that you get the most benefit from them. The most common problem is having too many desktops or too many applications in one desktop. Use these steps to configure your desktops initially. Over time, you will discover which desktops work for you and which do not. Keep tweaking your desktops until they suit the way you work.

Configure and Use Mission Control and Desktops (continued)

Change Desktops with a Gesture

1 Swipe on the trackpad to the left or right with three fingers. On the keyboard, you can press Control+ ← or Control+ →.

A As you swipe, the current space moves off the screen in the direction you swipe.

B The next space moves onto the screen in the direction you swipe.

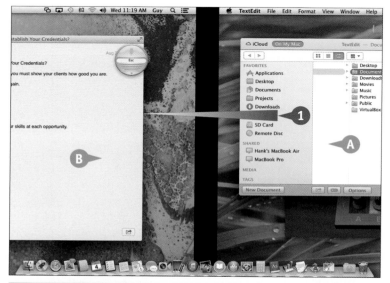

Change Desktops with Mission Control

1 Swipe up with four fingers on the trackpad or press F3 or Control+ ↑ on the keyboard.

2 Click the space you want to make active.

The desktop, application in Full Screen mode, or Dashboard on which you clicked becomes active.

Configure Desktops

1 Make the desktop you want to configure active.

2 If the icons for applications you want to add to the desktop do not appear on the Dock, launch the applications.

3 Control+click an application's Dock icon.

4 Click **Options**.

5 Select one of the options that follows.

C You can choose **All Desktops** to add the application to all desktops so it is available no matter which one is active.

D You can choose **This Desktop** to add the application to the active desktop.

E You can choose **None** to remove the application from all desktops so it behaves independent of the desktop you are using.

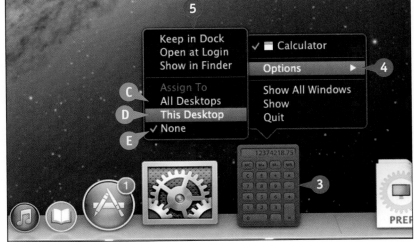

6 Repeat steps **2** to **5** until you configure all the applications you want to associate with the active desktop.

TIP

What happens when I open an application that is not part of the desktop that I am using?

If an application is available in only one desktop, when you open it from any source, such as the Dock or the Finder, you switch into the desktop with which that application is associated, if you have enabled that option in Mission Control preferences. If the application is not part of a desktop, it opens in the space you are currently using.

Manage Open Windows with Mission Control

Mission Control greatly helps with the inevitable screen clutter as you use MacBook Air and open window after window for documents and applications. For this purpose, Mission Control has three modes. You can hide all open windows to show the MacBook Air desktop. You can reduce all open windows to thumbnails so that you can quickly jump into a window you want to use. You can also see thumbnails for just the open windows within a specific application.

Manage Open Windows with Mission Control

Hide All Open Windows

1 Open several windows.

2 Press ⌘ + F3 .

A All the windows move off the MacBook Air screen.

Note: To return the windows to the desktop, press ⌘ + F3 again, or click one of the sides of the windows that you see at the edges of the desktop.

Show Thumbnails of All Open Windows

1 Make a desktop with open windows active.

2 Open Mission Control by swiping three or four fingers up the trackpad. On the keyboard, you can press F3 or Control+⬆.

B All windows shrink down so that they fit on the desktop.

3 Point to a window.

C The window is highlighted with a blue line.

4 Click a window to move into it.

Show All Open Windows for an Application

1 Open multiple windows within the same application.

2 Perform the gesture associated with App Exposé. For example, swipe down with four fingers.

Note: You can also press Control+`F3` or Control+`⬇` to give the App Exposé command.

D All windows currently open in the application appear as thumbnails at the top of the screen. You see the title of each window underneath its thumbnail.

E At the bottom of the screen, you see thumbnails for other files you have recently closed in the same application.

3 Point to a window or to a recent file.

F A blue highlight appears around the window or file.

4 Click the item you want to display.

Note: You can also press the arrow keys to move to a window and press `Return` to move into it.

TIPS

How can I get back to a recent file?
To browse recent files, swipe to the left or right across the thumbnails along the bottom of the screen. When you see the file you want to open, click it. The file opens and you can use it.

How can I change the set of windows that I am viewing?
With the windows for an application showing, hold down `⌘` and press `Tab`. The Application Switcher appears. Continue holding down `⌘` and press `Tab` until the application whose windows you want to see is highlighted with a white box. When it is, release the keys. All the windows open in that application appear.

Using and Configuring the Dashboard

The Dashboard offers an easy way to access *widgets*, small applications that provide very specific functionality. To use a widget, you activate the Dashboard, which fills the desktop and presents the widgets installed on it. Use the widgets you want; when you are done, close the Dashboard again. OS X includes a number of useful widgets by default, such as Weather, Calculator, Address Book, and Flight Tracker. There is even a widget to help you manage your widgets.

Using and Configuring the Dashboard

Open the Dashboard

1 Click **Launchpad** (⬜) on the Dock.

2 Click **Dashboard** (⚫).

Note: You can also open Dashboard by opening Mission Control and then clicking the **Dashboard** space.

Ⓐ The desktop and open windows move into the background and the Dashboard appears, displaying the widgets already on the Dashboard.

Ⓑ If a widget is informational, such as a clock widget, you can view the information it provides.

3 If the widget needs input, click the widget to make it active.

4 Point to the widget you want to configure.

The Info button (a lowercase *i*) appears.

5 Click **Info** (🛈).

6 Use the widget's configuration tools to change its settings.

7 Click **Done**.

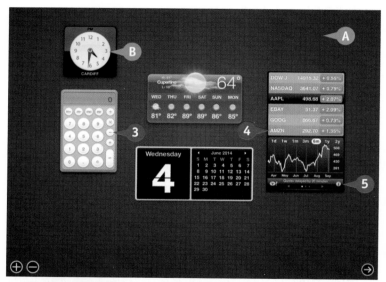

Configure the Dashboard

1 Open the Dashboard.

2 To change the location of widgets, drag them around the screen.

When you release the trackpad, the widget is saved in its new location and appears in that spot each time you open the Dashboard.

3 Click **Add** (⊕).

The Dashboard moves into configuration mode. You see all the widgets currently available for the Dashboard.

4 Browse the available widgets.

C If you have many widgets, you can search by clicking in the Search box and typing a search term.

D To find other widgets, click **More Widgets** and browse the selection on the Apple Dashboard Widgets page.

5 Click a widget to add it your Dashboard.

The widget is added to your Dashboard and it returns to its usable mode.

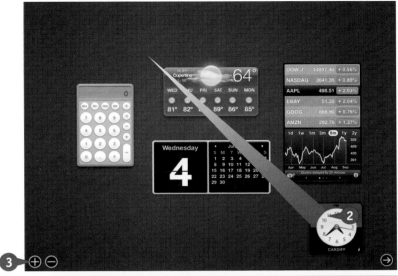

TIP

How can I remove widgets from the Dashboard?
To remove a widget from the Dashboard, open the Dashboard and click **Remove** (⊖). Click the **Delete** button (⊗) on the widget you want to remove. The widget is removed from the Dashboard, but remains on your MacBook Air so you can add it again later if desired. Click **Remove** (⊖) again when you finish removing widgets.

Work with Notifications

As you use your MacBook Air, you receive e-mail, reminders about appointments and tasks, information updates, and so on. Each application you use can send notifications to keep you informed about what is happening. There are two types of individual notifications. When Alert notifications appear on the screen, you have to take some action to clear them, such as clicking the Dismiss button. Banner notifications are more informational; they appear briefly on the screen and then go away automatically. You can view and work with groups of notifications in the Notification Center.

Work with Notifications

View Alert Notifications

1 View the information presented in the alert.

2 If you want to see the details of what you are being notified about, click the alert.

The application that sent the alert appears, and you can work with the item in detail.

3 If you want to dismiss the alert, click one of its buttons.

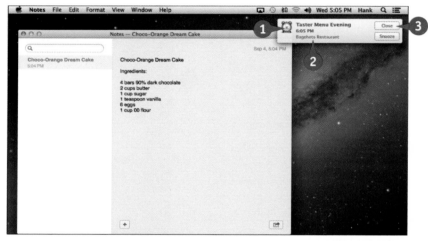

View Banner Notifications

1 View the information presented in the banner.

2 If you want to see the details of what you are being notified about, click the information.

The application that sent the alert appears, and you can work with the item in detail.

If you do not click the banner, after a few seconds, it disappears.

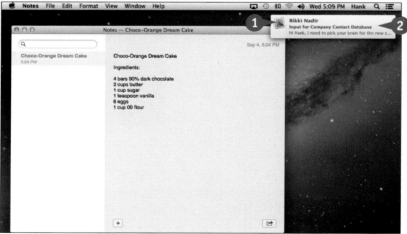

View Notifications in the Notification Center

1 Click the **Notification Center** button (▤).

Note: The color of the dot at the center of the Notification Center button is blue if you have notifications that you have not seen before. Otherwise, it is gray.

The Notification Center opens. You see the notifications you have from various applications, organized into groups with the application's name at the top the group.

2 Scroll up and down the list to review all the notifications.

3 Click a notification to display the related application and see all the item's details. For example, if you click a reminder notification, the Reminders application appears, and you can see all the information in that reminder.

4 To close a section, click the **Close** button (▨).

5 To close the Notification Center, click the desktop.

TIP

How can I change the order in which notifications are listed?

By default, groups of notifications are sorted so that the newest notifications appear at the top of the Notification Center. If you prefer to set the order manually, you can use the Notifications pane of the System Preferences Center, explained in the next section, to allow manual configuration. When that is set, drag sections up or down the list to change their order.

continued ▶

You can choose which applications can send notifications to you and which types of notifications each can send. To configure notifications, you use the Notifications pane in the System Preferences application. Here, you can set your Do Not Disturb period and choose who — if anyone — can interrupt it. As well as banners and alerts, OS X provides badge notifications and sound notifications. Badges are numbers that appear on an application's icon to show how many new items the application has. Sound notifications are sounds an application plays when events occur.

Work with Notifications (continued)

Configure Notifications

1 Control+click **System Preferences** (⬚).

2 Click **Notifications**.

3 Click **Do Not Disturb**.

4 Select the **From** check box (☐ changes to ☑) and choose the start time and end time for your Do Not Disturb period.

5 Choose other times to turn on Do Not Disturb.

6 Choose whether and which people can interrupt Do Not Disturb.

7 Click the **Sort Notification Center** pop-up menu (⬍) and select **Manually** if you want to be able to drag notifications up and down the list. Select **By time** if you want notifications always to be sorted based on when you received them.

8 Click the application for which you want to configure notifications.

9 Click **None**, **Banners** or **Alerts.**

10 Select the **Show notifications when display is off or locked** check box (☐ changes to ☑) to display notifications even when the display is off or locked.

11 Deselect the **Show in Notification Center** check box (☑ changes to ☐) if you do not want the application's notifications to appear in the Notification Center.

12 Click the pop-up menu (⬍) and select the number of recent notifications to display.

13 Deselect the **Badge app icon** check box (☑ changes to ☐) if you do not want badge notifications to appear on the application's icon.

14 Deselect the **Play sound for notifications** check box (☑ changes to ☐) to disable audible alerts.

15 Repeat steps **8** to **14** until you have configured notifications for all the applications shown.

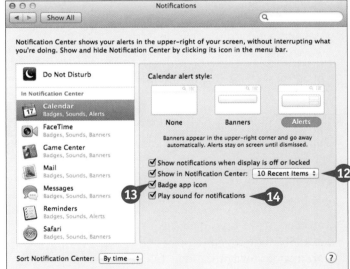

TIP

How do I disable all notifications?

If you want to hide all alerts and banners, open the Notification Center and scroll to the top. Set the Do Not Disturb switch to the On position. All banners and alerts will be hidden. To resume receiving these notifications, set the switch position to the Off position again.

Move to Locations on the Desktop

oving to specific locations is a critical skill to master because you need to do it for just about every task for which you will use your computer. The Mac desktop provides many ways for you to get to the specific folders you want to view and work with. Two of the most useful ways are the Sidebar and the Go menu. Starting from the Sidebar and using the Column view, you can quickly get to any location on the desktop. With the Go menu, you can easily jump to many locations that you commonly visit, along with locations typically hidden on the desktop.

Move to Locations on the Desktop

Go Places with Column View

1 Open a new Finder window.

2 Click **Column View** (▥) if the window is not already in Column view.

3 Select a starting point such as your Documents folder or a disk.

4 Click the first folder whose contents you want to view.

Ⓐ The contents of that folder appear in the column immediately to the right of the folder you selected.

5 Click the next folder you want to move into.

Ⓑ The contents of that folder appear in the column immediately to the right of the folder you selected.

Note: In Column view, folders have a right-facing arrow at the end of the column; files do not.

6 Keep selecting folders until you get to the specific folder or file you want.

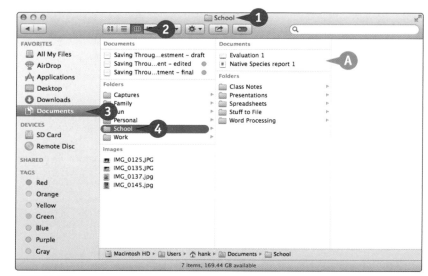

Go Places with the Go Menu

1 Click the desktop.

The Finder becomes active.

2 Click **Go** on the menu bar.

The Go menu opens.

3 Click the location you want to move to.

Note: To go to the Library folder, hold down Option and then click **Library** on the menu. To go to a folder not on the menu, click **Go to Folder** and type the path in the dialog that opens.

A Finder window opens, showing the location you selected.

Go Back to a Recent Folder

1 Click the desktop.

The Finder becomes active.

2 Click **Go** on the menu bar.

3 Point to **Recent Folders**.

The Recent Folders submenu opens.

4 Click the folder you want to open.

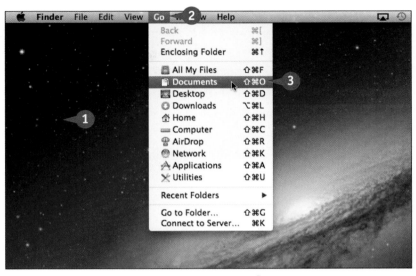

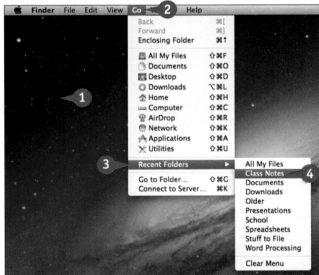

TIP

How can I navigate in the Finder using the keyboard?

The standard folders on the OS X desktop all have keyboard combinations that you can press to jump to them. The following list shows the keyboard combinations for jumping to some of the more useful locations:

All My Files (Shift + ⌘ + F)
Documents (Shift + ⌘ + O)
Desktop (Shift + ⌘ + D)
Downloads (Shift + ⌘ + L)

Home (Shift + ⌘ + H)
Computer (Shift + ⌘ + C)
AirDrop (Shift + ⌘ + R)
Network folder (Shift + ⌘ + K)

Applications (Shift + ⌘ + A)
Utilities (Shift + ⌘ + U)

Rename Files and Folders

You can change the name of your files or folders as you need to. Just as when you create them, you can change the names to be just about anything you want, using up to 255 characters. Each filename includes a file extension, the part after the period in the name. For example, a Microsoft Word document has a name such as Genealogy.docx, where .docx is the file extension. Unless you are sure what you are doing, avoid changing the file extension, because OS X uses it to associate the file with the application used to open it.

Rename Files and Folders

1 In a Finder window, select the folder or file whose name you want to change.

Note: Do not change the names of OS X system folders and files.

2 Press **Return**.

Ⓐ The name becomes highlighted to indicate that you can change it.

Note: Changing a file extension may change the application with which the file is associated. OS X hides file extensions so you do not inadvertently change them.

3 Type the new name of the folder or file.

4 Press **Return**.

The new name is saved.

Note: To change a file extension, Control+click the file and click **Get Info**. In the Info window, click ▶ next to **Name & Extension**, and then type the new extension. In the confirmation dialog, click **Keep**.

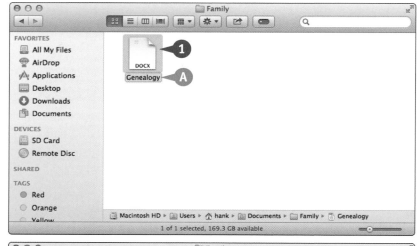

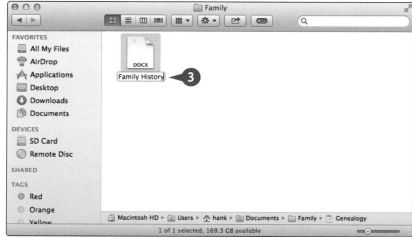

Compress Files and Folders

Files and folders require drive space to store their contents. You can compress them to reduce the space they consume. This is most useful when you transfer these files over a network, especially when you e-mail files as attachments. Not only do compressed files transfer more quickly, but also you can include all the relevant files in one compressed file to make them easier for the recipient to work with. See Chapter 12 to learn how to attach files to e-mail messages.

Compress Files and Folders

Compress Files or Folders

1 In a Finder window, select the files and folders you want to include in the compressed file.

2 Click **Action** (⚙) on the toolbar.

3 Click **Compress.**

OS X creates a compressed file called Archive.zip.

Note: If you compress one file, the Zip file's name is the same as the file you compress.

4 Change the name of the Archive.zip file.

Expand Compressed Files

1 In a Finder window, double-click a compressed file.

Ⓐ OS X expands the file. It stores the uncompressed files in a folder with the same name as the compressed file. If the compressed file contains a single file, OS X does not create a folder.

2 Open the expanded folder to work with the files and folders it contains.

Note: If you no longer need the compressed file, move it to the Trash.

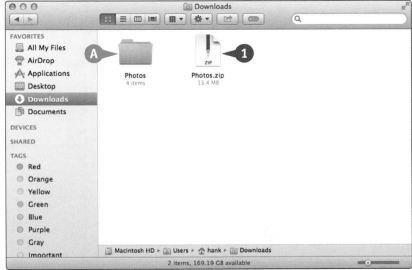

Find Files, Folders, and Other Information

As you use your MacBook Air, you create a lot of data in various documents, images, movies, and other kinds of files. You also interact with e-mail, web pages, and other sources of information. Over time, you might not remember where all this information is. OS X includes tools to help you find the information you need.You can search for files using the Search bar in Finder windows. You can also use Spotlight on the desktop to search many kinds of information at the same time.

Find Files, Folders, and Other Information

Find Files and Folders with Finder

1 In a Finder window, type the information you want to search for in the Search box.

A As you type, the Finder suggests options for how you want to search, such as Name matches or Kinds.

2 Click the option by which you want to search.

B Files and folders that meet your criteria appear in the window.

3 To make the search more specific, click the **Add** button (⊞).

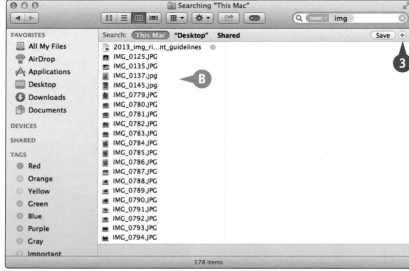

4 Click the arrows to select the criteria by which you want to narrow your search from the pop-up menu.

5 Select the condition.

6 Select other conditions on additional menus that appear.

7 Repeat steps **3** to **6** to add more conditions to your search.

The Finder window shows the files that meet your criteria.

Find Information with Spotlight

1 Click the **Spotlight** icon ( ).

The Spotlight bar appears.

2 Type the information for which you want to search.

C As you type, Spotlight displays matching search results.

3 Point to a result to see more information about it.

D A preview or other information appears.

4 To open one of the found items, click it.

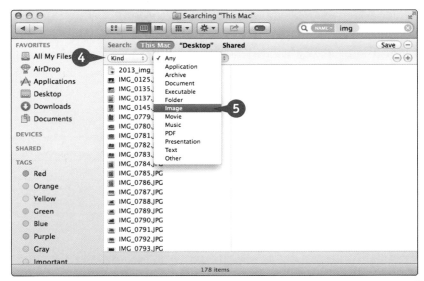

continued ▶ **61**

TIPS

How can I find information not stored on my MacBook Air?
Spotlight automatically searches for items on accessible network folders as well as on your MacBook Air. Beyond this, Spotlight can search the web for you too. In the search results, look for the Web Searches category. Select one of the results in that category to perform a web search for the term you entered.

How can I use keyboard shortcuts for Spotlight?
You can start a Spotlight search by pressing ⌘ + Spacebar . If you click outside the Spotlight window, it closes, but you can easily open it again by pressing ⌘ + Spacebar .

Find Files, Folders, and Other Information (continued)

If you enter a nonspecific search term, Spotlight may return too many results, and you may not find what you want. Use as specific a search term as you can at first, and make it more general if you do not find what you want. You can also configure the items included in searches and the order in which they appear. You can search for help using the OS X Help system or the help systems provided by third-party applications.

Find Files, Folders, and Other Information (continued)

E The item you clicked opens, and you can work with it.

5 To return to the search results, click the **Spotlight** icon again (🔍).

Note: To clear a Spotlight search, click **Clear** (⊗).

Configure Spotlight

1 On the Spotlight menu, click **Spotlight Preferences**.

F The Spotlight pane of the System Preferences application opens.

2 Deselect the check boxes for any categories you want to exclude.

3 Drag categories up or down the list to change the order in which they appear in the Spotlight results window.

4 Choose a keyboard shortcut for the Spotlight menu.

5 Choose a keyboard shortcut for the Show All command.

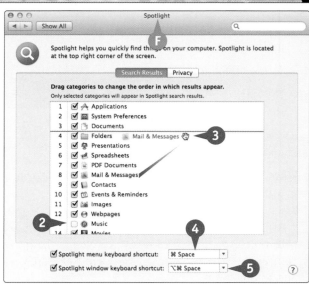

6 Click the **Privacy** tab.

This pane contains a list of folders Spotlight does not search.

7 Add folders or volumes to the list by clicking **Add** (➕) or by dragging them from the desktop or a Finder window into the list.

8 Click **Close** (⊗) to quit the System Preferences application.

Find Help

1 On the Finder menu, click **Help**.

2 Type the information related to the help you need.

As you type, the Mac Help system is searched.

3 To see where a menu item is, point to it.

G The menu opens and a large pointer indicates the menu item.

4 To read a help topic, click it.

H The Help window opens and you see the help topic you selected.

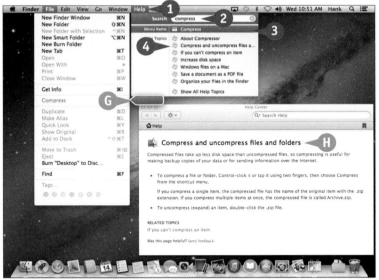

TIPS

What does the Show All in Finder option in the Spotlight results window do?

When you click **Show All in Finder** in the Spotlight results window, a Finder window appears, configured with the search information you entered in Spotlight. You can then add search criteria, save the search, and so on.

Do all applications use the Mac Help system?

All applications are supposed to provide a Help menu that you can use to get help. Apple applications use the Help system provided by OS X so that you can use the same tools to find help in any of these applications.

Create Smart Folders

A *Smart Folder* is a folder with built-in search criteria that make it automatically collect aliases to items that meet the criteria. For example, you can create a Smart Folder for a specific project that includes a key phrase that is part of all the file and folder names related to that project. Whenever you create a folder or file whose name includes that phrase, OS X automatically includes an alias to the folder or file in the project's folder. Each time you open the Smart Folder, you see aliases to all of the files and folders that currently meet its criteria.

Create Smart Folders

① With the Finder active, click **File** and then click **New Smart Folder**.

② Type the text or numbers for which you want to search.

ⓐ As you enter conditions, the Finder suggests options for how you want to search, such as Name matches.

③ Click the option by which you want to search.

Files and folders that meet your search criteria appear in the window.

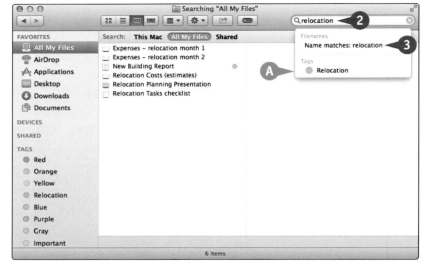

④ In the Search bar, click where the Finder should search.

⑤ Click **Add** (⊞).

A row of condition controls appears.

⑥ Click the arrows and select the criteria by which you want to narrow your search and then select the condition from the pop-up menu.

⑦ To make the search even more specific, click **Add** (⊞).

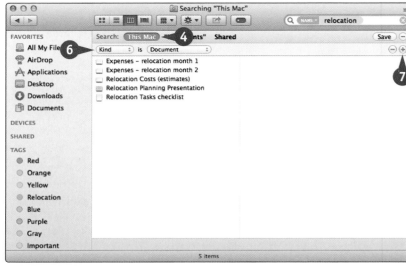

A new condition appears.

8 Click the arrows and select the attribute by which you want to search on the first pop-up menu.

9 Click here and select the operator from the pop-up menu.

10 Configure the rest of the parameters for the condition you created.

11 Repeat steps **7** to **10** to add more conditions to the search until you find all the content you want to include in the folder.

Note: To remove a condition, click **Remove** (⊖).

12 Click **Save**.

13 Type the name of the folder in the Save As field.

14 Click the arrows and select a save location from the pop-up menu.

15 Deselect the **Add To Sidebar** check box (☑ changes to ☐) if you do not want the folder to appear in the Favorites section of the Sidebar.

16 Click **Save**.

Whenever you open the Smart Folder — for example, by clicking its icon on the Sidebar — you see all the files and folders that currently meet its search criteria.

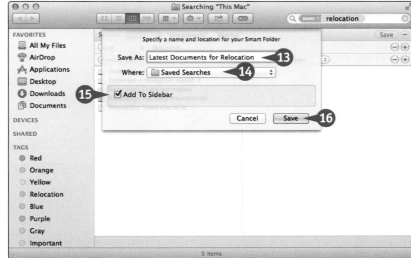

TIP

Where is the Saved Searches folder?
When you accept the default location in which to store your smart folders, they are saved in your Saved Searches folder. To access this folder, click the **Go** menu. Press and hold **Option**, and then click **Library**. You will see the Saved Searches folder in the Library folder. If you do not save your searches on the Sidebar, add the Saved Searches folder to your Dock or to the Sidebar to make moving back there easier.

Get Information About Files and Folders

Finder windows show essential information about the files and folders on your MacBook Air. To see more details about any file or folder, you can use the Finder's Get Info command. This command opens the Info window, which provides a lot of detailed information about what you have selected. The information in this window depends on the type of item you selected. For example, you see a different set of information when you select an application file than when you select a document.

Get Information About Files and Folders

1 In a Finder window, select a file or folder you want to get information about.

2 Click **File**.

3 Click **Get Info**.

The Info window opens. This window consists of several different sections that you can expand or collapse as needed.

4 Click a section's disclosure triangle to see the information it contains (▶ changes to ▼).

Note: In addition to viewing information about a file or folder, you can use the Info window to make changes to a file or folder. For example, the following steps show you how to change the application used to open a file. You can do other tasks as well, such as change the permissions for an item or enter comments or tags for searches.

Note: To view information about multiple items at once, use the Inspector window. Select the items, Control+click in the selection, press Option, and then select **Show Inspector**.

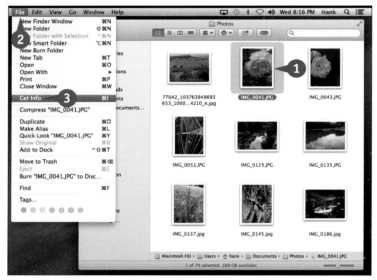

5 Click **Add Tags**.

The Tags list appears.

6 Click each tag you want to apply to the file.

Note: You can use the Inspector window to apply tags to multiple items at the same time.

7 Click the **Open with** disclosure triangle (▶ changes to ▼) to expand the section.

8 Click the **Open with** pop-up menu and select the application in which you want the document to open.

9 Click **Change All** to open all documents of the same type in the application.

10 When you are done viewing or changing information, click **Close** (●) to close the Info window.

Note: You can leave the Info window open as long as you want, and you can have many Info windows open at the same time, which makes comparing items easy.

What are Comments?

The Comments section appears at the top of the Info window. You can enter text in this field to associate that text with an item. When you search your MacBook, OS X includes this information in the search.

What is the Sharing & Permissions section used for?

Here, you see each person or group who has access to the item along with the permissions each has. You can use the controls in this section to change the access people or groups have to the item. First, click the **Lock** icon (●) and enter an administrator username and password. Second, use the pop-up menus to change privileges and **Add** (➕) or **Remove** (➖) to make changes.

Organize Your Files and Folders with Tags

You can organize your files and folders by giving them descriptive names and storing them in appropriate places. But OS X, its apps, and iCloud give you another means of organizing your files and folders: tags. OS X includes a set of default tags that you can customize to better describe your projects. Applying one or more tags to a file enables you to locate it more easily in the Finder, iCloud, or apps. You can use tags to pull together related files from across your MacBook's file system and your iCloud account.

Organize Your Files and Folders with Tags

Customize Your Tags

1 Click the desktop.

2 Click **Finder**.

3 Click **Preferences**.

4 Click **Tags**.

5 Click a tag you want to rename, and then type the new name.

6 Select the check box (☐ changes to ☑) to make the tag appear in the list in the Finder.

7 Drag the tags into the order in which you want them to appear.

8 Drag tags to the Favorite Tags list at the bottom to control which tags appear in Finder menus.

9 Click **Close** (⊗).

The Finder Preferences window closes.

Your customized tags appear in the Tags list in the Sidebar in the Finder.

Apply Tags to Files and Folders

1 If the Tags section of the Sidebar is not displayed, move the mouse pointer (🔖) over Tags and click **Show** when it appears.

2 Click the file or folder you want to tag.

3 Drag the file or folder to the appropriate tag in the Tags list in the Sidebar.

OS X applies the tag to the file or folder.

Note: You can also apply tags from the File menu or from the contextual menu.

View Files and Folders by Tags

1 Click the appropriate tag.

A The Finder window shows the tagged files and folders.

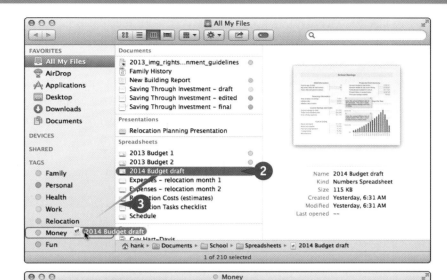

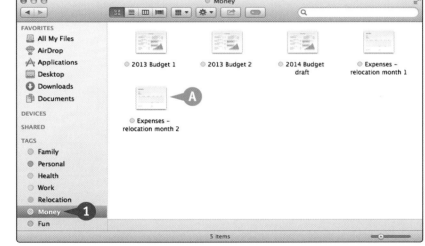

TIP

How do I apply tags to a new document I create?

1 In the app, click **File** and **Save** or press ⌘+S.

2 Type the file name.

3 Click **Tags** and then click the tag to apply.

4 Choose the folder.

5 Click **Save**.

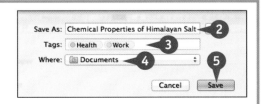

Understanding Applications and Documents

The main reason to use a computer is to run applications, which enable you to do all sorts of useful things, such as create text documents, analyze spreadsheets, edit and view photos and movies, browse the web, create presentations, send and receive e-mail, play games, and so on. Many types of applications are available for OS X, so you can choose applications that provide exactly the functionality you need. To enable you to use them easily, all applications share fundamental concepts and tools. Understanding them will help you use a wide variety of applications on your MacBook Air.

Applications

An *application* is a compilation of programming statements, more commonly called *code*, constructed according to a specific programming language. Applications give you an easy way to interact with the detailed code: You control what the application does using the menus and graphical elements of the user interface instead of having to create the lines of code anew each time you want to do something. Applications vary greatly in size, complexity, and purpose. For example, Microsoft Excel is a large application you can use to create spreadsheets containing billions of

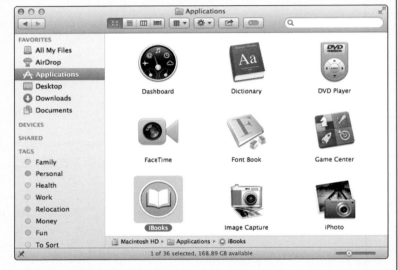

items of data, whereas a Dashboard widget is a tiny application that performs a limited task, such as showing you weather information.

Documents

Most applications work with documents. A document is much more than just a text file; documents can certainly contain text, but they can also be images, e-mails, and songs. Basically, a *document* is the content an application works with. So, for a text processor such as Microsoft Word, a document can include text and graphics. A graphics application, such as Photoshop, uses images as documents. The songs and video stored within iTunes can also be considered documents. If you open or save a file with an application, that file can be called a document.

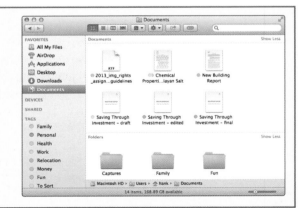

Windows

Chapter 2 explains the various kinds of windows you see on your MacBook Air. As that chapter mentions, applications provide windows through which you view documents, or controls and functions when an application does not work with documents — for example, in a game that runs full screen. An application's windows are whatever you see when you open and use that application. Most applications allow you to have many documents open at the same time, with each appearing in a separate window.

Standard Menus

Applications contain commands that you use to perform actions. For example, when you want to save changes to a document you are working on, you use the Save, Save As, or Save a Version command. Commands are organized into logical collections on menus. When you open a menu, you can see and choose the commands it contains. Most OS X applications have a set of standard menus that contain similar commands; these menus include the *Application* menu, which bears the application's own name, the File menu, the Edit menu, the Window menu, and the Help menu. These menus also contain sets of standard commands; for example, the application menu always contains the Quit command. Most applications also have other menus that give you access to the other available commands. Some applications, mostly games, do not include standard menus at all.

Application Preferences

Not everyone uses applications in the same way; everyone has her own preferences. Because of this, applications include preferences that enable you to configure various aspects of how the application looks and works. You can use preferences to enable or disable functions, change the appearance of the application's windows, and so on. In effect, these commands enable you to tailor the way they work to your preferences, thus the name for this type of command. You can set preferences by opening the application menu and choosing **Preferences**.

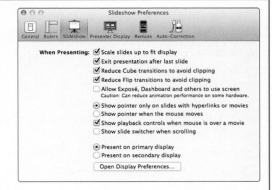

Install Applications from the App Store

The Mac App Store is an online service that provides a wide range of Apple-approved applications for OS X. You have to pay for most of the applications, but some are free. You use the App Store application to download, install, and update applications.

To use the Mac App Store, you need an Apple ID; you sign in to the store using your ID. Your Apple ID contains the payment information you use to purchase applications — for example, the credit or debit card associated with your Apple ID account. This makes the purchase process fast and convenient.

Install Applications from the App Store

Sign In to the Mac App Store

1 Click the **App Store** icon (🔲) on the Dock.

The App Store window opens.

2 In the Quick Links section, click **Sign In**.

3 Type your Apple ID.

4 Type your password.

5 Click **Sign In**.

You sign in to your account and are ready to shop in the App Store.

Browse for and Install Applications from the Mac App Store

1 Click one of the three tabs that enable you to browse for applications: **Featured**, **Top Charts**, or **Categories**.

2 Browse for applications of interest to you.

A You can search for applications by typing search terms in the search box.

3 Click an application's icon to get more information about it.

The application's information screen appears.

4 Read the information for the application; this includes a description, screenshots, user reviews, and so on.

5 To download and install the application, click the button showing the price or the word **Free**.

6 If the application has a license fee, click **Buy** at the prompt; skip this step for free applications.

Note: The App Store may prompt you to confirm the purchase.

OS X downloads and installs the application. You can then launch the application from the Launchpad.

TIP

How can I install applications I obtain through the App Store on more than one Mac without paying for them again?

To install the same application on a different Mac, launch the App Store application on that Mac. Sign in to the account under which you downloaded the application. Click the **Purchases** tab. Click the **Install** button for the application you want to install.

Install Applications from Distribution Files

Although the Mac App Store has many applications, it certainly does not have all the applications that are available. You can add other applications by downloading them from the web and installing them or installing them from a disc. Some applications include an installer program; to install the application, you open the installer and follow the on-screen instructions. Other applications use a drag-and-drop installation method that requires you to drag a folder or file into the Applications folder.

Install Applications from Distribution Files

Install Applications with an Installer

1 Download the application's installer from the Internet or insert the CD or DVD it came on in an optical drive connected to your MacBook Air or a drive you are using via Remote Disc.

2 Double-click the application installer's icon.

3 If prompted to accept the license agreement, click **Agree**.

4 Read the information on the first screen of the installer and click **Continue**.

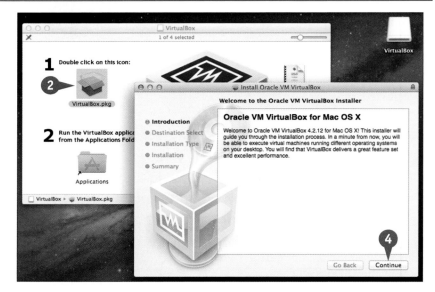

5 On the Install screen, click **Install**.

You are prompted to authenticate yourself as an administrator.

6 Type your username.

7 Type your password.

8 Click **Install Software**.

9 Click the button for closing the installer, such as **Close** or **Quit**.

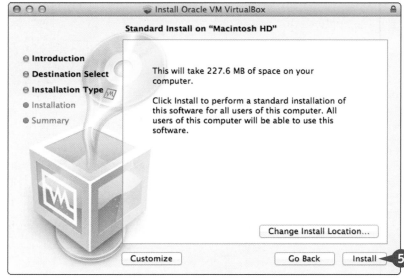

Install Applications with Drag and Drop

1 Download the application's installer from the Internet or insert the CD or DVD it came on in an optical drive connected to your MacBook Air or a drive you are using via Remote Disc.

Note: In most cases, the files are provided as a disk image, which OS X usually mounts automatically. If so, skip step **2**.

2 Double-click the disk image file ending in .dmg.

A OS X mounts the disk image.

3 Drag the application file to the shortcut representing the Applications folder.

OS copies the application to the Applications folder.

4 Click **Close** (⊗).

The Finder window closes.

5 Click **Launchpad** (▦) on the Dock.

The Launchpad screen appears.

6 Click the application's icon.

The application opens, and you can start using it.

TIP

How do I customize an install?

Most installer applications include a Customize button that enables you to customize the application's installation; for example, you can exclude features or resources you do not need. In most cases, you can ignore this and just perform a standard install. However, if your MacBook Air is low on drive space, you might want to use the customization options to see if you can skip features or resources you do not need.

Launch Applications with the Launchpad

The Launchpad provides quick, one-click access to your applications. When you install applications to the Applications folder or one of its subfolders, OS X adds them to the Launchpad automatically. To use an application, you simply open the Launchpad and click the application's icon. To locate applications quickly on the Launchpad, you can organize them in folders. Alternatively, you can simply search for an application by typing the first part of its name.

Launch Applications with the Launchpad

Open Applications from the Launchpad

1 Click **Launchpad** (🚀).

The Launchpad fills the screen. The Launchpad has pages, each of which contains a set of applications.

A The first page has OS X's default applications.

2 To move through the Launchpad's pages, swipe your fingers on the trackpad to the right or left, or press ◄ or ►.

B The applications on the page appear.

C The page you are currently viewing is indicated by the lighted dot just above the Dock.

Note: You can jump to a specific page by clicking its dot.

Note: To locate an app by name, simply start typing its name. As you type, the Launchpad displays only the apps that match.

3 To open an application, click its icon.

Access Applications in Folders

1 If the application you want to use is in a folder, click the folder's icon.

D The folder opens and you see the applications it contains.

2 Click the application you want to use.

The application launches.

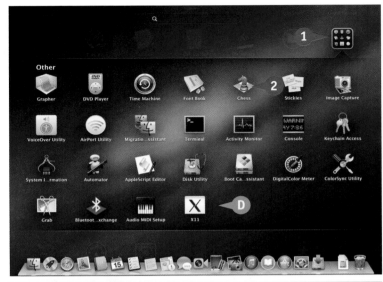

Organize the Launchpad with Folders

1 To create a folder, drag one application's icon on top of another one.

E OS X creates a new folder named after the type of applications you put in it.

2 To rename the new folder, click its name.

OS X highlights the name.

3 Type the new name.

4 Press Return.

TIPS

How can I remove applications?
When you no longer want an application on your MacBook Air, you can remove it. If the application included an uninstaller application, run the uninstaller application to remove the application from your MacBook Air. If it does not include an uninstaller, just drag the application's icon into the Trash. You cannot remove the applications that come with OS X.

How can I get an application that I have removed back?
To restore an application, you need to reinstall it. If you got it from the App Store, move to the **Purchases** tab and click **Install**. If you installed it from an install application, run the installer again. If you saved a copy of the disk image, use that to reinstall the application.

77

Launch Applications from the Desktop

The first step in using an application is to open it, which is also called *launching* it. You can do this in many ways, and as you use MacBook Air, you will no doubt develop your preferred method. It may be the Launchpad described in the last section. However, the Launchpad is just one way to open applications. You should try other ways to launch applications too; you have probably already used some of them. Over time, you will probably find that some methods work better for you than others.

Launch Applications from the Desktop

Open Applications from the Dock

1 Click an application's icon on the Dock.

A When the application has loaded, its windows appear. You can start using the application.

Open Applications from the Sidebar

1 Click the desktop.

The Finder becomes active.

2 Press ⌘+Shift+A.

A Finder window opens with the Applications folder displayed.

3 Click the application you want to add to the Sidebar.

4 Press ⌘+Control+T.

B The application's icon is installed in the Sidebar and is ready to use.

5 Repeat steps **1** and **2** for all the applications you want to be available in the Sidebar.

6 To launch the application, click its icon in the Sidebar.

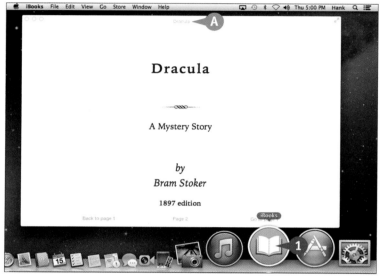

Open Applications from the Applications Folder

1 Click the desktop.

2 Click **Go** and then click **Applications**.

Note: You can also click **Applications** on the Sidebar to move into that folder.

C The Applications folder appears in a Finder window.

3 Scroll in the window until you see the application you want to open.

4 Double-click the application's icon.

Open Applications from Documents

1 Open a Finder window showing the folder that contains the document.

2 Double-click the document's icon.

The application with which the document is associated opens, and you see the contents of the document.

Note: To open the document with a different application, Control+click the document's icon, click or highlight **Open With**, and then click the appropriate application on the Open With submenu.

TIP

Why do some applications disappear from the Dock when I quit them?

Only applications whose icons are kept in the Dock appear there at all times. When you open an application that is not kept in the Dock, its icon appears on the Dock; when you quit the application, its icon disappears from the Dock. To keep the icon on the Dock, Control+click it, click **Options**, and then click **Keep in Dock**.

Control Applications

N̲o doubt you will find lots of applications to be very useful. Fortunately, you can have multiple applications running at the same time, such as Mail, Safari, iTunes, and so on. This means you do not have to waste time opening and closing applications; you can leave them running until you do not need them anymore. Once applications are running, you can control them in a number of ways. You can switch between them, hide them, minimize their windows, and eventually, quit them.

Control Applications

Switch Applications

1 Open several applications.

2 Press and hold ⌘, and then press Tab.

A The Application Switcher appears, showing an icon for each currently running application.

B The application you were last using is highlighted in the white box.

3 Click the application you want to display. Alternatively, continue to hold ⌘ and press Tab until the application you want to use is highlighted, and then release ⌘.

Hide Applications

1 Click *Application* and then click **Hide.**

OS X hides all the application's windows, and the menu bar displays the menus for the application you used before this one.

Minimize Application Windows

1 Click **Minimize** (▭).

OS X shrinks the window to a thumbnail and places it at the right end of the Dock.

Switch Applications with Mission Control

1 Swipe down on the trackpad with the gesture you configured for Mission Control to activate it. Alternatively, press **F3** or Control+⬆.

C Thumbnails of the Dashboard, your spaces, and the applications in Full Screen mode appear.

D Thumbnails of the applications that are open on the current desktop appear.

E The windows that are open in an application appear as individual thumbnails.

2 To move into an application, click its icon if it is Full Screen mode, or move onto the desktop on which its windows are shown and click the thumbnail into which you want to move.

Quit Applications

1 Click *Application*.

2 Click **Quit** *Application*.

Note: You can also quit an application by pressing ⌘+**Q**.

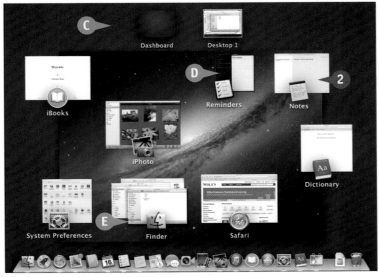

TIP

How do I handle an application that does not appear to be doing anything, although a spinning wheel appears on the screen?

Occasionally, an application hangs. Let some time pass to see if the application starts working again. If not, click **Apple** () and click **Force Quit**. Click the application having problems and then click **Force Quit**. Click **Force Quit** again. You lose any unsaved changes, so do this only as a last resort.

Save Documents

After creating a new document, you save it to a location and assign it a name. When you subsequently change the document, you need to save the changes. If an application quits before you save changes, you may lose all the changes you have made, so you should get in the habit of saving documents frequently. OS X supports *versioning* of documents, which means you can save multiple versions of a document in the same file and return to earlier versions as needed. But only some applications support versioning; not all applications that run on OS X do.

Save Documents

Save New Documents

1 Open the application with which you want to create a new document.

Note: Some applications automatically create a new document when you open them. In other applications, you click **File** and then **New** to create a new document.

2 Click **File**.

The File menu opens.

3 Click **Save**.

The Save As dialog opens.

4 In the Save As field, type a name for the document.

Note: If the Save As field shows the filename extension — for example, *.docx* for a Word document — leave it as is.

5 Click in the Tags field.

The Tags list appears.

6 Click each tag you want to apply.

7 Click **Expand Dialog** (▼).

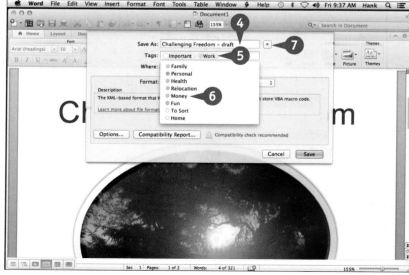

The dialog expands so that you see more details.

8 Select the location in which you want to save the file.

Note: You can choose save locations from the Where pop-up menu just under the Tags field.

A In many applications, you can click the Format pop-up menu to change the format used for saving the file.

B You can show the filename extension by deselecting the **Hide extension** check box (☑ changes to ☐).

The filename extension is appended to the filename.

9 Click **Save**.

The application creates the document file in the location, and you can work in the document.

Save an Existing Document

Note: This section applies only to applications that do not support OS X's Version feature.

1 Open a document and work with it using its associated application.

2 Click **File**.

3 Click **Save**.

The application saves the document in its current state, and the new version replaces the previous version you saved.

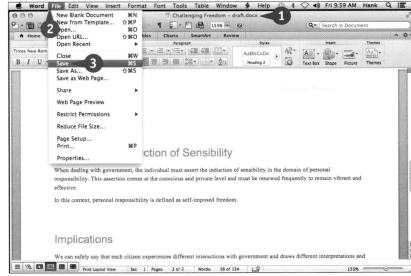

TIP

Can my documents be saved automatically?
If an application supports OS X's Version feature, it saves your documents automatically. Open the application's Preferences dialog and look for the save preferences. Set them to save frequently so as to reduce the number of changes you will have to redo if the application crashes.

Work with Versions of Documents

Applications that support OS X's Version feature automatically save documents as you change them. Each time an application saves a document, it creates a version. Applications create versions at least every hour, and more frequently when you are making "significant" changes to the document. You can also save a version at any time. Versions are useful because they enable you to go back to a previous edition of a document. OS X saves hourly versions for 24 hours. Daily revisions are available for a month, after which time weekly versions are available.

Work with Versions of Documents

Save a Version of a Document

1 Click **File**.

2 Click **Save**.

The current version of the document is saved and becomes available in the document's version history.

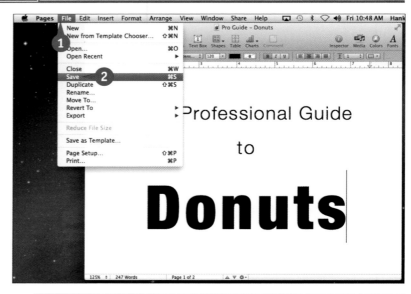

Restore a Previous Version of a Document

1 Open the document for which you want to recover a version.

2 Click **File**.

The File menu opens.

3 Click **Revert To**.

The Revert To submenu opens.

4 Click **Browse All Versions**.

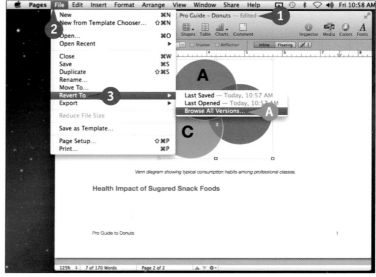

The available versions of the document fill the screen.

Ⓐ On the left, you see the current version of the document.

Ⓑ On the right, you see the saved versions, with the most recent facing you and the older versions behind it. The date and time shown under the document is for the frontmost version.

Ⓒ To the right is the timeline history of the document from the frontmost version back to the oldest version (from bottom to top).

⑤ To move back to a previous version, click in the windows behind the current one or click the timeline.

Ⓓ The version you selected comes to the front.

⑥ To compare the versions, scroll up and down in each window.

⑦ To restore the frontmost version, click **Restore**.

The version you selected replaces the one you were working on.

Note: To return to the version of the document you were working on, click **Done**.

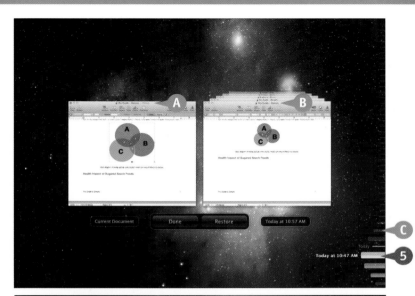

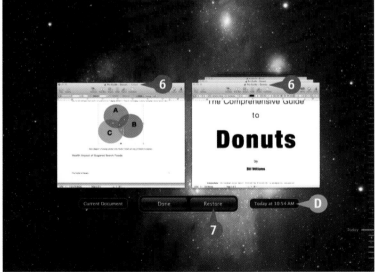

TIP

How does versioning relate to Time Machine?
Time Machine automatically backs up files every hour. So, the most amount of working time at risk is one hour. Versioning also saves documents every hour, and also saves them when a significant amount of changes have been made. So if a problem occurs with the current version of a document and you made changes over the past hour, try reverting to a previous version instead of restoring from Time Machine.

Expand an Application to Full Screen Mode

Almost all Apple applications, and some third-party applications, support OS X's Full Screen mode. In this mode, the application fills the entire desktop, giving you the maximum amount of room. OS X even hides the menu bar to make as many pixels available for you as possible.

Expand an Application to Full Screen Mode

1 Click the Dock icon for the application you want to use. For example, click **iPhoto** ().

The application opens.

2 Click **Full Screen** ().

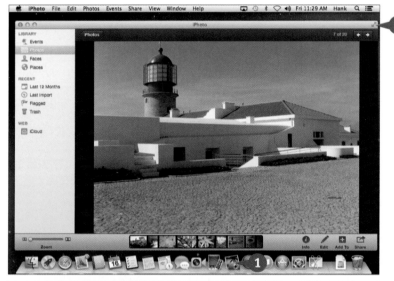

The application fills the screen.

A To access the application's menu bar, point to the top of the screen and the menu bar will appear.

3 To exit Full Screen mode, press **Esc**.

Note: You can also exit Full Screen mode by moving the mouse pointer () to the top of the screen and then clicking **Exit Full Screen** () on the menu bar that appears.

Work with Multiple Application Windows

M any applications allow you to have multiple windows open at the same time. For this to be effective, you must understand how to easily move between the windows open in the application you are using. Like so many other tasks, there are multiple ways to work with more than one window at a time.

Work with Multiple Application Windows

Managing Windows with App Exposé

1 Swipe three or four fingers — depending on your trackpad setting — down the trackpad.

Note: On the keyboard, you can press Control+ ⬇ + F3 .

A App Exposé shows you thumbnails of all the open windows in the application at the top of the screen.

B Thumbnails of the windows and related files appear at the bottom of the screen.

2 Click the window you want to display.

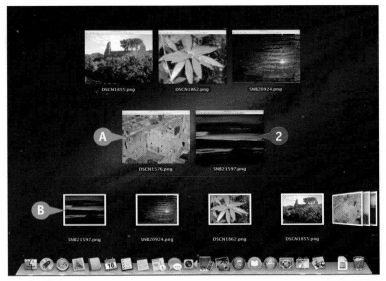

Managing Windows with the Windows Menu

1 Click **Window**.

C The check mark indicates the current window.

D A diamond indicates a minimized window.

2 Click the window you want to display.

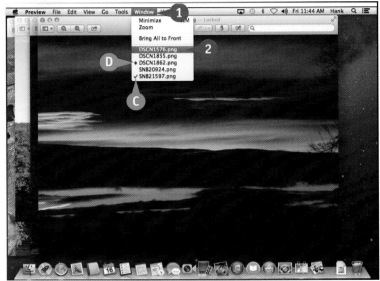

Set Finder Preferences

The Finder is the application that controls the OS X desktop, how files and folders are managed, and many other aspects of the way your MacBook Air operates. Like most applications, the Finder has a set of preferences you can configure to change the way it looks and works. You change Finder preferences using its Preferences command. The Preferences window has several tabs that you use to configure specific aspects of how the Finder looks and behaves.

Set Finder Preferences

1 Click the **Finder** menu and select **Preferences** to open the Finder Preferences window.

2 Click the **General** tab.

3 Select the **Hard disks** check box, the **External disks** check box, the **CDs, DVDs, and iPods** check box, or the **Connected servers** check box (☐ changes to ☑) if you want icons for these items to appear on the desktop.

4 Click the **New Finder windows show** pop-up menu (⬍) and select the default location for new Finder windows. For example, click **Documents** to open your Documents folder.

5 If you want each folder to open in a new tab in the current window rather than in a new window, select the **Open folders in tabs instead of new windows** check box (☐ changes to ☑).

6 If you want folders to spring open when you drag icons onto them, select the **Spring-loaded folders and windows** check box (☐ changes to ☑). Drag the slider to set the timing.

7 Click the **Tags** tab.

Note: You can apply tags to files and folders to help you identify and organize them more easily. To apply a tag, Control+click the file or folder, and then select the color of the tag you want to apply.

8 Type a name for each tag in the field next to its color.

9 Drag the tags into your preferred order.

Note: When you apply a tag to a file or folder, the color appears for quick reference.

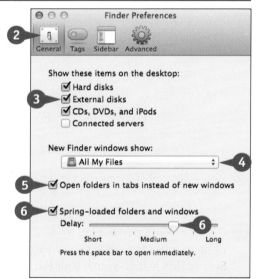

10 Click the **Sidebar** tab.

11 Select each item to choose whether it appears in the sidebar (□ changes to ☑) or not (☑ changes to □).

Note: You can access all the items in Finder windows even if you do not display them in the Sidebar.

12 Click the **Advanced** tab.

13 Select the **Show all filename extensions** check box (□ changes to ☑) if you want the Finder always to display all filename extensions.

14 Select the **Show warning before changing an extension** check box (□ changes to ☑) to receive a warning when you change a filename extension. This is normally helpful.

15 Select the **Show warning before emptying the Trash** check box (□ changes to ☑) if you want to confirm the Trash should be emptied.

16 Select the **Empty Trash securely** check box (□ changes to ☑) if you want the Trash to be emptied securely, making things you delete harder to recover.

17 Click the **When performing a search** pop-up menu (⬒) and select the default search scope. Choose **Search This Mac** to search your MacBook Air, **Search the Current Folder** to search the active folder, or **Use the Previous Search Scope** to repeat your last search.

Note: You can change the scope of any search regardless of the default scope setting.

18 Click **Close** (⊗).

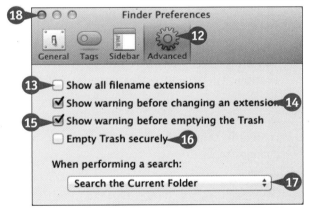

TIPS

Which folder should I use as my start folder for new Finder windows?

Choose whichever folder you find most convenient — for example, the folder you keep your most important documents in. Click the **New Finder windows show** pop-up menu (⬒) and select **Other**. In the dialog that opens, click the folder you want to use, and then click **Close**.

What is another way to apply tags to folders and files?

Open a Finder window showing the folder or file you want to label. Press ⌘+ⓘ. The Info window opens. Expand the General section. Click the tag color that you want to apply. You can apply as many tags as you want.

Explore the System Preferences Application

The System Preferences application enables you to configure many different aspects of how your MacBook Air looks and works. By using System Preferences, you can make OS X look and work the way you prefer. System Preferences is one application organized in many different panes, with each pane used to configure a specific aspect of your MacBook Air. You open the pane you want to use to configure a specific area. For example, you use the Dock pane to configure the Dock, and the Network pane to specify how the MacBook Air connects to a network.

Explore the System Preferences Application

Open and Use System Preferences

1. Click **Apple** (🍎) on the menu bar.

   The Apple menu opens.

2. Click **System Preferences**.

A. The System Preferences application opens, showing an icon for each pane it contains.

3. Click the icon for the pane you want to open.

B. The pane you chose appears.

4. Use the controls on the pane to make changes to the way OS X works.

5. When you finish making changes in the pane, click **Show All**.

   The open pane closes and you see all the icons again.

Show Panes Alphabetically

1 Click **View** on the menu bar.

The View menu opens.

2 Click **Organize Alphabetically**.

C System Preferences displays the icons organized alphabetically instead of by category.

Note: Click **View** and then click **Organize by Categories** to switch back to Category view.

Search for a Pane

1 To search for a pane, type text in the search bar.

D As you type, a highlight appears on each pane that meets or is related to your search criteria.

2 Click the relevant topic.

E You can also click a highlighted icon to display its pane.

System Preferences displays the pane containing the settings.

How can I change settings when they are disabled?

You must be an administrator to make some changes to settings using the System Preferences application. To determine who can change settings, look at the lower-left corner of a pane. If no lock icon appears, any user can change the pane. If a closed lock appears (🔒), click it and verify that you are an administrator by entering your username and password. If an open lock appears (🔓), you can already make changes.

Why do I see a section called Other in my System Preferences application?

Some software you install, such as software for configuring hardware devices, includes a pane installed on the System Preferences application that you use to configure that software or hardware. OS X places all these additions in the Other category.

Change General Preferences

Using the General pane, you can configure the color of buttons, menus, and windows along with the color used when something is highlighted to show that it is selected. You can also configure how scrolling in windows works. You also use the Appearance pane to determine how many items are stored on Recent menus. You can also control how font smoothing works. *Font smoothing* makes the edges of large letters and numbers look smoother on the screen — they sometimes can look pixelated or "jaggy."

Change General Preferences

Choose Finder Appearance and Colors

1 Open the System Preferences application and click **General**.

2 Click the **Appearance** pop-up menu (▣), and select **Blue** to see the default button, menu, and window colors.

Note: Click **Graphite** for a more subdued color for these items.

3 Click the **Sidebar icon size** pop-up menu (▣) and select **Small**, **Medium**, or **Large**.

4 Click the **Highlight color** pop-up menu (▣) and select the highlight color that appears for a selected file or folder.

5 To create your own highlight color, click **Other** on the **Highlight color** pop-up menu.

The Colors window opens.

6 Click the type of color picker you want to use, such as the **Color Wheel**.

Ⓐ The controls for the color picker you selected appear in the window.

7 Use the controls to choose the color you want to use.

8 Click **Close** (⊗).

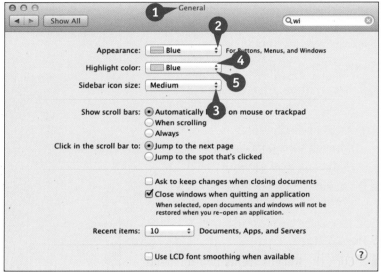

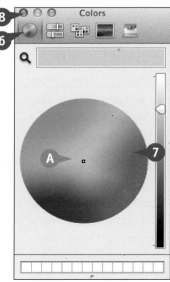

Configure Scroll Tools and Document Behavior

1 In the Show scroll bars area, select **Automatically based on mouse or trackpad**, **When scrolling**, or **Always** (◯ changes to ◉).

2 In the Click in the scroll bar to area, select **Jump to the next page** or **Jump to the spot that's clicked** (◯ changes to ◉).

3 Select the **Ask to keep changes when closing documents** check box (☐ changes to ☑) if you want to be prompted when you close a document without saving changes first.

4 Select the **Close windows when quitting an application** check box (☐ changes to ☑) if you want all the open windows in an application to close when you quit an application.

Set Recent Items and Font Smoothing

1 Click the **Recent items** pop-up menu (⬍) and select the number of items you want to show on each of the Recent menus.

2 To apply font smoothing, select the **Use LCD font smoothing when available** check box (☐ changes to ☑).

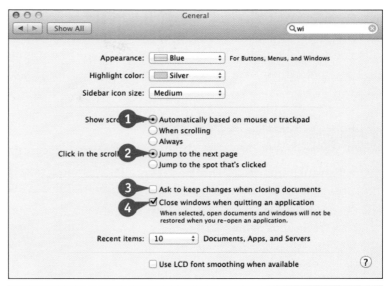

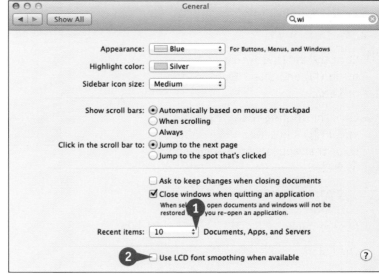

TIP

Which color picker is the best?

The Colors window has different color pickers that change the way you choose colors. The easiest to use is the crayons picker because you simply choose colors by clicking a crayon. The other pickers offer more control and specificity. For example, you can use the color wheel picker to select any color in the spectrum by dragging the intensity bar up or down and then clicking in the wheel to choose a specific color. Other pickers offer different tools.

Set a Desktop Picture

As you use your MacBook Air, you look at the desktop quite often. So why not look at something you want to see? To change what your desktop shows, you set the desktop picture. This picture fills the background on the desktop and you see it behind any open windows. Although it is called a desktop picture, you are not limited to pictures. You can use just about any kind of graphic file as a desktop picture.

Set a Desktop Picture

Set a Default Image as the Desktop Picture

1 Open the System Preferences application and click **Desktop & Screen Saver**.

2 Click the **Desktop** tab.

3 Choose a source of images in the left pane of the window, such as the **Desktop Pictures** folder.

Ⓐ The images in that source appear in the right pane of the window.

4 Click the image that you want to apply to the desktop.

That image fills the desktop.

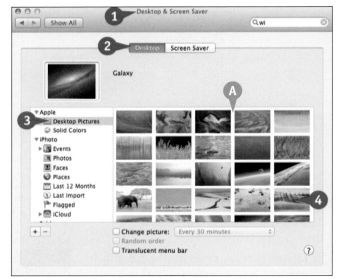

5 To have the image change automatically, select the **Change picture** check box (☐ changes to ☑).

6 Click the pop-up menu (⬍) and select how often you want the picture to change.

7 If you want images to be selected randomly rather than by the order in which they appear in the source, select the **Random order** check box (☐ changes to ☑).

8 If you want the menu bar to show the background through it, select the **Translucent menu bar** check box (☐ changes to ☑).

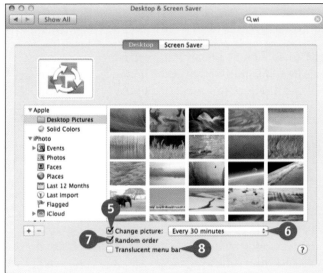

Set a Photo as the Desktop Picture

1 Open the System Preferences application and click **Desktop & Screen Saver**.

2 Click the **Desktop** tab.

3 Click the disclosure triangle (▶) to the left of iPhoto (▶ changes to ▼) to expand the sources it contains.

4 Click the source of photos to use.

Ⓑ The images in the selected source appear in the right pane of the window.

5 Click the pop-up menu (⬍) near the top of the window to choose how you want photos to be scaled to the screen.

6 To have the image change automatically, select the **Change picture** check box (☐ changes to ☑).

7 Click the pop-up menu (⬍) and select how often you want the picture to change.

8 If you want images to be selected randomly rather than by the order in which they appear in the source, select the **Random order** check box (☐ changes to ☑).

9 Click Close (⊗).

Ⓒ OS X applies a new desktop image according to the timing you selected.

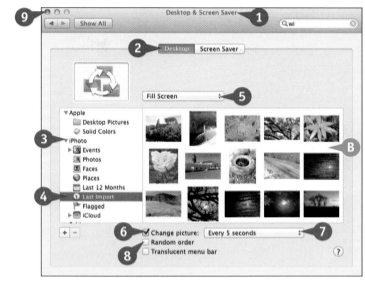

TIPS

What is the Pictures folder source?
The Pictures folder is a folder in your user account's Home folder. By default, various applications store image files in the Pictures folder, so if you choose this folder in the source list, you see all the images the applications have added so far.

What if the location of the photos I want to use as the desktop picture does not appear on the source list?
You can choose any folder as a source of desktop pictures by clicking **Add** (➕) at the bottom of the source list. Use the resulting dialog to navigate to and select the folder containing the images you want. After you click the **Choose** button, that folder appears as a source in the list.

Choose a Screen Saver

Your MacBook Air can display various screen savers when you are not using the screen. While screen savers can provide entertainment, they are most useful for preventing other people from seeing what is displayed on-screen. You can require a password to stop the screen saver, which is a good security measure.

Choose a Screen Saver

Create a Photo Slideshow Screen Saver

1 Open the System Preferences application and click **Desktop & Screen Saver**.

2 Click the **Screen Saver** tab.

3 Click the slide show screen saver you want to use.

Ⓐ You see the selected screen saver run in the right pane of the window.

4 Click the **Source** pop-up menu (🔅) and select the source of images for the screen saver.

5 Select the **Shuffle slide order** check box (☐ changes to ☑) if you want to display the photos in random order.

6 Click the **Start after** pop-up menu (🔅) and select the amount of idle time to allow before the screen saver activates.

7 If you want the time to appear on the screen saver, select the **Show with clock** check box (☐ changes to ☑).

8 Click **Hot Corners**.

9 Click the pop-up menu at the screen corner that you want to set as the hot corner for the screen saver and then click **Start Screen Saver**.

10 Click **OK**.

11 Point to the hot corner you set.

You see the screen saver in action.

12 Press a key or drag on the trackpad to stop the screen saver and go back to the System Preferences application.

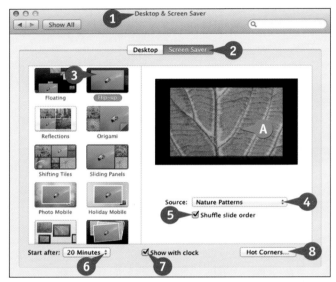

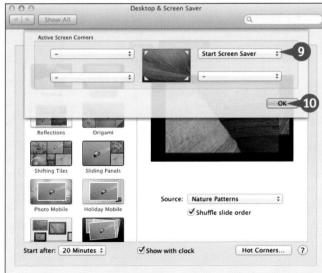

Choose a Default Screen Saver

1 Open the System Preferences application and click **Desktop & Screen Saver**.

2 Click the **Screen Saver** tab.

3 Click the screen saver you want to use from the lower part of the list in the left part of the window.

B You see the selected screen saver run in the right pane of the window.

4 Click the **Start after** pop-up menu and select the amount of idle time to allow before the screen saver activates.

5 If you want the time to appear on the screen saver, select the **Show with clock** check box (☐ changes to ☑).

6 Click **Screen Saver Options**.

The Screen Saver Options dialog opens.

7 Choose settings to configure the screen saver.

8 Click **OK**.

9 Click **Hot Corners** and then set the hot corner for the screen saver.

10 Point to the hot corner.

You see the screen saver in action.

11 Press a key or drag on the trackpad to stop the screen saver and go back to the System Preferences application.

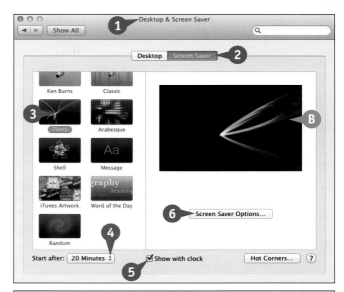

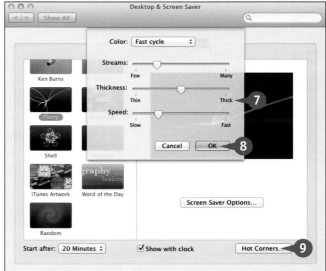

TIP

How can I manually activate the screen saver?

Use the hot corner you set. When you move the pointer to that corner, the screen saver starts. This is especially useful if you have set your MacBook Air to require a password to stop the screen saver. You can start the screen saver and your MacBook Air immediately becomes secured because it is protected with a password.

Set and Configure the Clock

OS X displays the current time at the right end of the menu bar for your reference; it also stamps all the files and folders you use with the time and date they were created, when they were changed, and when they were last opened. So it is important to make sure your MacBook Air has the correct time set. You can set the time and date either manually or automatically using a time server.

Set and Configure the Clock

Set the Clock Automatically

1. Open the System Preferences application and click **Date & Time**.

2. Click the **Date & Time** tab.

3. Select the **Set date and time automatically** check box (☐ changes to ☑).

4. Click the pop-up menu and then click the time server you want to use. If you live in the United States, click **Apple Americas/U.S.**

5. Click the **Time Zone** tab.

6. To have the OS X determine your location automatically based on your Wi-Fi connection, select the **Set time zone automatically using current location** check box (☐ changes to ☑) and skip the rest of these steps. To manually set your location, deselect the **Set time zone automatically using current location** check box (☑ changes to ☐) and select the time zone you want to set on the Time Zone menu.

Note: If you select the automatic option, the rest of the controls are disabled.

Ⓐ The time zone you select is indicated by the light band on the map and the text next to Time Zone.

7. Open the **Closest City** pop-up menu and choose a city in the same time zone as your location.

When your MacBook Air is connected to the Internet, it sets the time and date automatically.

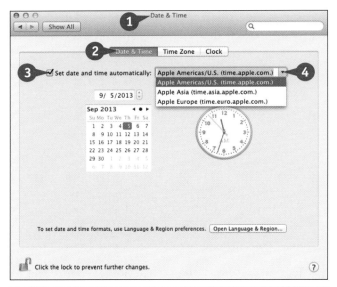

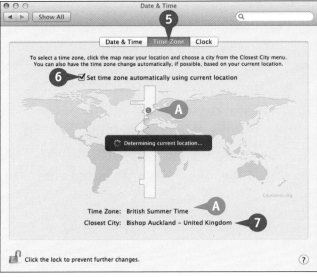

Configure the Clock's Options

1 Open the System Preferences application and click **Date & Time**.

2 Click the **Clock** tab.

3 If you want to see the clock on the menu bar, select the **Show date and time in menu bar** check box (☐ changes to ☑).

4 To see the time in the digital format, select **Digital** (◌ changes to ◉); to see it in analog format, select **Analog**.

5 If you want to see seconds in the time display, select the **Display the time with seconds** check box (☐ changes to ☑).

6 To flash the colon between the hour and minutes at each second, select the **Flash the time separators** check box (☐ changes to ☑).

7 To use the 24-hour format, select the **Use a 24-hour clock** check box (☐ changes to ☑).

8 To show the AM/PM indicator, select the **Show AM/PM** check box (☐ changes to ☑).

9 To show the day of the week, select the **Show the day of the week** check box (☐ changes to ☑).

10 To include the date, select the **Show date** check box (☐ changes to ☑).

11 To hear an announcement of the time, select the **Announce the time** check box (☐ changes to ☑).

12 Click the pop-up menu (⬍) and select **On the hour**, **On the half hour**, or **On the quarter hour**.

13 Click **Customize Voice** and use the resulting sheet to select and configure the voice.

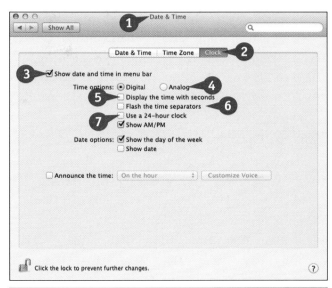

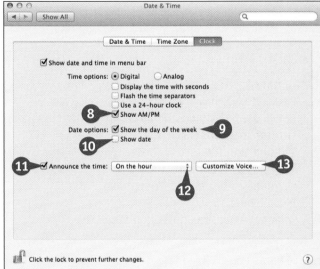

TIPS

What if I take my computer to a different time zone?

If you prefer to set the time manually, change it using the steps on this page. If you use the automatic setting, your MacBook Air updates the time and date based upon the Wi-Fi network to which it is connected.

Save Energy

The Energy Saver pane in System Preferences provides several options you can use to minimize your MacBook Air's power draw, thereby maximizing your work time on the battery. Your options include dimming the display on battery power and adjusting the time before the display goes to sleep. You can also turn on the Power Nap feature, which enables your MacBook Air to wake up periodically to check for new information, and set up a schedule for your MacBook Air to sleep and wake.

Save Energy

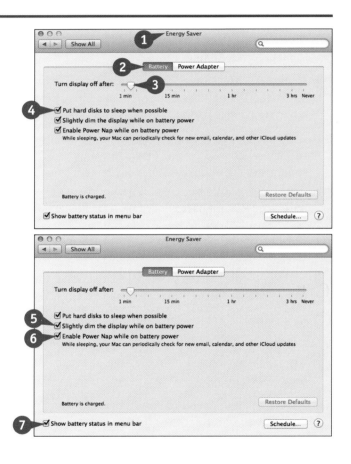

1. Open the System Preferences application and click **Energy Saver**.

2. Click the **Battery** tab.

3. Drag the **Turn display off after** slider to set the idle time before your MacBook Air turns off its display.

Note: The display uses a lot of power. You should set it to sleep after a couple of minutes of inactivity to conserve battery power.

4. Select the **Put hard disks to sleep when possible** check box (☐ changes to ☑) to have OS X put the disk to sleep when it is not in use.

5. Select the **Slightly dim the display while on battery power** check box (☐ changes to ☑) the display to dim slightly while running on battery power.

6. Select the **Enable Power Nap while on battery power** check box (☐ changes to ☑) to use the Power Nap feature.

7. Select the Show battery status in menu bar check box (☐ changes to ☑) if you want to see the battery icon (🔋) in the menu bar.

8 Click the **Power Adapter** tab.

9 Drag the **Turn display off after** slider to set the idle time before your MacBook Air turns off its display.

10 Select the **Prevent computer from sleeping automatically when the display is off** check box (☐ changes to ☑) if you want to prevent OS X from putting your MacBook Air to sleep automatically when the display is off.

11 Select the **Put hard disks to sleep when possible** check box (☐ changes to ☑) to have OS X put the SSD to sleep when it is not in use.

12 Select the **Wake for Wi-Fi network access** check box (☐ changes to ☑) if you want to enable devices connected to your MacBook Air through the Wi-Fi network to be able to wake it up.

13 Select the **Enable Power Nap while plugged into a power adapter** check box (☐ changes to ☑) if you want to use Power Nap while running on the power adapter.

14 Click **Schedule**.

15 Use the **Start up or wake** controls to have your MacBook Air automatically start up or wake up at a specific time.

16 Use the lower controls to have your MacBook Air automatically sleep, restart, or shut down at a specific time.

17 Click **OK**.

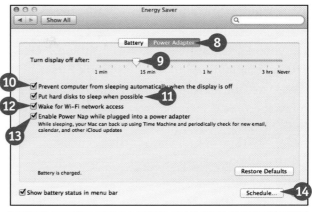

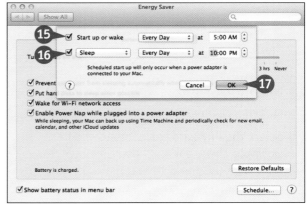

TIP

How else can I make my battery last longer?

Put your MacBook Air to sleep whenever you are not using it; close its lid, press the Power button, or click **Apple** (🍎) and then click **Sleep**. Because the display is a major power drain, lower its brightness by pressing F1 until the screen is as dim as possible while you can still see it comfortably. Turn off Wi-Fi or Bluetooth when you are not using them.

Configure the Display

OS X automatically sets your MacBook Air's bright and beautiful display to its default resolution. This resolution, also called the *native resolution*, is normally the best choice for general use, but you can change the resolution if you prefer. You can also change the resolution for any external display you connect to your MacBook Air. When you change the resolution, OS X changes the size of each pixel, or picture element, that makes up the display's images. Larger pixels make the screen's contents appear zoomed in; smaller pixels make the screen's contents appear zoomed out, so more content fits.

Configure the Display

Configure the Display's Resolution

1. Control+click **System Preferences** ( ) on the Dock.

2. Click **Displays**.

3. Click the **Display** tab.

4. Select **Best for display** (changes to) to use the native resolution. If this setting works for you, skip to step **8**.

5. Select **Scaled** (changes to).

6. Click a resolution.

   The MacBook Air's screen updates to the selected resolution. The current resolution is highlighted on the list.

Note: Notice how much more screen space the Displays pane takes in this figure. This is because the display is set to a lower resolution.

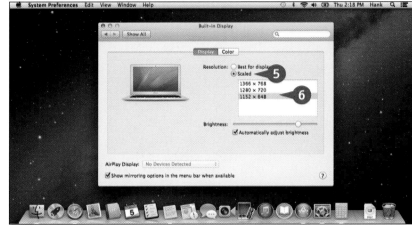

7 Experiment with resolution settings until you find the highest resolution still comfortable for you to see.

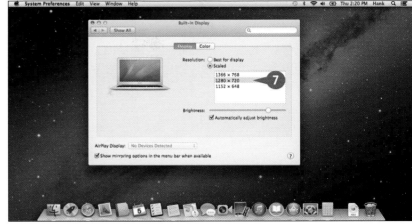

8 Drag the **Brightness** slider to the right to make the screen brighter, or to the left to make it dimmer.

9 To have OS X automatically adjust brightness based on the lighting conditions in which you are using the computer, select the **Automatically adjust brightness** check box (☐ changes to ☑).

TIPS

How else can I set screen brightness?
The MacBook Air includes two keys that you can use to change the screen's brightness. Press F1 to lower the brightness or F2 to increase it. These do the same thing as the Brightness slider on the Displays pane. Each time you press one of the keys, an indicator appears on the screen to show you the relative brightness level you have set.

How do I use the Color tab?
The Color tab is used to configure a color profile for the display. You will not likely need to do this unless you are doing very precise color printing work, in which case, you can configure a screen profile to match your printer output.

103

Control Sound

From sound effects to music and movies, sound is an important part of OS X. Additionally, you may want to use sound input for audio and video chats, to record narration for movies, and so on. The Sound pane of the System Preferences application is your primary stop for managing audio settings on your MacBook Air. Here, you can configure sound effects, choose output settings, and select the input device you want to use.

Control Sound

Configure Sound Effects

1 Open the System Preferences application and click **Sound**.

2 Click the **Sound Effects** tab.

3 Click a sound on the alert sound list.

4 Click the **Play sound effects through** pop-up menu, and select the device through which effects should play.

5 Drag the **Alert volume** slider to set the alert volume.

6 To hear sound effects for system actions, such as when you empty the Trash, select the **Play user interface sound effects** check box (☐ changes to ☑).

7 If you want audio feedback when you change the volume level, select the **Play feedback when volume is changed** check box (☐ changes to ☑).

Configure Sound Out

1 Open the System Preferences application and click **Sound**.

2 Click the **Output** tab.

3 Select the output device for sound.

4 Drag the **Balance** slider to set the left-right balance.

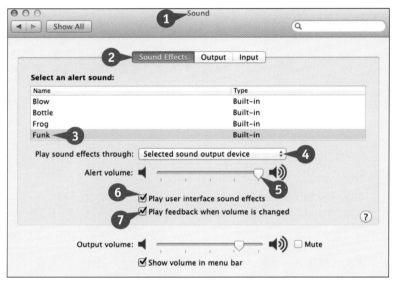

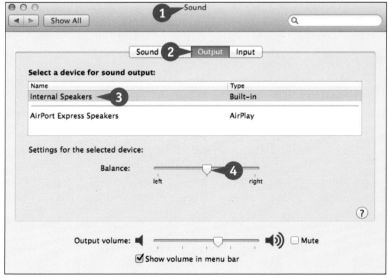

Control System Volume

1 Open the System Preferences application and click **Sound**.

2 Click the **Output** tab.

3 Drag the **Output volume** slider to the right to increase the volume or to the left to decrease it.

4 To mute all sounds, select the **Mute** check box (☐ changes to ☑).

5 To configure the volume menu on the menu bar, select the **Show volume in menu bar** check box (☐ changes to ☑).

Configure Sound Input

1 Open the System Preferences application and click **Sound**.

2 Click the **Input** tab.

3 Click the input device you want to use.

4 Play the sound you want to input.

5 Drag the **Input volume** slider to the left to reduce the level of input sound or to the right to increase it.

6 Keep trying levels until the gauge looks about right, about three-fourths of the length of the bar.

7 If the area you are in is noisy, select the **Use ambient noise reduction** check box (☐ changes to ☑).

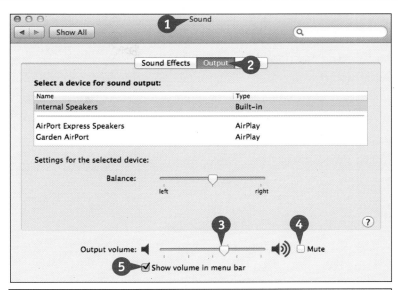

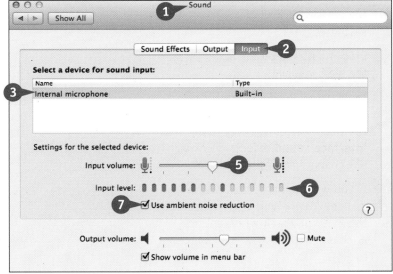

TIP

How can I use external speakers?
You can connect external speakers to your MacBook Air's Headphone/Audio Out port. These can be powered computer speakers or you can use headphones. When you have speakers connected, click the **Output** tab and click the speakers you want to use. Sound will play from those speakers. You can use the controls to configure how it plays. See Chapter 8 for details.

Create and Configure User Accounts

OS X is a multiuser system, so you can create a user account for each person who uses your MacBook Air. Each person who uses it then has a unique desktop, folders, files, and preferences so that the MacBook Air is tailored specifically to her. For yourself, you will already have created an Administrator account, which gives you the power to perform administrative tasks, such as those discussed in this chapter. For most other users, you should create a Standard user account. This type of account can access all the MacBook Air's resources, but it cannot perform administrator tasks.

Create and Configure User Accounts

Create a User Account

1. Open the System Preferences application and click **Users & Groups**.

A. The Users & Groups pane appears. The accounts list on the left side of the window shows the accounts that currently exist.

2. Click **Add** (➕).

3. Click the **New Account** pop-up menu (🔄) and select the type of account. For example, click **Standard**.

4. Type a name for the account.

   OS X creates a shortened account name based on what you enter.

5. Edit the account name as needed.

6. Click **Password** and type the password for the user.

Note: Instead of choosing a password yourself, you can have Password Assistant suggest one. See the tip in this section for details.

7. Click **Verify** and type the password again.

8. Optionally, type a password hint to help the user remember the password.

9. Click **Create User**.

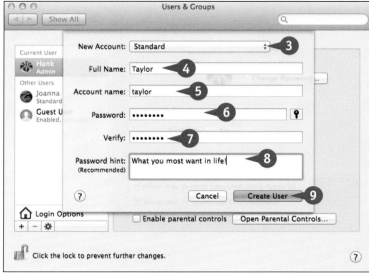

OS X creates the user account and assigns it a default picture.

Ⓑ The user account appears in the list of accounts.

⑩ Click the image well, which contains the default picture OS X has assigned to the account.

⑪ Click the picture you want to use for the account.

Ⓒ Instead of using one of the default pictures, you can click **iCloud** to use one of the pictures you have stored in iCloud.

Note: You can also drag a picture to the image well from iPhoto, a Finder window, or your desktop.

Ⓓ You can also click **Camera** and use the camera to take a picture of the person for whom you are creating the account.

⑫ Click **Edit**.

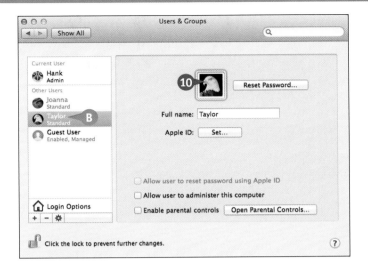

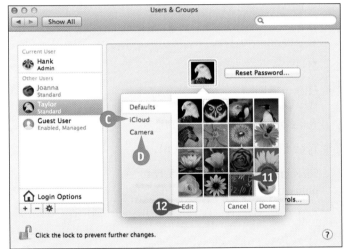

continued ▶

TIP

How can I create a hard-to-crack password?

① Click **Password Assistant** (🔑) in the New Account sheet.

② In the Password Assistant window, click the **Type** pop-up menu (⬆) and select the password type.

③ Drag the **Length** slider to adjust the password length.

④ Click the **Suggestion** pop-up button (▼) and select the suggested password you want to use.

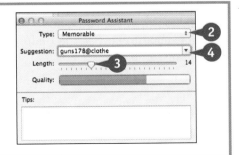

Y ou should have at least two user accounts for yourself. One should be an Administrator account that you use for your regular computing. This can be the account you created when you first set up your MacBook Air. The other account should be an Administrator account that you create but do not use so that it remains in the default state. You use this second account during troubleshooting.

Create and Configure User Accounts (continued)

13 Drag the **Size** slider to the right to zoom in on the image of the user's icon, or to the left to zoom out.

14 Drag the image within the selection box until the part of the image you want to use is enclosed in the box.

15 Click **Done**.

E The image appears on the user's account record.

16 If the user has an Apple ID, click **Set**.

17 Type the user's Apple ID.

18 Click **OK**.

19 Select the **Allow user to reset password using Apple ID** check box (☐ changes to ☑) if you set an Apple ID and want the user to be able to reset his OS X user account password based on his Apple ID.

F You can select the **Allow user to administer this computer** check box (☐ changes to ☑) to change a Standard user to an Administrator user.

20 Tell the username and password you created to the person so he or she can start using your MacBook Air.

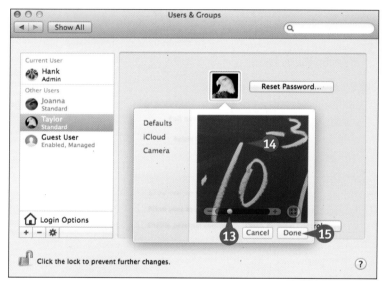

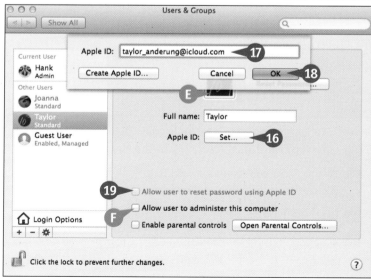

Configure Login Items for a User Account

1 Log in under the user's account.

Note: You must be logged into an account to set Login Items for it.

2 Open the System Preferences application and click **Users & Groups** to open the Users & Groups pane.

3 Click the **Login Items** tab.

4 Select **Hide** check boxes (☐ changes to ☑) for any items you want to be hidden by default.

5 Click **Add** (➕).

6 Navigate to locate and select the application or types of file, such as a document, that you want to open automatically.

7 Click **Add**.

The next time the user logs in, the items you configured open automatically.

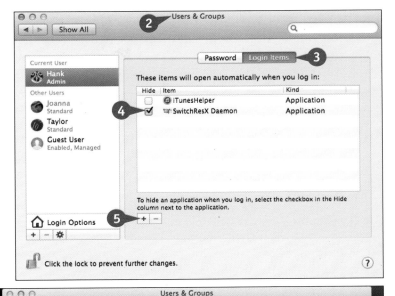

Must I set a password for a user account?
No. If you leave the Password and Verify fields empty, you see a warning that an account without a password is not secure. If you are sure that is not a problem for you, clear the warning prompt and finish setting up the user. The user is able to log in to the MacBook Air without entering a password, which can mean that anyone who has access to the MacBook Air can use it. This leaves your computer vulnerable. If you need to let others use your MacBook Air temporarily without using a password, have them use the Guest account.

Protect Users with Parental Controls

When you need to limit a user account, you can use the parental controls built into OS X. You can use parental controls to tailor any user's access to OS X features and the Internet. Further, you can set up a user account such that the user can use the MacBook Air only during times you specify.

Protect Users with Parental Controls

1 Open the System Preferences application and click **Parental Controls**.

2 Select the Standard user account for which you want to configure Parental Controls.

3 Click **Enable Parental Controls**.

4 Click the **Apps** tab.

Ⓐ You can select the **Use Simple Finder** check box (☐ changes to ☑) to make OS X display a simplified version of the Finder for the user. Simple Finder is helpful for some beginners.

5 To limit a user's access to specific applications, select the **Limit Applications** check box (☐ changes to ☑).

6 Click the **Allow App Store Apps** pop-up menu (⬍) and select the level of apps you will allow the user — for example, click **up to 12+** or **All**.

7 Deselect the check boxes (☑ changes to ☐) for the groups or individual applications you do not want the user to be able to use.

8 Select the **Prevent the Dock from being modified** check box (☐ changes to ☑) if you want to prevent the user from changing the Dock.

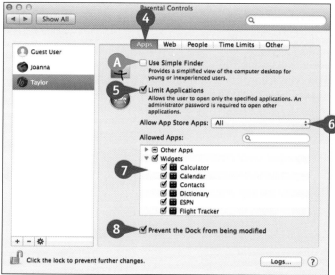

9 Click the **Web** tab.

10 To attempt to prevent access to adult websites, select **Try to limit access to adult websites automatically** (◻ changes to ◉).

11 To limit access to only specific websites, select **Allow access to only these websites** (◻ changes to ◉). In the dialog that opens, click **Add** (＋) and type the URLs to allow.

12 Click the **People** tab.

13 Deselect the **Allow joining Game Center multiplayer games** check box (☑ changes to ◻) if you do not want the user to be able to join multiplayer games in Game Center.

14 Deselect the **Allow adding Game Center friends** check box (☑ changes to ◻) if you want to prevent the user from adding friends.

15 To limit e-mail with Mail, select the **Limit Mail to allowed contacts** check box (◻ changes to ☑).

16 If you want to receive an e-mail requesting permission to e-mail someone not on the Allowed Contacts list, select the **Send requests to** check box (◻ changes to ☑) and enter your e-mail address.

17 To limit messaging with Messages, select the **Limit Messages to allowed contacts** check box (◻ changes to ☑).

18 Click **Add** (＋) and use the Contacts sheet to add contacts to the Allowed Contacts list.

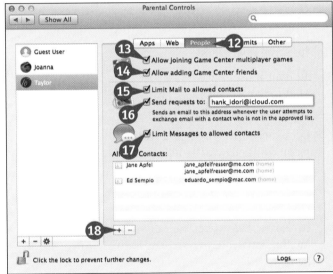

TIPS

What is the Time Limits tab for?
You can use the Time Limits tab to limit the amount of time the user can access the MacBook Air. You can configure time on weekdays and weekends. You can also configure "bedtimes" during which the user is unable to access MacBook Air.

What is the Other tab for?
On the Other tab, you can disable the MacBook Air's camera, disable dictation, hide profanity in the Dictionary application, limit printer administration, disable password changes, and prevent CD or DVD burning.

Set Login Options

By default, the OS X login window displays a list of users in which you click your user name, but you can configure it to display an empty username field instead for greater security. You can also choose whether to display the Sleep, Restart, and Shut Down buttons, and control whether the Input menu and password hints appear. Beyond these options, you can set up automatic login to save yourself the need to log in. You can also turn Fast User Switching on to enable multiple users to be logged into the MacBook Air at the same time.

Set Login Options

Configure Automatic Login

1. Open the System Preferences application and click **Users & Groups**.

2. Click **Login Options**.

3. Click the **Automatic login** pop-up menu (🛟) and choose the name of the user that you want to be automatically logged in.

4. Type the user's password.

5. Click **OK**.

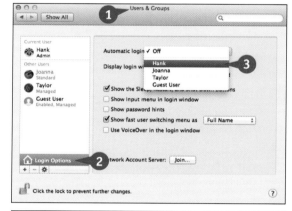

Configure the Login Window

1. Open the System Preferences application and click **Users & Groups**.

2. Click **Login Options**.

3. In the Display login window as area, select **List of users** or **Name and password** (○ changes to ◉).

4. Deselect the **Show the Sleep, Restart, and Shut Down buttons** check box (☑ changes to ☐) if you want to remove these buttons from the login window.

5. Select the **Show Input menu in login window** check box (☐ changes to ☑) if you want to be able to change the input type while logging in.

6. Select the **Show password hints** check box (☐ changes to ☑) to show a hint when a user forgets her password.

7. Select the **Use VoiceOver in the login window** check box (☐ changes to ☑) if you want to have the MacBook Air read the text in the Login window.

Configure and Use Fast User Switching

1 Open the System Preferences application and click **Users & Groups**.

2 Click **Login Options**.

3 Select the **Show fast user switching menu as** check box (☐ changes to ☑).

4 Click the pop-up menu (▤), and select **Full Name** to see the current user's full name at the top of the Fast User Switching menu, **Account Name** to see the user's account name, or **Icon** to see a silhouette.

The Fast User Switching menu appears on the menu bar.

5 Click the **Fast User Switching** menu.

A All the user accounts on MacBook Air appear. A check mark indicates a user is currently logged in.

6 Click the user to switch to.

7 Enter the user's password.

8 Press **Return**.

The user is logged in and his or her desktop appears. The previous user remains logged in; select that user's account on the Fast User Switching menu to move back to it.

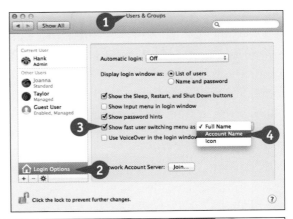

TIP

What happens to running applications when another user logs in using fast user switching?
Because a user does not log out when another one logs in using fast user switching, the applications and processes running under a user account continue to run in the background, even while another user is using the MacBook Air. As soon as the previous user logs back in, the results of the activity that was ongoing appear, such as new e-mails and web pages.

Set Up Internet Accounts

Before you can use the Mail application, you need to set it up with the details of your e-mail account. Similarly, if you use online calendars, contacts, or social networking, you need to set up the accounts for the Calendar application, the Contacts application, or the social-networking application, such as Facebook, Twitter, LinkedIn, or Flickr. You can set up your accounts in the individual applications, but it is usually easier to manage them centrally using the Internet Accounts pane in the System Preferences application. After you set up an account here, other applications that need to access the account can pick up the details without you having to enter them again.

Set Up Internet Accounts

1 Open the System Preferences application and click **Internet Accounts**.

A On the Accounts list, you see the accounts already set up. You may have set them up yourself using the process explained here, or you may have set them up using other applications, such as Mail.

Note: If you click an account to select it, the account's configuration information and tools appear in the right pane. Click **Add** (![+]) to start adding an account, and then click the account type.

2 Click the account type you want to add.

Note: If the account you are creating is not one of those listed, select **Other**.

3 Type your name as you want it to appear in the account.

4 Type the e-mail address for the account.

5 Type the account's password.

6 Click **Set Up**.

The application checks the information you entered.

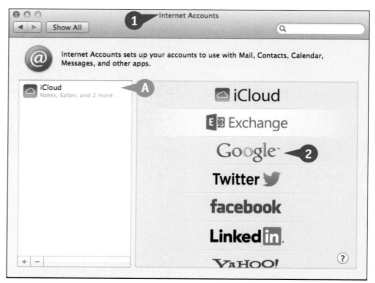

114

If the information is valid, a configuration sheet appears. If not, you are prompted to correct it.

7 Click each service (☐ changes to ☑) you want to use.

Note: The services available vary depending on the account type, but they may include Mail, Contacts, Calendar, Reminders, Messages, and Notes.

8 Click **Done**.

B The account appears in the Accounts list.

Other applications can now use its information.

I do not see the accounts I created in my e-mail application. Why not?

Applications have to be written to obtain account information from the System Preferences application. All of Apple's applications that need it have this capability, but applications from other sources may not. If not, use that application's tools to create and manage accounts in it.

How can I change an account?

Click the account in the Accounts list to display its information in the right pane. Select the check boxes for the services to turn them on (☐ changes to ☑) or deselect them to turn the services off (☑ changes to ☐). Click **Details** and use the resulting sheet to change the account's information. To delete an account, select it and click **Delete** (☐) at the bottom of the Accounts list.

PART II

Getting Connected

A MacBook Air really shines when it is connected to the Internet. As you move around, you need to know how to keep connected without risking the computer or its data. You will also want to connect devices to your MacBook Air. In this part, you learn how to get and keep your MacBook Air connected.

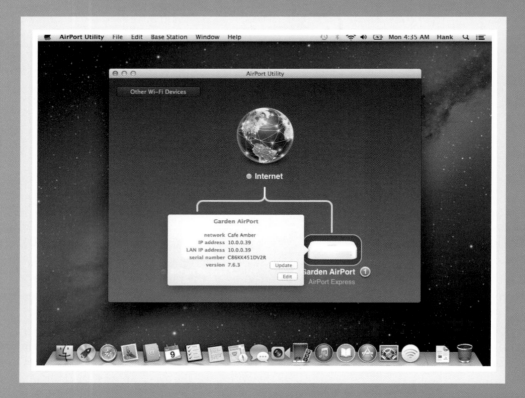

Understanding Networking Concepts

Networking is vital to getting the most out of your MacBook Air. OS X manages most of the details of networking your MacBook Air for you, but it is helpful to understand essential networking concepts as you create your own network.

Network

Simply put, a *network* is two or more devices connected together. A network enables the devices on it to communicate with each other. Devices communicate using various *protocols* to provide different services. For example, the Transmission Control Protocol/ Internet Protocol, or TCP/IP, is the basic "language" that devices speak over the

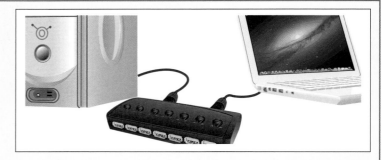

Internet. There are other protocols for a variety of services, but the data for all of these services is communicated over a network. Networks can be large or small, simple or complicated, but they all have the same basic purpose.

Internet

The Internet is the largest existing network because it literally spans the globe, and billions of devices and people are connected to it. The Internet makes communication and information available way beyond anything that was possible before it came to be. For example, you can use the Internet for e-mail, searching the web, chatting online, and transferring files.

Connecting your MacBook Air to the Internet is just about as important as being able to charge its battery.

Local Network

A *local network*, also known as a local area network or *LAN*, is a network that covers a defined physical space. LANs can be quite large, such as a LAN in a business or school, or fairly small, such as a LAN in a home. A LAN connects devices so they can communicate with one another and also connect to outside networks — most

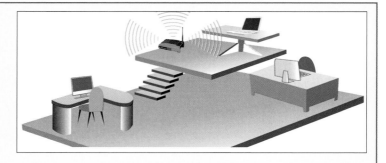

important, to the Internet. This chapter focuses on helping you create a small LAN, such as the ones many people use in their homes. The principles of larger LANs are the same, but the details can get much more complicated.

Ethernet

Ethernet is both a physical means of connecting devices — for example, an Ethernet cable — and the protocol used to communicate over the physical connection. Ethernet can support various communication speeds, including Fast Ethernet at 100 megabits per second (Mbps) and Gigabit Ethernet at 1 gigabit per second (Gbps). You

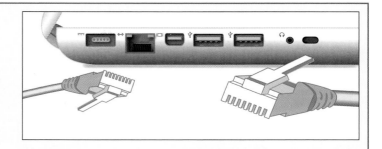

can use a Thunderbolt-to-Gigabit Ethernet adapter or a USB-to-Ethernet adapter to connect your MacBook Air to an Ethernet network. In addition to their speed, Ethernet connections offer other benefits, including simplicity and security. The primary downside to Ethernet is it requires cables to make the physical connection between the devices.

Wi-Fi Network

Wi-Fi is a general term for a set of wireless communication standards and technologies defined in the Institute of Electrical and Electronics Engineers (IEEE) 802.11 specifications. Like Ethernet networks, Wi-Fi enables devices to communicate, but it uses radio transmissios instead of physical wires to connect devices. This offers ease of configuration and makes it possible to move

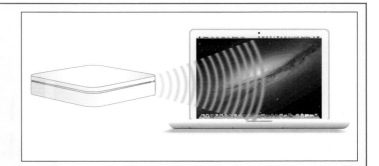

around while remaining on a network. The downsides of Wi-Fi are that it is neither as secure nor as fast as Ethernet networks and is prone to interference from other devices operating in the same band.

AirPort

Apple uses the term *AirPort* for its implementation of Wi-Fi in its wireless base stations, which include AirPort Express, AirPort Extreme, and AirPort Time Capsule. The application used to configure one of these devices is called AirPort Utility. In earlier versions of OS X, the wireless networking capability

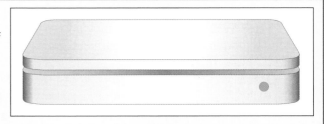

of Macs was called AirPort too, but in OS X 10.7, or Lion, Apple changed the name to Wi-Fi. AirPort is fully compatible with standard Wi-Fi technologies, such as those used for Windows PCs and networking equipment.

continued ▶

Switch/Hub/Router/Access Point

All networks need a device that controls the flow of information among the various computers, printers, and other resources on the network. These devices are called switches, hubs, routers, or access points. They can support Ethernet, Wi-Fi, or both kinds of networks. This chapter focuses on the AirPort base stations from Apple, because they offer powerful features and integrate closely with OS X. However,

because your MacBook Air supports standard Wi-Fi technology, you can use it with other kinds of devices as well. Some of the key features of routers are the capability to share an Internet connection among many devices and to shield those devices from Internet attacks.

Internet Service Provider

To connect to the Internet, you need the services of an Internet Service Provider, or ISP for short. The ISP provides the means that you use to connect your network to the Internet using various connection

technologies, such as cable; Digital Subscriber Line, commonly referred to as DSL; or even satellite.

Internet Account

To access the Internet, you need an Internet account with an ISP. If you access the Internet through a business or school, that organization acts as your ISP. The cost and technical details, such as the connection speed and the amount of server space you get, vary depending on the specific ISP you use. Typically, an ISP requires you to have only one Internet account for your network. All your computers and devices can

connect through your account using your network. You are responsible for maintaining your network and the Internet router, whereas the ISP is responsible for ensuring that the connection from your router to the ISP's equipment is working. Depending on the type of Internet access you use, you might need a username and password to connect to your account, or it might be based on your physical location, as with a cable connection.

IP Address

Each device that connects to the Internet must have an Internet Protocol address, or IP address, that identifies it. An IP address consists of a set of four numbers with periods between each number, as in 169.155.12.3. In most networks, you do not need to worry about the details of IP addresses because the router uses Dynamic Host Control Protocol, DHCP, to automatically assign addresses to devices as needed. You just need to be able to recognize whether or not a device has a valid IP address, which is usually pretty clear because when you do not have one, you cannot connect to the Internet.

Internet Services and Applications

The reason to connect devices to the Internet is to access the services delivered over it. To access these services, you use Internet applications, such as the Mail application for sending and receiving e-mail and the Safari application for browsing the web. Many kinds of services are available on the Internet, and many different applications use each of those services, but you will likely end up using just a few of them. Because OS X includes powerful and easy-to-use Internet applications, they are a good place to start.

Internet Dangers

Although the Internet offers amazing capabilities, it also holds risks and threats. The dangers of Internet life include the annoying, such as pornography and spam, and the truly dangerous, such as viruses, hacking, or identity theft. Fortunately, with some basic precautions and common sense, you can protect yourself from most Internet dangers relatively easily.

Local Network Services

Similar to the Internet, you can take advantage of services that you can provide over your local network. These include file and printer sharing, screen sharing, and messaging. Configuring and using local network services is pretty straightforward because these services are built into OS X.

Obtain an Internet Account

To connect your network or MacBook Air to the Internet, you must have an Internet account. The most common high-speed technologies for homes are cable and DSL. Satellite and cellular connections are also available. Some communities provide free wireless networks that you can use. Before you decide on an Internet account, research the options available where you live, including the monthly cost, installation costs or startup fees, and length of contract of each option. Verify that potential providers support Macs.

Obtain an Internet Account

Determine Your Options

1 If cable service is available to you, contact the cable provider to get information about Internet access.

2 If you have access to a computer connected to the web, go to dsl.theispguide.com.

3 Use the tools to search for DSL access in your location.

4 Contact DSL providers that serve your area to get details about their service, including the monthly cost. Make sure you have potential providers check your actual phone number to ensure that DSL is available.

Note: If cable or DSL is available to you, skip to step **1** in the next section. Satellite is the best option only when cable or DSL is not available.

5 If cable or DSL is not available, access the web and move to www.dbsinstall.com.

6 Follow the links on the DSL provider's website to search for satellite providers of Internet access.

Choose, Obtain, and Install an Internet Account

1 Compare your options.

If you have only one option for a broadband connection, the choice is made for you, and you can skip to step **3**.

2 If you have a choice between cable and DSL, consider which is best for you based on cost, the provider's reputation for service, and other factors.

3 Contact the provider you want to use to obtain an account and schedule installation.

The provider activates your account, and if you choose to have the provider install the router, they schedule an appointment with you. Some providers provide a self-install kit for you to set up.

TIPS

What about dialup Internet accounts?
Internet accounts that you access over a standard phone line and dialup modem are available just about everywhere, though you need to add a USB modem to be able to use one with your MacBook Air. Dialup is very slow and unreliable, and you must connect each time you want Internet access.

If I need an Internet account to connect, why can I use Wi-Fi at public places without an account?
In public places, the organization that controls that place can make a wireless network available to you. Through that network, you can access the organization's Internet account. In some cases, you can do this for free. In others, you need to purchase access from the organization providing the network.

Set Up a Local Network

After you have a working Internet connection, you are ready to build a local network. You can include both wired and wireless devices on the network. The heart of any network is the switch or router you use. The best router choice for most Mac users is an AirPort Extreme or an AirPort Time Capsule because OS X has built-in support for administering the AirPort networks they provide. Also, these base stations shield your network from Internet attacks. The rest of this chapter assumes you are using one of these devices and that you have a working Internet connection and router.

Set Up a Local Network

Install an AirPort Extreme or Time Capsule

1 Connect the output cable of the router to the WAN (wide area network) port on the AirPort.

2 Connect power to the AirPort.

Note: An AirPort Time Capsule is an AirPort Extreme that includes a hard drive. This chapter refers to all three types of AirPort — AirPort Extreme, AirPort Express, and AirPort Time Capsule — as "AirPort" for simplicity.

3 Log in to your MacBook Air.

As long as you have not disabled Wi-Fi, the MacBook Air can communicate with the AirPort wirelessly. You can also connect the MacBook Air directly to one of the Ethernet ports on the AirPort using an Ethernet cable and adapter.

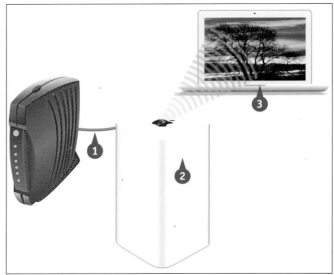

Configure an AirPort

Note: The specific screens and options you see in AirPort Utility depend on the type of AirPort you are configuring and its current status. These steps show a new AirPort Time Capsule.

1 Click **Wi-Fi** (📶) on the menu bar.

2 Click the new AirPort.

The AirPort Utility application opens and connects to the AirPort.

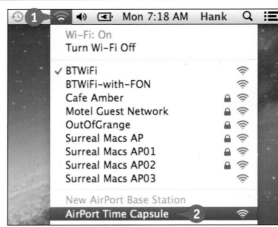

3 In the Network Name box, either accept the default name or type the name you want to use for the network.

4 In the Base Station Name box, either accept the default name or type the name you want to give the AirPort.

5 Deselect the **Use a single password** check box (☑ changes to ☐) if you want to use separate passwords for accessing the network and the AirPort. Otherwise, leave this check box selected (☑) to use a single password for both.

6 Enter the password for the wireless network you are creating in the Password box.

7 Type the password again in the Verify box.

8 Click **Next**.

AirPort Utility prompts you to create a guest Wi-Fi network.

Note: A guest network connects to the Internet but not to the computers and devices on your network. You would use a guest network to give your guests Internet access.

9 If you want to create a guest network, select the **Enable guest network** check box (☐ changes to ☑) and type a name for it in the box.

10 Click **Next**.

AirPort Utility announces the new network is available.

11 Click **Done**.

The Wi-Fi network is ready to use.

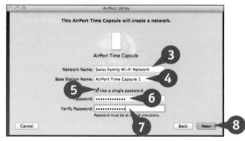

TIPS

What do the lights next to devices in AirPort Utility mean?

The status light next to each device shows you how the device is functioning. A green light means everything is working correctly. A flashing orange light indicates a problem. No light indicates the device is currently not communicating.

What does the Other Options button do?

By default, a new AirPort is set up to provide a wireless network. If you click the Other Options button, you can choose to add the device to another network or to replace an existing device. In most cases, the default choice is what you want to use for a new network.

continued ▶

You can use AirPort Utility to manually configure an AirPort. This is useful when you want to change something about how the AirPort works, such as the name or password of the wireless network. You can configure many different options using AirPort Utility. Some of these options are mostly useful for larger networks; for a home network or other small network, you usually need to set only a few options. This section shows you how to run AirPort Utility and change some of the more useful options.

Set Up a Local Network (continued)

Use AirPort Utility to Configure an AirPort

1 Click **Launchpad** (🚀) on the Dock.

2 Type **a**.

Launchpad displays only the items that include a word starting with *a*.

3 Click **AirPort Utility** (📶).

The AirPort Utility application opens and shows you the devices with which it can communicate.

4 Click the device you want to configure.

The Details pane opens.

Ⓐ If the Update button appears, you can click it to update the AirPort's firmware to the latest version. Updating is usually a good idea, because updates can eliminate bugs or add features.

5 Click **Edit**.

Note: The administrative password is the password you must enter before you can change the AirPort's configuration. It is a good idea to use a different base station password from the password for connecting to the network the AirPort provides.

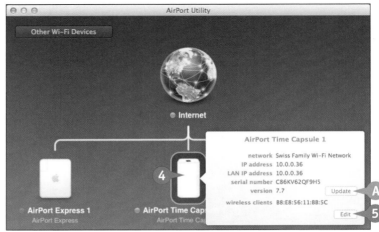

6 Click the **Base Station** tab.

7 If necessary, change the AirPort's name by typing a new name in the Base Station Name box.

8 To set an administrative password for the AirPort, enter it in the Base Station Password box.

9 Type the password again in the Verify box.

10 Select the **Remember this password in my keychain** check box (☐ changes to ☑).

11 Click the **Wireless** tab.

12 If necessary, type a new name for the wireless network the AirPort provides.

13 Click the **Wireless Security** pop-up menu (⬍) and select the security type to use.

Note: WPA2 Personal is normally the best security type for a home network.

14 Type the password for the wireless network.

15 Type the password again in the Verify box.

16 Select the **Remember this password in my keychain** check box (☐ changes to ☑).

17 Select the **Enable Guest Network** check box (☐ changes to ☑) if you want to create a guest network.

18 Type the name for the guest network.

19 Click the **Guest Network Security** pop-up menu (⬍) and select the security type.

Note: Choose **None** if you want your guest network to be open to anyone within wireless range.

20 Enter the password for the guest network if you chose to use security.

21 Click **Update**.

AirPort Utility applies the changes to the AirPort and restarts it.

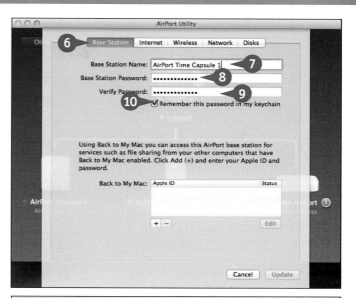

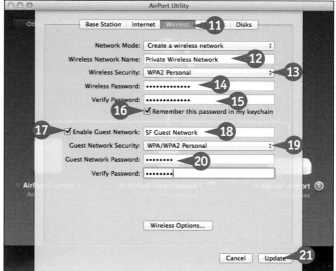

TIP

What is the difference between an AirPort Extreme and an AirPort Express?
The AirPort Express is designed mostly for home use and can play streaming audio through speakers you connect to it. The AirPort Extreme is designed for both home use and business use and cannot play streaming audio.

127

Protect Your MacBook Air from Internet Attacks

The Internet connects you to an unlimited number of people and organizations. This opens you up to Internet attacks ranging from attempts to steal your data or identity to suborning your computer to launch attacks on other computers. You also need to be mindful of the threat from viruses. Fortunately, you can protect yourself with relatively simple steps. An AirPort Extreme or AirPort Time Capsule protects you from most attacks automatically. If you ever connect your MacBook Air directly to your router, such as for troubleshooting, make sure you turn on its firewall before doing so.

Protect Your MacBook Air from Internet Attacks

Enable NAT on Your AirPort

1 Click **Launchpad** (⟦⟧) on the Dock.

2 Click **AirPort Utility**.

3 Click the AirPort you want to configure.

4 Click **Edit**.

5 Click the **Network** tab.

6 Click the **Router Mode** pop-up menu (⟦⟧) and select **DHCP and NAT**.

7 Click **Update**.

AirPort Utility applies the changes to the AirPort and restarts it.

Note: When NAT is active, the only IP address exposed to the Internet is the AirPort's. This shields the devices connected to the Internet through the AirPort from Internet attacks because devices outside your AirPort cannot identify the devices on the network; they see only the AirPort, which cannot be hacked like a computer can.

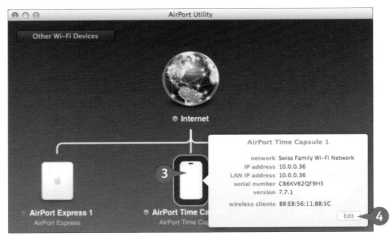

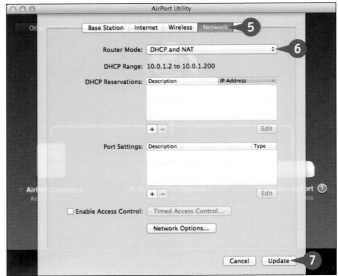

Enable the OS X Firewall

1 Open the System Preferences application and click **Security & Privacy**.

2 Click **Firewall**.

3 Click **Turn On Firewall**.

Note: You must authenticate yourself to configure the firewall.

The firewall starts up and protects your MacBook Air.

Note: Chapter 9 explains performing more advanced configuration of the firewall.

Protect Your MacBook Air from Viruses

1 Get and install an antivirus application.

Note: Most OS X antivirus software is commercial, but you can download a free virus scanner called ClamXav 2 from http://clamxav.com.

2 Configure the antivirus application so that it updates its virus definitions and scans your MacBook Air automatically (see the instructions for the particular application you use).

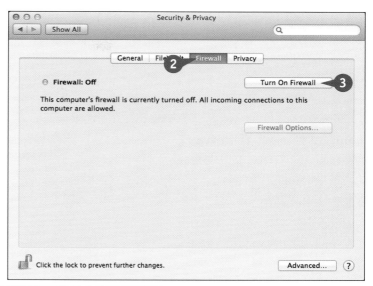

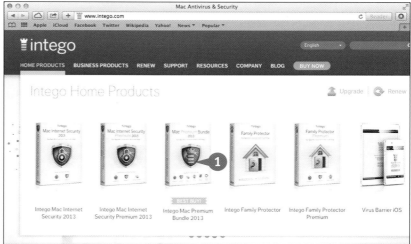

TIP

What other options are there for a wireless network?

If you click the Wireless Options button on the Wireless tab, you can set up a network on the 5GHz channel, which can sometimes help you avoid interference with nearby wireless networks. 5GHz requires your computer or device to have 802.11n or 802.11ac capability; if it cannot see the network, it lacks such capability. You can also manually change the channel of both the regular 2.4GHz channel and the 5GHz channel to avoid interference. You can also hide the network by preventing it from broadcasting its name.

Connect to the Internet with Wi-Fi

With a Wi-Fi connection, you can use the Internet from wherever you are — on the couch at home, in the yard, or anywhere your cellular phone or cellular modem can connect to the cellular network. You use the same steps to connect to a Wi-Fi network outside your LAN, to a Personal Hotspot network or Portable Hotspot network on your cellular phone, or to your cellular modem.

Connect to the Internet with Wi-Fi

Connect to a Wi-Fi Network

1 Open the System Preferences application.

2 Click **Network**.

Ⓐ The left pane shows the available network interfaces.

3 Click **Wi-Fi**.

Ⓑ The Wi-Fi controls appear in the right pane.

4 Click **Turn Wi-Fi On** if it is not on already.

5 Click the **Network Name** pop-up menu (⬍).

6 Click the network you want to join.

7 Type the password.

Ⓒ You can select the **Show password** check box (☐ changes to ☑) to display the password's characters. This can be helpful with complex passwords.

8 Select the **Remember this network** check box (☐ changes to ☑) if you will use this network again.

9 Click **Join**.

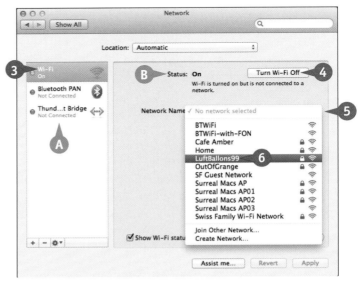

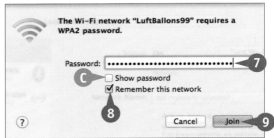

The MacBook Air connects to the Wi-Fi network, and you return to the System Preferences application window. The status of the network becomes Connected.

10 Select the **Show Wi-Fi status in menu bar** check box (☐ changes to ☑) to make the Wi-Fi menu appear on the menu bar.

11 Click **Apply** if this button is enabled.

12 Click **Close** (⊗).

13 Open Safari and go to a web page.

The web page opens, showing that the MacBook Air is connected to the network and the Internet through Wi-Fi.

If the web page does not open, troubleshoot the problem.

Note: See the section "Troubleshoot an Internet Connection" for information on how to troubleshoot connection problems.

Use the Wi-Fi Menu

1 Click **Wi-Fi** (📶).

The Wi-Fi menu opens.

Ⓓ The number of waves on the Wi-Fi menu shows the signal strength. More waves mean a stronger connection.

2 Click the network you want to join.

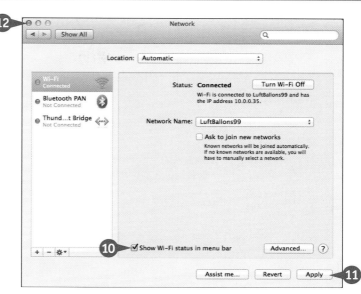

TIP

How can I connect directly to another Mac using Wi-Fi?

Click **Wi-Fi** (📶) on the menu bar and select **Create Network**. Name the network, and then click the **Security** pop-up menu (⬍) and select **128-bit WEP**. Type a 13-character password and click **OK**. Other Mac users can connect to your network using the same steps they use to connect to a network provided by an AirPort.

Connect to the Internet with Ethernet

U sing a Thunderbolt-to–Gigabit Ethernet adapter or a USB-to-Ethernet adapter, you can connect your MacBook Air to a wired network that shares an Internet connection. This gives your MacBook Air access to the Internet through the wired network. You may need to choose settings in the Network pane in System Preferences to make the connection work. This section assumes you are using an AirPort. If you have a different network configuration, the details might be slightly different.

Connect to the Internet with Ethernet

Connect the MacBook Air to an Ethernet Network

1 Connect an Ethernet cable to one of the available ports on the AirPort.

2 Connect the other end to the Ethernet port on the Thunderbolt-to–Gigabit Ethernet adapter or USB-to-Ethernet adapter.

3 Connect the adapter to your MacBook Air.

Configure the MacBook Air to Access the Internet over an Ethernet Network

1 Open System Preferences.

2 Click **Network**.

Ⓐ The Network pane appears.

3 Click **Ethernet** in the left pane.

Ⓑ The status should be Connected. If it is not, the cable is not connected correctly or the AirPort is not working.

4 Click the **Configure IPv4** menu (⯭) and select **Using DHCP**.

5 Click **Apply** if this button is enabled.

6 Click **Close** (⊗).

The System Preferences application closes.

7 Click **Safari** (⚪) on the
Dock.

Safari opens.

8 If Safari does not load a web
page automatically, type a
URL in the address bar and
press `Return`.

C Safari displays the website
when the MacBook Air has
successfully connected to the
network via Ethernet. If it
does not, troubleshoot the
problem.

Note: See the section
"Troubleshoot an Internet
Connection" for information on
troubleshooting connection
problems.

Note: For detailed information
about using Safari, see
Chapter 11.

TIPS

Why use Ethernet when wireless is available?
Wireless connections are great because you are
not tethered to one spot. But Ethernet
connections typically provide better
performance than wireless connections and do
not suffer interference issues. Additionally, an
Ethernet connection is more secure because a
device has to be physically connected to the
network to use it.

**Can I have more than one connection active at a
time?**
A MacBook Air can have multiple connections to
networks active at the same time. You can use the steps
in this section to configure your MacBook Air for
Ethernet access and the steps in the previous section to
configure it for wireless access. OS X chooses the
connection to use at any point in time based on how
you configure it and the connections available.

Using AirDrop to Share Files

The AirDrop feature enables you to share files easily and instantly with nearby Macs. AirDrop automatically locates other AirDrop-capable Macs running OS X Lion or later versions that have Wi-Fi on, that are in range of your MacBook Air, and whose users have their AirDrop folder selected. Your AirDrop folder displays an icon for each Mac using AirDrop; to share files with the person using that Mac, you simply drop the file on that Mac's icon. Likewise, people can share files with you by dropping them on your MacBook Air's icon on their Macs.

Using AirDrop to Share Files

Use AirDrop to Share Files

① Open a Finder window.

② Click **AirDrop**.

③ Ask the people with whom you want to share a file to select AirDrop on their computers.

Ⓐ Your AirDrop icon appears at the bottom of the window.

Ⓑ Each Mac on the same network as your MacBook Air with an AirDrop window active appears above your icon. The Mac's name appears, bearing the image for the active user account.

④ Drag the file you want to share onto another user's icon. You can drag it either from the desktop or from another Finder window.

Note: You can share multiple files at the same time by selecting them and dragging them to the other user's icon.

A confirmation dialog opens.

⑤ Click **Send**.

If the person accepts the file you sent, you get no feedback. If the person declines the file, you see a message to that effect.

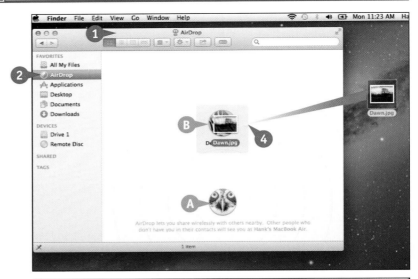

Receive Files via AirDrop

When someone sends you a file via AirDrop, you see a notification showing the source computer's name, the file name, and a preview of its content.

1 Respond to the notification.

C To save the file in your Downloads folder, click **Save**.

Note: Never accept a file unless you are absolutely sure about the computer sending the file to you. If you accept files from people you do not know, your Mac and its data could be in jeopardy.

D To save the file in your Downloads folder and open it, click **Save and Open**.

If you click **Save** or **Save and Open**, you see the file's icon "jumping" from the AirDrop folder to the Downloads icon on the Dock.

E To prevent the file from being moved onto your computer, click **Decline**.

2 If you accepted the file, you can work with it.

TIPS

Why can I not see other Macs in the AirDrop window when I know they are on the same network?
AirDrop must be selected in at least one Finder window on each computer. If a user closes the AirDrop window, you no longer see her icon in the window. As soon as she selects AirDrop, her icon reappears in your AirDrop window. Each Mac must also have AirDrop-compliant hardware.

How can I keep AirDrop available without using up screen space on a Finder window just for AirDrop?
Open a Finder tab and click **AirDrop**. Open other tabs in the Finder window to use them to access files and folders. AirDrop is available, even if the tab is hidden by others.

Share Files on a Local Network

Just like services you access over the Internet, you can provide services over a local network. These include sharing files, printers, and an Internet connection; and iTunes sharing and streaming. Any computers that connect to the network, whether they use Ethernet or Wi-Fi, can access any of the services you make available. File sharing is one of the most useful local network services because you can easily share resources among multiple computers. You can configure your MacBook Air to share files with others, and you can access files being shared with you.

Share Files on a Local Network

Share Files with Others

1 Open the System Preferences application.

2 Click **Sharing**.

Ⓐ The left pane lists the services you can provide over a local network. When you select a service, the tools you use to configure it appear in the right part of the window.

3 Type a name for your MacBook Air in the Computer Name box.

This is the name others on the network choose to access your MacBook Air.

Note: This is the name AirDrop uses for your MacBook, too.

4 Select the **File Sharing** check box (☐ changes to ☑).

File sharing starts.

Ⓑ By default, OS X shares the Public folder for each user account.

5 To share a specific folder, click **Add** (➕).

6 Move to and select the folder you want to share.

7 Click **Add**.

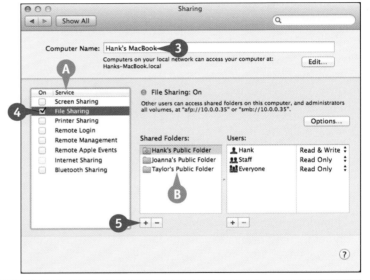

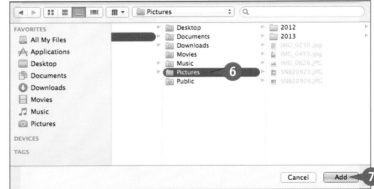

C The folder you selected appears on the Shared Folders list.

8 Click the folder in the Shared Folders list.

9 In the Users list, click the user for whom you want to set access. For example, click **Everyone**.

10 Click the **Access** pop-up menu (▼).

11 Click the access level, such as **Read & Write**.

Note: See the first tip in this section for an explanation of access levels.

12 To configure more users, click **Add** (➕) at the bottom of the Users list.

The Select Users sheet appears.

13 Choose the users for whom you want to configure access.

14 Click **Select.**

The users appear on the Users list.

15 Repeat steps **8** to **11** to configure the user's access to the shared folder.

16 Repeat steps **5** to **14** to share other folders and configure users to access your shared files.

TIP

What are the permissions I can assign to folders that I share?
Assign **No Access** to prevent people from accessing an item at all. Assign **Write Only (Drop Box)** to enable people to place items within the shared folder, but not to view or change its contents. Assign **Read Only** to enable people to view items but not change them. Assign **Read & Write** to enable people to view items, change their contents, and create new items.

continued ▶

When you connect to a local network, your MacBook Air automatically identifies resources on the network that are sharing files. It displays these resources in the Shared section of the Sidebar so that you can access them easily. When you connect to a sharing resource, what you can do with the content of that resource is determined by the permissions that you have been granted for it. For example, if you have Read & Write access, you can use a shared folder just like one you created. If you have Read Only access, you can see its contents, but you cannot change those contents.

Share Files on a Local Network (continued)

Access Files Being Shared with You

1 Open a Finder window.

D The Shared section of the Sidebar shows all the computers sharing files on the network.

2 Click the computer whose files you want to access.

3 Click **Connect As**.

4 To connect as a guest, select **Guest** (not shown) and skip to step **9**.

Note: By default, the Public folder in each user's Home folder is available to everyone on the network.

5 To connect as a registered user, select **Registered User** (◯ changes to ◉).

6 Type the username of the account under which you want to connect.

7 Type the password for the username you typed in step **6**.

8 Select the **Remember this password in my keychain** check box (☐ changes to ☑).

9 Click **Connect**.

Your MacBook Air connects to the resource under the user account you entered.

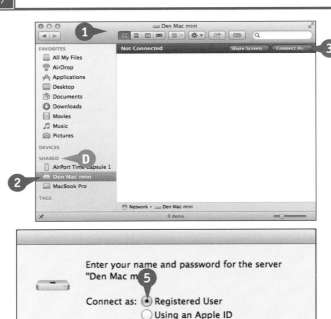

138

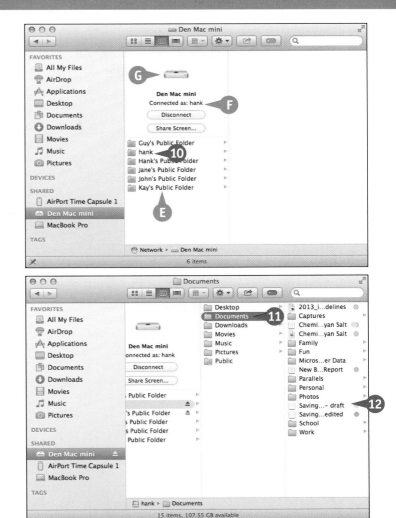

E The Finder window that appears shows the resources available to you based on the kind of access the user account you used has.

F The user account under which you are logged in is shown here.

G At the top of the window, you see the Sharing icon indicating that the resource you are using is stored on a different computer on the network.

10 Open a shared resource.

11 Open folders on the shared resource.

12 Double-click files to open them.

13 To copy a file or folder from the shared resource to your MacBook Air, drag it from the shared resource folder onto a folder stored on your MacBook Air.

TIPS

When are the files that I share available to others?
For people to access files you are sharing, your MacBook Air must be awake and connected to the network. If a MacBook Air is configured to go to sleep automatically, people lose access to shared files when it sleeps unless you select the **Wake for Wi-Fi Network Access** check box (☐ changes to ☑) on the Power Adapter pane in Energy Saver preferences. Likewise, if your MacBook Air is no longer connected to the network, its files are not available.

How can I share files with Windows computers?
Turn on File Sharing by selecting its check box. Click **Options**. Select the **Share files and folders using SMB (Windows)** check box (☐ changes to ☑). Select the check box next to each user (☐ changes to ☑) and type the password for that user's account. The user can access the files by typing **smb://*ipaddress***, where *ipaddress* is the current IP address of your MacBook Air; this address appears in the Sharing pane.

Share Screens on a Local Network

With screen sharing, you can control another Mac on your local network just as if you were sitting in front of it. For example, you can share the screen of a different Mac on your network and run an application on that Mac as if it were installed on your MacBook Air. This is also useful for helping other users on your network because you can take control of the other computer to solve problems. Like file sharing, you must configure screen sharing permissions on each computer to determine who can access this feature.

Share Screens on a Local Network

Configure Screen Sharing on a Mac

1 On the Mac whose screen you want to share, open System Preferences and click **Sharing**.

2 Select the **Screen Sharing** check box (☐ changes to ☑).

3 Click **Computer Settings**.

4 Select the **Anyone may request permission to control screen** check box (☐ changes to ☑) if you want to allow anyone to request to share your screen.

5 Select the **VNC viewers may control screen with password** check box (☐ changes to ☑) and enter a password if you want people using Virtual Network Computing connections to be able to control your MacBook Air.

6 Click **OK**.

7 Select **All users** (☐ changes to ◉) to allow anyone who can access your MacBook Air over the network to share its screen, or select **Only these users** (☐ changes to ◉) to create a list of user accounts that can share your screen.

Ⓐ To create a user list, click **Add** (➕). The User Account sheet appears. Select the user accounts with which you want to share your screen and click **Select**.

Ⓑ The readout below Screen Sharing: On shows the VNC address and computer name for your Mac.

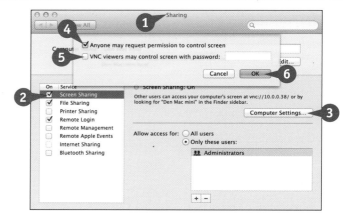

Share Another Computer's Screen

1 Open a Finder window.

2 Click the Mac whose screen you want to share.

3 Click **Share Screen**.

4 Select **As a registered user** (□ changes to ◉).

5 Type your user name for the other Mac.

6 Type your password for the other Mac.

7 Select the **Remember this password in my keychain** check box (□ changes to ☑) if you want to store the password for future use.

8 Click **Connect**.

Note: If a Screen Sharing dialog opens offering you the choice between sharing the display and logging in, click **Share Display**.

C Within the Screen Sharing application's window, which has the other computer's name as its title, you see the other computer's desktop.

9 Within the Screen Sharing window, you can control the shared Mac.

10 When you finish using Screen Sharing, click **Screen Sharing** and then click **Quit Screen Sharing** to quit the application.

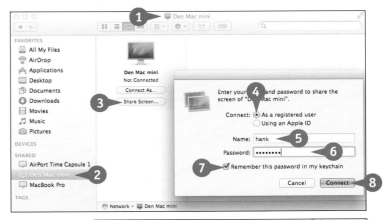

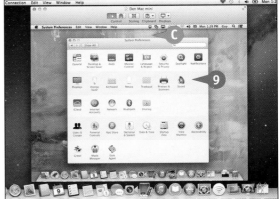

TIP

How can I share another computer's screen if that computer is not on my local network?

You can use the Screen Sharing feature in the Messages application to share screens with your chat contacts or view their screens. If you have an iCloud account, you can use the Back to My Mac feature to access your own Macs across the Internet. On the iCloud pane of the System Preferences application, register your iCloud username and password on each computer among which you want to share screens, and then select the **Back To My Mac** check box (□ changes to ☑) to enable it.

Troubleshoot an Internet Connection

You can troubleshoot your Internet connection if you have problems with it. If an error message appears, determine if the problem is a network issue or if it is related just to one computer by trying the same action on a different computer on the same network.

Troubleshoot an Internet Connection

Troubleshoot a Network Problem

1. Check the status lights on the router to make sure it is working.

   If the router appears to be working, go to step 2. If not, go to step 7.

2. Check the status of the AirPort.

   If the status lights indicate the base station is working, go to step 3. If not, go to step 7.

3. Use a thin, blunt object such as the end of a straightened paper clip to press the Reset button on the back of the AirPort.

4. Try the task that you had a problem with.

   If it is successful, you are done; if not, continue with the next steps.

5. If the router's power light is on but the connection light is not, contact the ISP to make sure service is available. If it is not, you need to wait until service is restored.

6. When you are sure that your Internet service has been restored, restart the AirPort again.

7. Try the task that you had a problem with.

   The problem should be solved.

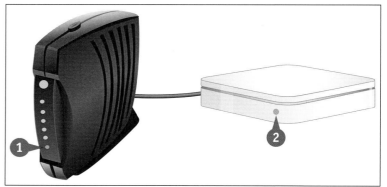

Troubleshoot a MacBook Air Problem

1 Open System Preferences and click **Network**.

2 Check the status of the various connections.

If the status is Not Connected for a connection, you need to reconfigure that connection using the steps outlined in the section "Connect to the Internet with Wi-Fi" or the section "Connect to the Internet with Ethernet."

3 If the status is Connected, click the **Apple** icon (🍎).

4 Hold down Option and click **Restart**.

Note: Option+clicking **Restart** makes OS X restart without displaying the confirmation dialog.

5 After the MacBook Air restarts, try the activity again.

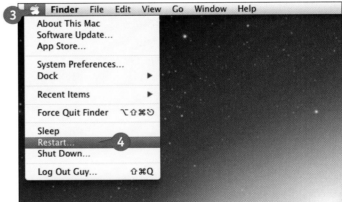

TIPS

How can I get help diagnosing a problem?
Open the Network pane of the System Preferences application. Click **Assist Me**. At the prompt, click **Diagnostics**. Follow the on-screen steps to diagnose the issue. When the application finds a problem, it identifies it and provides some hints about how to solve it. However, using the steps outlined in this section is usually faster because they include most of what the application tells you to do.

What can I do if none of these steps helped?
Visit www.apple.com/support. Search for the problem you are having. Disconnect everything from your network, turn on your computer's firewall, and then connect that computer to the router. If it works, the problem is related to the network; add devices one by one until you find the source of the problem. If the connection does not work, you need help from your ISP.

Expand Storage Space with an External Hard Drive

Your MacBook Air includes a drive on which you store the operating system, applications, and your own files and folders. You can connect an external hard drive to provide more storage space or to back up your files using the OS X Time Machine feature. To get an external hard drive ready to work with your MacBook Air, you first connect the drive to the computer. You then optionally use the Disk Utility application to format and partition the hard drive.

Expand Storage Space with an External Hard Drive

Connect and Power an External Hard Drive

1 Connect the hard drive to a power source and turn it on.

2 Use the appropriate cable to connect the hard drive to the compatible port on the MacBook Air.

Note: Most hard drives include the cable you need to connect to MacBook Air. However, some do not. Check the package information to make sure the cable is included. If it is not, you have to buy a cable separately.

The hard drive is ready to format and partition.

Format and Partition an External Hard Drive

1 Click **Launchpad** () on the Dock.

The Launchpad screen appears.

2 Type **d**.

Launchpad narrows the selection of applications to those beginning with *d*.

3 Click **Disk Utility** ( ).

Disk Utility opens.

Ⓐ The left pane shows all available disks.

④ Click the external hard drive.

⑤ Click the **Partition** tab.

Ⓑ You see the number of partitions the disk currently has.

Note: A new disk typically has one partition.

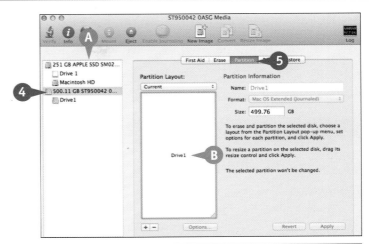

⑥ Click the **Partition Layout** pop-up menu (🔽) and select the number of partitions you want to create on the disk.

Ⓒ Disk Utility divides the space available into the number of partitions you selected, naming the partitions Untitled 1, Untitled 2, and so on.

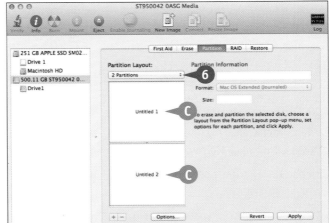

TIPS

What kind of drive works with a MacBook Air?

All current models can work with USB 2.0, USB 3.0, or Thunderbolt drives. For Time Machine, make sure the drive is at least twice as large as the drive in your MacBook Air. You can also use either Mac- or Windows-compatible hard drives.

Which interface is best?

USB 2.0 is the least expensive, but also the slowest. USB 3.0 is faster and a bit more expensive. Thunderbolt is the fastest; you pay a premium for that speed. Another option is to use a FireWire drive with a Thunderbolt-to-FireWire adapter; this is especially useful if you already have a FireWire drive. If you are going to use the drive for active projects, you want the fastest interface you can get, so go with Thunderbolt.

continued ▶

With an external hard drive, you can use the OS X Time Machine feature to back up your important data. You can also back up to an AirPort Time Capsule using Time Machine. Should something happen to the data on your MacBook Air or to the MacBook Air itself, you can easily recover the data from the external drive or the AirPort Time Capsule so that you do not lose files that you can never recover, such as your photos. For more information about Time Machine, see Chapter 17.

Expand Storage Space with an External Hard Drive (continued)

7 Click the top partition.

D The Partition Information section shows the information for the partition.

8 Type a name for the partition in the Name box.

9 Click the **Format** pop-up menu (⬍) and select **Mac OS Extended (Journaled)**.

10 Enter the size of the first partition in the Size box and press **Return**.

Disk Utility names and resizes the partition.

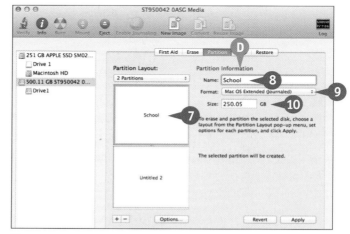

11 Click the next partition.

12 Repeat steps **8** to **10** to name, format, and size the partition.

13 Repeat steps **11** and **12** until you have configured each partition.

14 Click **Apply**.

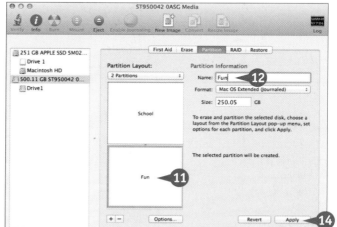

The partition warning appears.

Note: Partitioning a disk erases all the data it contains, so make sure you do not need its data before continuing.

15 Click **Partition**.

16 If the Time Machine dialog appears, click **Decide Later**.

Note: See Chapter 17 for information about configuring Time Machine.

17 Press ⌘+Q to quit Disk Utility.

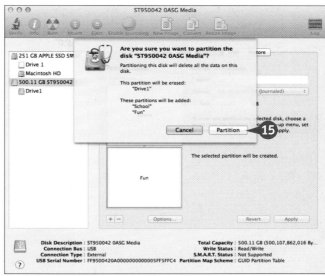

18 Open a Finder window.

E You see the partitions on the external drive, and they are ready to be used just like the MacBook Air's internal drive.

Note: Before disconnecting a hard drive from MacBook Air, click **Eject** (⏏) next to its icon in the Sidebar or press ⏏ and wait for the disk icon to disappear from the Sidebar.

TIPS

Why can I not partition a new hard drive?
Some drives come in a format incompatible with OS X, and the partition process fails while displaying an error message. Before you click **Apply** on the **Partition** tab of the Disk Utility application in step **14**, click **Options**. On the resulting sheet, click **GUID Partition Table** and then click **OK**. The sheet closes. Continue with the rest of the steps as described.

What is a partition and how many should I create on my drive?
Partitions are logical volumes, which means that they behave as if each partition is its own drive, even though they are on the same physical device. You can create partitions for various purposes, such as to organize data. You should use only one or two partitions on a drive to avoid ending up with a lot of partitions too small to be usable.

Connect and Use an External Display

Your MacBook Air screen is as large as will fit within its slim body, but you may sometimes need more screen space to spread out your documents and work with multiple windows at the same time. To add screen space to your MacBook Air, you can connect an external display to it. This enables you to use the MacBook Air's internal display and the external display at the same time. You can use both as a single large desktop, or you can mirror the displays, which means that each shows the same thing.

Connect and Use an External Display

Connect the External Display

1 If required, purchase the Mini DisplayPort adapter needed for the external display.

2 Plug the small end of the adapter into your MacBook Air.

3 Connect the other end of the adapter to the display.

4 Connect the display to a power source, and power it up.

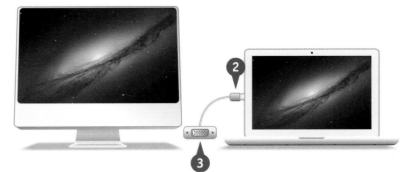

Configure the External Display

1 Open the System Preferences application and click **Displays**.

A Displays pane opens on the MacBook Air display and on the external display.

2 Click the **Arrangement** tab on the Displays pane on the MacBook Air screen.

3 Drag the external display's thumbnail to match the physical location of the display compared to MacBook Air.

4 If you want the external display to be the primary display, drag the menu bar from the MacBook Air display's thumbnail onto the external display's thumbnail.

5 If you want the displays to show the same information, select the **Mirror Displays** check box (☐ changes to ☑) and skip the rest of these steps.

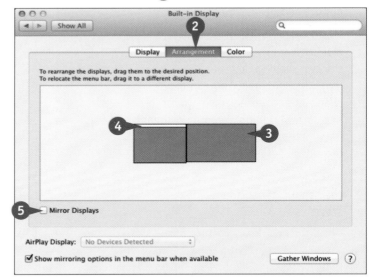

6 Click the **Displays** window on the external display.

7 Click the **Display** tab.

8 Select **Best for display** (⭕ changes to ⦿) if you want OS X to set the resolution. Otherwise, select **Scaled** (⭕ changes to ⦿) and then click the resolution to use.

9 If the **Refresh Rate** pop-up menu (⬍) appears, click it, and select the highest rate available.

10 Click the **Color** tab.

11 Select the color profile for the display you are using.

12 Click **Close** (⬛) or press ⌘ + **Q** to quit the System Preferences application.

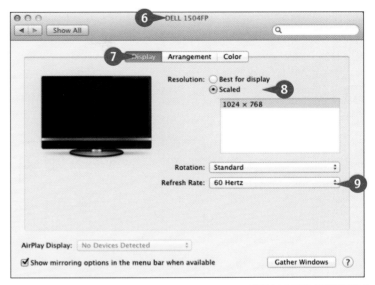

You now can use the external display. When video mirroring is off, the two displays act as a single, large desktop area. You can move windows onto either display. For example, you might keep a document on which you are working on one display and Mail on the other.

When video mirroring is on, you see the same information on both screens.

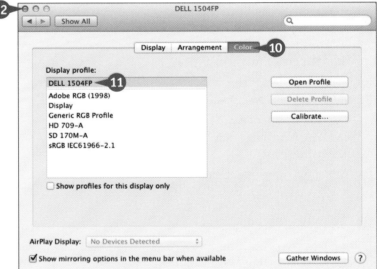

TIP

What kind of external display should I get for my MacBook Air?

The three most important considerations are interface, size, and cost. An Apple Thunderbolt Display gives you a huge screen with great performance and connectivity, but it is expensive. HDMI and DVI displays give a digital picture, whereas VGA translates the signal to analog.

Larger displays are better because they give you more working space. They also tend to be more expensive, although that depends on the specific brand you choose.

Using an Apple TV to Display on an HDTV

With a second-generation or later Apple TV, you can wirelessly broadcast your MacBook Air's display on the device to which the Apple TV is connected. This is great for watching movies or videos on a big-screen TV, enjoying a shared web-browsing session, or giving presentations from your MacBook Air to a group of people.

To broadcast to an Apple TV, your MacBook Air uses AirPlay. This technology enables Macs and iOS devices to send a signal to an Apple TV for it to display on a television.

Using an Apple TV to Display on an HDTV

Set Up the Apple TV for AirPlay

1 Connect the Apple TV to a power outlet and to your television.

2 Connect the Apple TV to a wireless network.

3 Open the Apple TV's Settings screen.

4 Select **AirPlay**.

5 Turn AirPlay on if it is not on already.

Broadcast from a MacBook Air to an Apple TV

1 Click **Wi-Fi** (<svg>) on the menu bar.

The Wi-Fi menu opens.

2 Click the network to which you connected the Apple TV in step **2** in the previous section.

Note: Your MacBook Air and the Apple TV must be on the same network for AirPlay to work.

3 Open the Displays pane of the System Preferences application. For example, Control+click **System Preferences** () on the Dock and then click **Displays**.

4 Click the **AirPlay Display** pop-up menu (⬍).

5 Click the Apple TV you want to use.

Your MacBook Air's desktop appears on the television to which the Apple TV is connected. By default, the same image appears on your MacBook Air and on the television.

6 Select the **Show mirroring options in the menu bar when available** check box (☐ changes to ☑).

7 Click **AirPlay** (🖥) on the menu bar.

The AirPlay menu opens.

8 To match the MacBook Air's desktop to the Apple TV, click the Apple TV's name on the menu.

Your MacBook Air's display adjusts to match the resolution of the Apple TV.

9 When you want to stop broadcasting to the Apple TV, click **Disconnect AirPlay Display**.

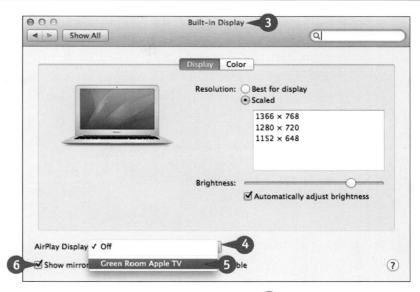

TIP

Why do I not see any AirPlay devices available on my MacBook Air?
First, check the network configuration of each device to make sure all devices are on the same network. Second, the network you are using may not support the protocols AirPlay uses; in some public areas, networks are designed to prevent streaming of content. If you cannot use a different network, see if the available one can be reconfigured to support AirPlay.

Connect and Use Bluetooth Devices

Although your MacBook Air comes fully equipped for mobile computing, you will likely want to connect other devices to it sometimes. When you want to connect a device such as a keyboard, a mouse, or speakers, a wireless technology called Bluetooth is often the easiest and most flexible choice. To connect and manage Bluetooth devices, you use the Bluetooth pane in the System Preferences application. To connect a Bluetooth device for the first time, you pair the device with your MacBook Air. Once you have paired the devices, you can quickly disconnect and reconnect the device as needed.

Connect and Use Bluetooth Devices

1 Turn on the Bluetooth device.

2 Place the Bluetooth device in discovery mode.

Note: Consult the Bluetooth device's documentation for instructions on placing the device in discovery mode.

3 Click **Bluetooth** (🔵) on the menu bar.

The Bluetooth menu opens.

4 Click **Open Bluetooth Preferences**.

The System Preferences application opens, showing the Bluetooth pane.

Note: If the readout in the left pane says *Bluetooth: Off*, click **Turn Bluetooth On**.

Ⓐ The Devices list shows the Bluetooth devices available.

5 Click **Pair** for the Bluetooth device you want to use.

Note: Pairing with some devices may require you to type a code on your MacBook Air's keyboard or on the device itself.

B The Connected readout appears when your MacBook Air has established the connection. You can now use the Bluetooth device.

C You can click **Remove** () if you want to remove the device's pairing from your MacBook Air. This action unpairs the device.

6 Click **Close** (⊗).

The System Preferences app closes.

7 When you want to disconnect the Bluetooth device, click **Bluetooth** (❋) on the menu bar.

8 Highlight the device's name.

9 Click **Disconnect**.

OS X disconnects the device.

TIP

Why does my Bluetooth device not appear in the Bluetooth pane even after I turn on discovery mode?

If you have previously paired the Bluetooth device with another computer or device, you may need to unpair it from that device before your MacBook Air can discover it. For example:

- In OS X, open the Bluetooth pane in the System Preferences application, move the mouse pointer (🔺) over the device in the Devices list, and then

click **Remove** (⊗). Click **Remove** in the confirmation dialog that opens.

- In iOS, touch **Settings** on the Home screen to display the Settings app, and then touch **Bluetooth**. In the Devices list, touch the **Info** button (ⓘ), touch **Forget This Device**, and then touch **Forget Device** in the confirmation dialog.

Connect and Use External Speakers

Your MacBook Air has speakers built in, but they are limited by their tiny size. With iTunes, streaming video, and all the other great applications for which sound is vital, you will likely want to use external speakers with your MacBook Air. You can use a variety of speakers with MacBook Air. The easiest arrangement is usually to use *powered speakers*, also called *computer speakers*. You can also play back audio through speakers connected to an AirPort Express or Apple TV, or connect your MacBook Air to a receiver that drives speakers or connect a pair of analog headphones.

Connect and Use External Speakers

1 Connect the speaker input to the Audio port.

2 Make the connections between the speakers, such as between the left and right speaker and the subwoofer.

3 Connect the speakers to power and turn them on.

4 Open the System Preferences application and click **Sound**.

The Sound pane appears.

5 Click the **Output** tab.

6 In the Select a device for sound output list, click the speakers you want to use.

Note: The Audio port appears as Headphones in the Select a device for sound output list even when you attach a set of speakers.

7 If controls for the speakers appear, use them to improve the sound.

For example, you might be able to set a balance level and system volume level.

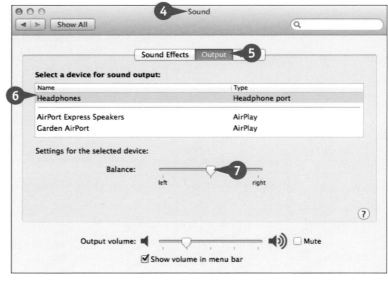

8 Play sound with an application such as iTunes.

Note: For more information about iTunes, see Chapter 18.

9 Use the application's controls to set the specific volume level.

10 Adjust the volume level and other settings using the speaker system's controls.

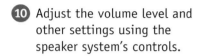

Does a MacBook Air support digital audio?	How can I play audio on an Apple TV or other devices?
Yes. The Audio port on the MacBook Air supports both analog and digital audio. Use a TOSLINK adapter to connect the Audio port to the digital audio cable. When you connect the other end to the speaker system, you can enjoy the benefits of digital, such as surround sound coming from multiple speakers.	You can use AirPlay to broadcast your MacBook Air's audio to an Apple TV, to AirPort Express base stations to which you have connected speakers, or directly to AirPlay-enabled speakers. Set up the AirPlay device and then choose the AirPlay device on the Output tab or in the AirPlay menu in iTunes or another audio source.

Connect to and Use a USB Hub

M any devices use USB to connect to a computer. The MacBook Air has only two USB ports, so you can connect only two devices to it at a time — at least, using direct connections.

For situations in which you want to connect more than two USB devices to your MacBook Air at the same time, you can use an external USB hub. You connect the hub to your MacBook Air and then connect USB devices to the ports on the hub. Your MacBook Air can access these devices just as if they are connected to its USB port. Usually, it is best to get a USB hub with an external power supply, but for travel you may prefer a hub that draws power from the MacBook Air.

Connect to and Use a USB Hub

Obtain an External USB Hub

1 Visit your favorite retailer, either online or in the real world.

2 Look for a USB 2 or USB 3 hub with as at least as many ports as the number of devices you want to connect at the same time.

3 Purchase a hub.

Install a USB Hub

1 Connect the input port on the hub to a USB port on the MacBook Air.

2 Connect the hub to a power source, if required.

3 Connect USB devices to the hub.

The devices are ready to use.

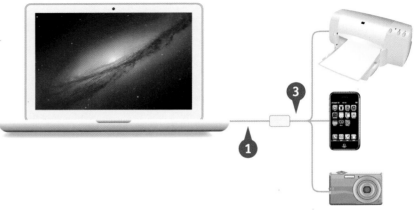

Connect to and Use Ethernet Devices

Your MacBook Air is designed to be wireless when it comes to connecting to many devices — most important, local networks and the Internet. But Ethernet, a wired technology, offers tempting benefits over wireless connections. Ethernet is faster, and so achieves the best network performance. Ethernet is also more secure than wireless because you have to be physically connected to a network to access it.

To connect to a network or a device with Ethernet, you can use a Thunderbolt-to–Gigabit Ethernet adapter or a USB-to-Ethernet adapter. Use an Ethernet cable to connect the adapter to an AirPort, network switch or router, or other Ethernet device, such as a printer.

Connect to and Use Ethernet Devices

1 Connect a Thunderbolt-to–Gigabit Ethernet adapter to the Thunderbolt port on your MacBook Air, or connect a USB-to-Ethernet adapter to a USB port.

2 Connect an Ethernet cable to the Ethernet adapter.

3 Connect the other end of the cable to an Ethernet device, such as an AirPort Extreme Base Station.

4 If your MacBook Air does not establish an Internet connection automatically through the Ethernet cable, open the Network pane in the System Preferences application and configure it.

For example, whereas many Ethernet networks use DHCP, for others you may need to click the **Configure IPv4** pop-up menu (⬍), select **Manually**, enter network details, and then click **Apply**.

Connect to the Internet with Wi-Fi

When you are away from your home network, you can easily connect to the Internet via wireless networks that use the Wi-Fi standards. Many public places, hotels, restaurants, and other businesses provide Wi-Fi networks you can use, either by paying a fee or simply by agreeing to abide by their terms and conditions. Connecting to the Internet using Wi-Fi is a two-step process. First, you establish the connection between your MacBook Air and the network. Second, you register your MacBook Air to access the Internet over the network.

Connect to the Internet with Wi-Fi

Connect to a Wi-Fi Network

1 Click the **Wi-Fi** menu (🛜).

Note: If the lock icon appears along the right side of the window for a network, it is secured and you need a password to join it.

2 Click the wireless network you want to join.

The MacBook Air connects to the network. Depending on the kind of network you are connecting to, you are prompted to join the network by providing required information or by accepting fees or terms and conditions.

3 Type in the required information.

4 Click **Accept** or **Login**.

Typically, you see the home page for the network's provider.

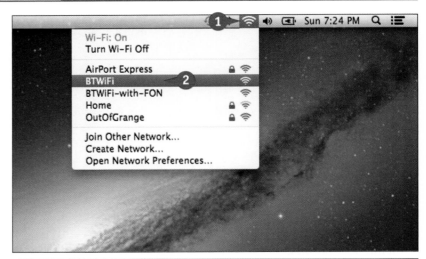

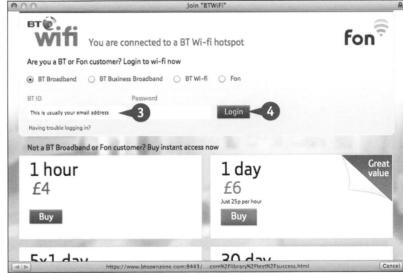

5 Go to any web page.

If the page appears, the MacBook Air is connected to the Internet, and you can skip the remaining steps.

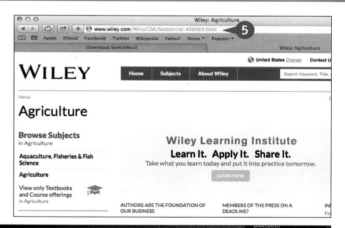

6 If a page does not appear, Control+click **System Preferences** (⬛) on the Dock.

The contextual menu opens.

7 Click **Network**.

The System Preferences application opens and displays the Network pane.

8 Click the **Network Name** pop-up menu (🔼) and select a different network.

What does Wi-Fi stand for?

Wi-Fi stands for "wireless fidelity." It applies to a set of standard protocols used to ensure that wireless devices and the software they use are compatible. The technical specifications fall under the Institute of Electrical and Electronics Engineers (IEEE) 802.11 series. The MacBook Air's wireless capabilities are Wi-Fi or 802.11 compatible so that you can connect to any network or device that uses these standards.

What if there is only an Ethernet connection available?

Some places, such as hotel rooms or meeting rooms, have only an Ethernet connection available. In that situation, you have three options: connect wirelessly through an AirPort Express Base Station connected to the Ethernet network, connect using an Ethernet cable and a Thunderbolt-to-Gigabit Ethernet adapter or a USB-to-Ethernet adapter, or connect wirelessly with a broadband wireless modem. You can find more information on the first and third methods later in this chapter.

Connect to the Internet via AirPort Express

An AirPort Express Base Station is a small, portable wireless base station that you can use to easily create your own wireless networks. For example, if you happen to stay in a hotel that offers only wired Internet access in its rooms, you can use an AirPort Express to quickly create a wireless network for your MacBook Air and your other devices, avoiding multiple access fees.

To set up a temporary wireless network with an AirPort Express, you first connect the device to the wired network. Then you configure the AirPort Express to provide a wireless network.

Connect to the Internet via AirPort Express

Connect the Base Station to the Network

1 Using an Ethernet cable, connect the Ethernet WAN port on the AirPort Express to the wired network.

Note: WAN is the acronym for *wide area network*, a network that covers a much larger area than a local area network, or LAN.

2 Connect the AirPort Express to a power outlet.

Note: This task assumes that the wired network provides an Internet connection using Dynamic Host Configuration Protocol, or DHCP, which automatically configures the network settings. Most such wired networks use DHCP for simplicity.

Configure and Access a Wireless Network

1 On the **Wi-Fi** menu (📶), select AirPort Express.

The AirPort Utility application opens and connects to the base station.

2 Type the name you want to give to the wireless network that the base station will provide.

Note: The AirPort Utility application suggests default names for the network and base station.

3 Type the name by which you will identify the base station itself.

4 Type the network's password in the Password and Verify fields.

5 Click **Next**.

AirPort Utility completes the network configuration and starts providing a wireless network and Internet connection. The MacBook Air connects to the new network automatically.

6 Click **Done**.

The base station provides the wireless network. You can quit the AirPort Utility.

Note: If the provider's network now prompts you to log in, type your login information and click **Login** or **Join**, as appropriate. If it is fee-based access, you usually have to select the period and fee you want to use.

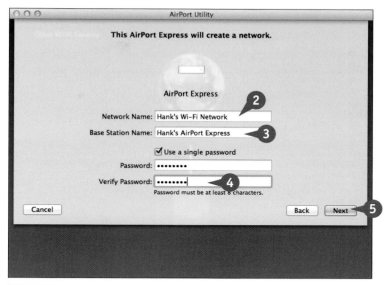

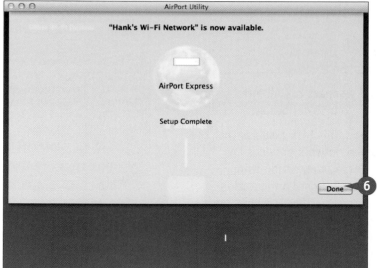

TIP

How do I correct base station errors?
Click **Launchpad** (📱) on the Dock, type **air**, and then click **AirPort Utility** (📶), select the base station, and click **Edit**. Use the resulting sheet to make changes to the base station's configuration. For example, on the Network tab, you might need to change the Router Mode to DHCP and NAT. After you make changes, click **Update**.

Connect to the Internet with a Wireless Modem

If you travel a lot, consider getting a broadband wireless modem. This is a device that can connect to the Internet anywhere within the network's coverage area. You can choose between a wireless modem that connects to your MacBook via USB and a MiFi device that provides a mobile hotspot to which your MacBook and other devices connect via Wi-Fi. *MiFi* stands for "my Wi-Fi." With a broadband wireless modem, you use the same network every time you connect, so you do not have to find and sign onto networks in various locations. You also pay only a single access fee.

Connect to the Internet with a Wireless Modem

Obtain a Broadband Wireless Modem

1. Explore the major cell phone company websites to determine which ones offer suitable modems.

2. Choose between a modem that connects via USB and a MiFi device that acts as a mobile hotspot.

3. Check the modem and accompanying software are OS X compatible.

4. Check the cost of the modem.

5. Check the data allowance and the "overage" charges for exceeding the allowance.

6. Choose a suitable contract — for example, two years.

7. Check the coverage area for the provider.

8. Purchase the modem and account that makes the most sense to you.

9. If required, install the software for the broadband wireless modem using the modem's installer application.

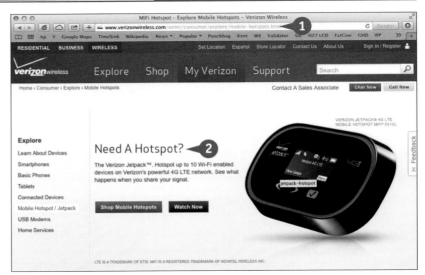

Use a Broadband Wireless Modem to Connect to the Internet

1 Turn the device on.

2 If necessary, launch the broadband wireless modem's connection application.

Note: If you are using a MiFi device, you do not need to run any software on your MacBook Air. After you power up the device, it starts providing the network after its startup process is complete.

3 Click **Wi-Fi** (📶).

The Wi-Fi menu opens.

4 Click the wireless modem.

5 If prompted, enter the network's password.

6 Select the **Remember this network** check box (☐ changes to ☑).

7 Click **Join**.

The MacBook Air connects to the wireless network and provides you with an Internet connection.

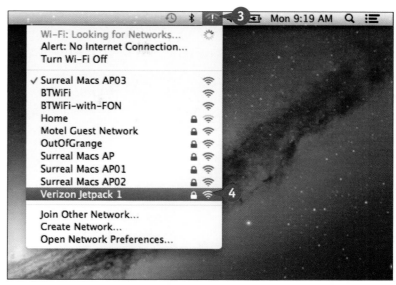

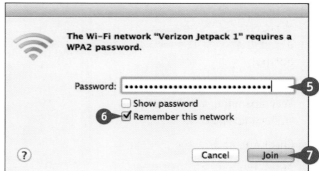

TIP

Why not use a wireless modem all the time?

If a broadband wireless modem provides sufficient connection speeds in the locations you use your MacBook Air the most, you can use it as your primary Internet connection and avoid getting another account with a cable or DSL provider. If you decide to do this, make sure you get an account with a data allowance large enough for all your Internet activity — ideally, an unlimited data allowance — so you do not have to pay overage charges, which tend to be extortionate. Another consideration is that, even though performance can be fast, a broadband wireless modem is still significantly slower than a cable or DSL connection.

Manage Your MacBook Air's Power

Your MacBook Air needs power to operate, just like any other electronic device. Because it has an internal battery, the MacBook Air does not need to be connected to an electrical outlet to run. As you travel with your MacBook Air, you need to manage its power so it does not run out at an inconvenient time.

You can take three steps to manage power on your MacBook Air. First, you can configure the MacBook Air to use as little power as possible. Second, you can monitor the MacBook Air's power status. Third, you can build a power toolkit.

Manage Your MacBook Air's Power

Configure the MacBook Air to Minimize Power Use

1. Click **Battery** (🔋) on the menu bar.

2. Click **Open Energy Saver Preferences**.

3. Click **Battery**.

4. Set the controls to configure the MacBook Air to use as little power as possible when running on the battery.

Note: See Chapter 6 for details on choosing Energy Saver preferences.

5. Click **Close** (⊗).

   The System Preferences window closes.

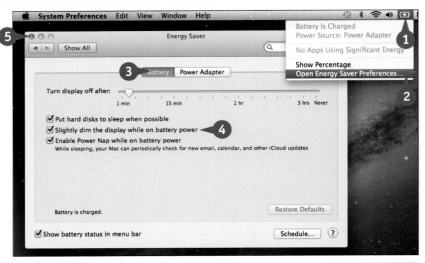

Monitor the Battery Power

1. Look at the battery icon (🔋) in the menu bar.

   As battery power is used, the filled part of the icon shrinks to give you a relative idea of how much battery power remains.

2 To access more detailed information, open the battery menu by clicking the battery icon (⌨).

A The Apps Using Significant Energy list alerts you to apps that are using a lot of power.

3 To display the percentage of charge remaining next to the battery icon, click **Show Percentage**.

Build a MacBook Air Power Toolkit

1 When you travel with your MacBook Air, bring its power adapter with you so that you can recharge it when an electrical outlet is available.

2 If you frequently travel on long plane flights, purchase an airline power adapter or inverter to connect your MacBook Air to the power outlets provided in some airplanes.

Note: Some airline inverters power the MacBook but do not charge its battery.

TIP

What are some other tips to extend my working time on the road?

- Close the lid to put your MacBook Air to sleep when you are not using it.
- Dim the screen as far as is tolerable by pressing F1.
- Turn off Wi-Fi and Bluetooth when you do not need them.
- Run as few power-hungry applications as possible. Click **Battery** (⌨) on the menu bar and look at the Apps Using Significant Energy list to identify power hogs.
- Carry an external battery pack and plug in your MacBook Air when the battery is low.
- If you have an iPod, iPhone, or iPad, use it to listen to music or watch video instead of iTunes on your MacBook Air.

Protect Your Data with FileVault

$\mathbf{I}$t is likely you have a lot of personal and sensitive information on your MacBook Air that you do not want others to access. To protect yourself against identity theft or other security breaches, you can use the OS X FileVault feature to encrypt your data securely. You must also turn off the Automatic Login feature, because this bypasses FileVault. FileVault encrypts your data so that it cannot be used without a password. Even if someone steals or accesses your MacBook Air, he cannot access its data without the password, so he cannot see or use your data.

Protect Your Data with FileVault

1 Control+click **System Preferences** (🖼️).

2 Click **Security & Privacy**.

3 Click **FileVault**.

4 Click **Unlock** (🔒), type your password in the authentication dialog, and click **Unlock**.

5 Click **Turn On FileVault**.

The Accounts dialog opens, showing a list of user accounts on your MacBook Air.

Ⓐ A check mark indicates the user account is already set to unlock FileVault.

6 Click **Enable User** for a user you want to add, type the user's password, and then click **OK**.

7 Repeat step **6** until you have enabled all the users you want to be able to unlock FileVault.

8 Click **Continue**.

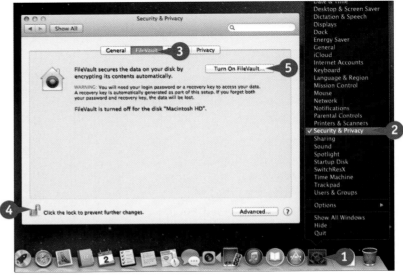

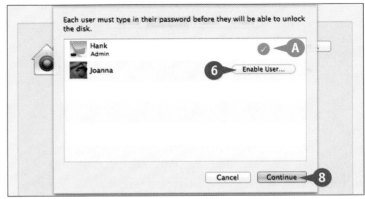

9 Make a note of your recovery key. Jot it down on paper and place it in a safe location. Memorize the key if you can.

10 Click **Continue**.

11 Click **Store the recovery key with Apple** (⊙ changes to ⊙).

12 Choose your security questions and answers, which are required for you to get the key from Apple.

13 Click **Continue**.

14 Click **Restart**.

Your MacBook Air restarts and the encryption process begins. This process can take several hours. You can monitor the process on the FileVault tab.

Note: When you are logged into your user account, your data is available. Make sure you log out whenever you are not using MacBook Air if any risk exists of someone you do not know or trust accessing it. Only when you are logged out is your data encrypted.

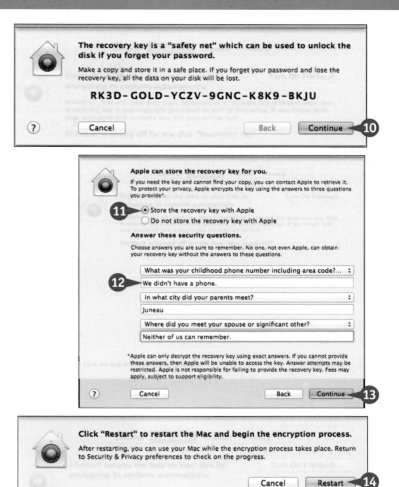

TIPS

Should I enable all the users on my MacBook Air to unlock FileVault?

This depends. You should enable only those users you want to be able to start up the MacBook Air. If you want to control startup yourself, and then allow other users to use the computer, do not enable those other users. For example, you might choose not to enable young children to unlock FileVault.

What happens if I forget my password?

You have to use the recovery key to be able to access your data. If you cannot locate the key, contact Apple to get it, assuming you enabled that option. If you or Apple cannot get to your recovery key, *all* the data on your MacBook Air is lost. So make sure you keep your key in a safe location, and you should store it with Apple too.

Tighten Security and Set Up the Firewall

OS X includes a firewall for protecting your MacBook Air from network and Internet threats. To secure your MacBook Air against threats from your own network, turn on the firewall and set it to accept only essential connections. When you connect your MacBook Air to a public network, set the firewall to block all incoming connections. For greater security, you can require a password to wake the MacBook Air from sleep or to stop the screen saver. You can disable automatic login to avoid others bypassing FileVault. And you can choose which sources of apps to allow.

Tighten Security and Set Up the Firewall

1 Control+click **System Preferences** (🖫).

2 Click **Security & Privacy**.

3 Click **General**.

4 Select the **Require password** check box (☐ changes to ☑) to require a password to start using MacBook Air after it goes to sleep or the screen saver activates.

5 Click the **Require password** pop-up menu (🔢) and select **immediately** or **a short time**.

6 Select the **Disable automatic login** check box (☐ changes to ☑) to disable automatic login.

Note: Disable automatic login when you set up FileVault to encrypt your data.

7 In the Allow apps downloaded from area, select **Mac App Store**, **Mac App Store and identified developers**, or **Anywhere** (◯ changes to ◉).

8 Click **Firewall**.

The Firewall pane opens.

9 Click **Turn On Firewall**.

10 Click **Firewall Options**.

Ⓐ Select the **Block all incoming connections** check box (☐ changes to ☑) when you want to block all incoming connections to your MacBook Air.

⑪ In the list of applications, click an application's pop-up menu (⬍) and select the **Allow incoming connections** or **Block incoming connections** check box (◯ changes to ◉), as needed.

⑫ Deselect the **Automatically allow signed software to receive incoming connections** check box (☑ changes to ☐) if you want to prevent developer-signed applications from receiving incoming connections unless you specifically allow them.

⑬ Select the **Enable stealth mode** check box (☐ changes to ☑) if you want to turn off responses to network requests.

⑭ To add an application to the list, click **Add** (⊞).

⑮ Click the application you want to add.

⑯ Click **Add**.

⑰ Click **OK**.

⑱ Click **Close** (◉).

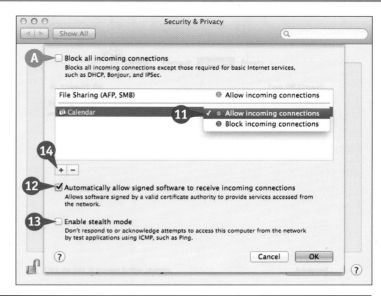

TIP

Which setting should I choose in the Allow Apps Downloaded From area?
Select **Mac App Store** (◯ changes to ◉) to restrict yourself and other users to installing only apps from the App Store. This is the safest choice. Select **Mac App Store and identified developers** (◯ changes to ◉) if you want to be able to install apps from Apple-registered third-party developers as well. Select **Anywhere** (◯ changes to ◉) if you want to be able to install any apps, even if they are poorly programmed or dangerous.

Find Directions with Maps

The Maps app on your MacBook Air can pinpoint your location by using known wireless networks. You can view your location on a road map, a satellite picture, or a hybrid that shows street annotations on the satellite picture. You can easily switch among map types to find the most useful one for your current needs. Maps can give you directions to where you want to go. Maps can also show you current traffic congestion in some areas to help you identify the most viable route for a journey.

Find Directions with Maps

Open Maps and Find Your Location

1 Click **Maps** (🗺️) on the Dock. The Maps screen appears.

2 Click **Current Location** (➚ changes to ➚).

A A blue dot shows your current location.

Change the Map Type and Zoom In or Out

1 Tap **Standard**, **Hybrid**, or **Satellite**.

Note: Standard view shows a street and road map. Satellite view shows satellite images. Hybrid view adds street and place names to the satellite images.

2 Tap and pinch out with two fingers on the trackpad to zoom in.

Note: You can tap and pinch in with two fingers to zoom out.

Note: You can rotate the map by placing two fingers on the trackpad and turning them to the left or right. To return the map to its default northward orientation, click the compass arrow (🧭).

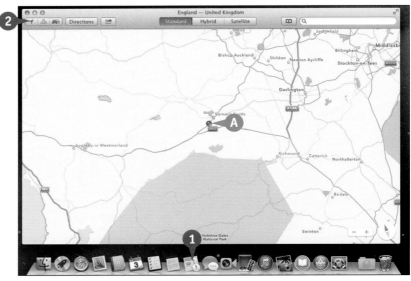

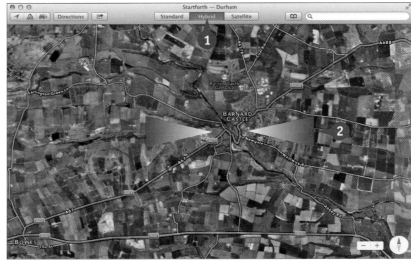

Get Directions

1 Click **Directions**.

Ⓑ The Directions pane opens.

2 Type your start point.

Note: If Maps displays a panel of suggestions for the start point or end point you type, click the appropriate suggestion.

Note: You can type a contact's name, or part of it, and then click that contact in the panel of suggestions to use the contact's address as the starting point or ending point.

3 Type your end point.

Maps displays suggested routes.

Ⓒ The green pin marks the starting point.

Ⓓ The red pin marks the ending point.

Ⓔ The current route appears in darker blue.

Ⓕ The current route's details appear in the Directions pane.

Ⓖ You can click another route or its time box to display its details.

4 Click one of the directions to zoom in on that part of the route.

TIP

How do I get directions for walking?

Click **Walking** (🚶) in the Directions panel to display the distance and time for walking the route. Be aware that walking directions may be inaccurate or optimistic. Before walking the route, check that it does not send you across pedestrian-free bridges or through rail tunnels.

Explore with Maps

M aps is not only great for finding out where you are and for getting directions to places, but it can also show you 3D flyovers of the places on the map. After switching on the 3D feature, you can zoom in and out, pan around, and move backward and forward.

Explore with Maps

1 Click **Maps** (🗺) on the Dock.

Note: If Maps does not appear on the Dock, click **Launchpad** (🚀) on the Dock and then click **Maps** (🗺) on the Launchpad screen.

The Maps screen appears.

2 Display the area of interest in the middle of the screen. For example, click and drag the map, or search for the location you want.

3 Click **Flyover** (🏙 changes to 🏙).

The map changes to Flyover view.

4 Double-tap or pinch outward with two fingers to zoom in.

Note: You can pinch in with two fingers to zoom out.

5 Tap and drag to scroll the map.

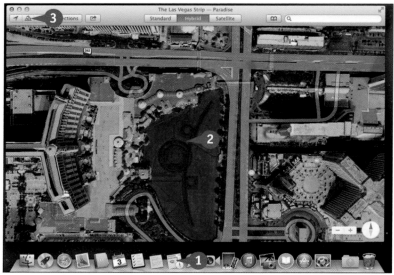

6 Place two fingers on the trackpad and twist clockwise or counterclockwise.

The view rotates, and you can explore.

Note: Pan and zoom as needed to explore the area.

A The red end of the compass arrow (![]) indicates north. You can tap this icon to restore the direction to north.

7 Click **Flyover** (![] changes to ![]).

The map returns to normal view.

TIP

What does Flyover do with the Standard map?
When you tap **Flyover** (![] changes to ![]) to switch on Flyover with the Standard map displayed, Maps tilts the map at an angle, as you might do with a paper map, and displays outlines of buildings if they are available. For most purposes, Flyover is most useful with the Satellite map and the Hybrid map.

PART III

Enjoying the Internet

A MacBook Air is ideal for using the Internet. With iCloud, you can store your information online where all your devices can access the same data. Safari is OS X's excellent web browser. Using Mail, you can send, receive, and organize e-mail. To communicate with people near and far, you use FaceTime and Messages for text, audio, and even video chats.

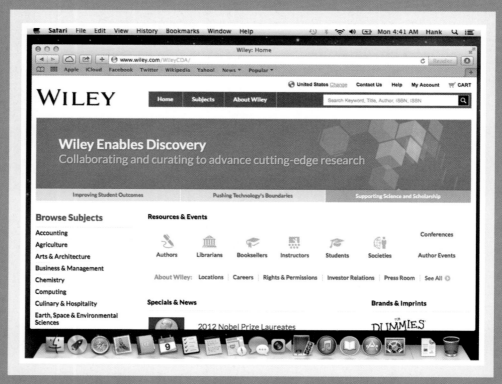

Explore iCloud

An iCloud account gives you access to a number of useful services and online applications. Because your iCloud account is integrated with OS X, iCloud extends your MacBook Air's desktop onto the Internet.

You can use iCloud to keep information and documents in sync among several devices, such as your MacBook Air, other Macs, an iPhone, an iPad, and even a Windows PC. An iCloud account provides you with online e-mail, calendars, contacts, documents, photos, and more. You can access this through applications on your MacBook Air and through your iCloud website.

iCloud

iCloud gives you an online storage space you can access from many devices, keeping your information and documents in sync. For example, you can start a document in the Pages application on your MacBook Air and save it to iCloud. You can make changes to the document in the Pages app on an iPad; those changes are also saved to iCloud, from where they are copied back to your MacBook Air. Pages on the Mac has fuller features than Pages on the iPad, but the latter can still edit the document's content enough to be highly useful.

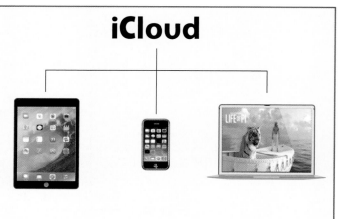

iCloud Account

To use iCloud, you must have an iCloud account. If you already have an Apple ID, you also have an iCloud account. If you do not, creating an iCloud account is simple. You can use many of iCloud's services for free, so you have no reason not to try it to see if it will be useful to you. After you have an iCloud account, you configure each of your devices to use it.

iCloud Website

In addition to being able to access iCloud data and services from your MacBook Air and other devices, you can use the iCloud website to access your information through the online applications it provides. This is very useful for those times you might not have one of your devices with you. You can log into your account from any compatible web browser and check your e-mail, create an event on your calendar, and so on.

E-Mail

iCloud gives you an e-mail account, with an e-mail address on the @icloud.com domain; older accounts may use the mac.com and me.com domains. You can send and receive e-mail from your iCloud account, just like you do with other e-mail accounts that you may have, using an e-mail application such as Mail; using an iPhone, iPad, or iPod touch; or working directly from the Mail application on your iCloud website. You can also create e-mail aliases that enable you to use multiple addresses at the same time.

Calendars and Contacts

Similar to e-mail, iCloud enables you to store contact and calendar information on the cloud so that you can access it through applications on your MacBook Air and iPads, iPhones, and iPod touches. You can also use the online applications to work with this information from any computer using a compatible web browser.

Notes

The Notes feature in iCloud provides an easy way to sync the notes you create in the Notes app on your MacBook, iPad, iPhone, or iPod touch. When you create a note in your iCloud account, your MacBook and iOS devices sync it automatically, so you always have your latest information at hand. You can also edit notes on the iCloud website by using a web browser.

Reminders

In addition to your e-mail, contacts, calendars, and notes, your iCloud account can sync the reminders you create in the Reminders app. You can keep multiple lists of reminders, sync them among your MacBook and iOS devices, and update your to-do list anywhere you go. You can edit your reminders on the iCloud website by using a web browser.

Find My Mac

The Find My Mac feature, which appears on iCloud as Find My iPhone, can pinpoint the current location of your MacBook Air through its network connection. This can be helpful if your MacBook is lost or stolen because you can identify where it is and you can take steps to protect the information stored on it, such as by erasing its drive.

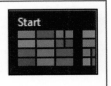

iCloud and Windows PCs

iCloud works with Windows PCs, too. If you also use a Windows PC, you can configure its applications, such as Outlook, to access your iCloud account so that you can share information on a PC. You can download the iCloud Control Panel, the software necessary to configure iCloud on a Windows PC, from www.apple.com/icloud/setup/pc.html.

Set Up an iCloud Account on Your MacBook Air

To use iCloud services, you need an iCloud account. An iCloud account is free, although some services or upgrades require a fee. If you have an Apple ID already, you also have an iCloud account, so you just need to set up your account on your MacBook Air.

To obtain or set up an iCloud account, you use the iCloud pane in the System Preferences application. This pane enables you to create a new account, log in, and configure your account.

Set Up an iCloud Account on Your MacBook Air

1 Control+click **System Preferences** (■) on the Dock.

The System Preferences contextual menu opens.

Note: You can also click **Apple** (■) to open the Apple menu, select **System Preferences** to display the System Preferences window, and then click **iCloud**.

2 Click **iCloud**.

The System Preferences application opens and displays the iCloud pane.

Note: If you need to get an iCloud account, click **Create an Apple ID** and complete the steps in the Create an Apple ID dialog that appears.

3 Type your Apple ID.

4 Type your password.

5 Click **Sign In**.

6 Deselect the **Use iCloud for mail, contacts, calendars, reminders, notes, and Safari** check box (☑ changes to ☐) if you do not want your information synced on the cloud.

7 Deselect the **Use Find My Mac** check box (☑ changes to ☐) if you do not want to be able to use Find My Mac to locate your MacBook Air.

8 Click **Next**.

The iCloud pane displays controls for configuring your account further, as discussed later in this chapter.

9 Click **Close** (⊗).

The System Preferences window closes.

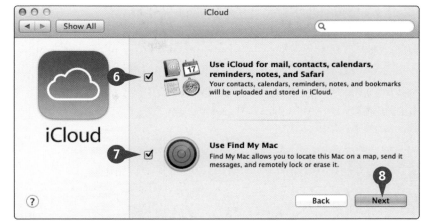

TIPS

How do I switch iCloud accounts?

To switch to a different iCloud account, open the iCloud pane and click **Sign Out**. You are prompted to keep or delete the information that has been synced on your MacBook Air, such as contacts, calendars, and so on. After you have chosen to delete or keep each type of information, you return to the iCloud pane and can sign in to a different account.

How can I stream music to all my devices?

The iTunes Match service matches as many as possible of the songs in your iTunes library with existing iCloud versions and uploads the other songs to iCloud. From there, each of your devices can access, download, and play that music. This is useful because you do not have to bother with selecting only parts of your music collection to sync on a device. All your music is available all the time. You must subscribe to iTunes Match for a fee; see www.apple.com/itunes/itunes-match/ for more information.

Access iCloud via a Web Browser

As well as using iCloud on your MacBook Air and your iOS devices, you can also access your iCloud account and data using the applications and tools on Apple's icloud.com website. All you need to use the iCloud website is your Apple ID, your password, and a computer running a compatible web browser, such as Safari, Firefox, Internet Explorer on a Windows PC, or Google Chrome. After signing in to the iCloud website, you can work with your e-mail, contact information, calendar appointments, reminders, and notes. You can also use the Find My iPhone feature to locate your Macs and iOS devices.

Access iCloud via a Web Browser

1 Open a web browser and go to www.icloud.com.

The iCloud Login page appears.

2 Type your Apple ID.

3 Type your password.

4 Select the **Keep me signed in** check box (☐ changes to ☑) if you want to remain logged into your account.

Note: Use the **Keep me signed in** feature only on your own computer, not on anybody else's computer or a public computer.

5 Click **Sign In** (➡) or press `Return`.

iCloud signs you in.

Icons for the available iCloud applications appear.

6 Click the icon for the application you want to use. For example, click **Reminders** to use the Reminders application.

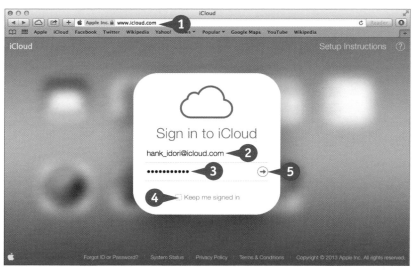

The application you selected opens.

7 Work with the online application.

Note: The iCloud applications work very similarly to the OS X desktop applications.

8 To switch to a different application, click **iCloud**.

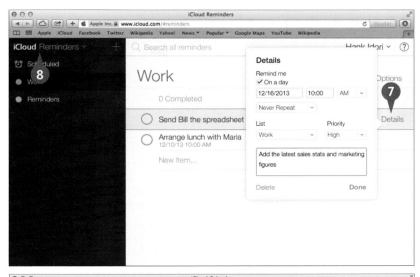

The iCloud navigation panel appears, showing the application icons.

9 To switch to a different application, click its icon.

10 To leave the iCloud website, click your user name. The Account menu opens.

11 Click **Sign Out**.

iCloud signs you out and displays its sign-in screen again.

TIPS

How can I configure my iCloud account?
Click your name in the upper-right corner of the iCloud window and then click **Account Settings** on the pop-up menu. The Account dialog appears. Here you can add a photo, set the language and time zone, and choose which notifications to receive. Clicking your Apple ID displays the My Apple ID website, where you can reset your password and perform various administrative moves.

How can I add more disk space to my account?
Your iCloud account includes 5GB of storage space by default. This is typically enough for e-mail, calendars, and contacts. If you store a lot of documents on the cloud and need more room, open **System Preferences**, click **iCloud**, and then click **Manage**. Click **Buy More Storage** and follow the on-screen instructions to increase the amount of online storage available to you. Note that content from the iTunes Store, App Store, iTunes Match, and Photo Stream does not count against your storage space.

Sync Information Across Your Devices with iCloud

You can use your iCloud account to keep your essential information synced on each of your Macs and your iOS devices. For example, you sync your contacts to your Mac and your iPhone, put your reminders on your iPad, and ensure that all your favorite bookmarks are available when you need them.

To get started, you need to configure each computer and iOS device to sync via iCloud. After you do that, the sync process happens automatically and you do not even have to think about it.

Sync Information Across Your Devices with iCloud

1 Click **Apple** (🍎).

The Apple menu opens.

2 Click **System Preferences**.

The System Preferences window opens.

3 Click **iCloud**.

The iCloud pane appears.

Note: If necessary, sign in to your iCloud account as described in the section "Set Up an iCloud Account on Your MacBook Air."

4 Select the check box (☐ changes to ☑) for each item you want to sync.

5 Deselect the check box (☑ changes to ☐) for each item you do not want to sync.

When you remove an item, OS X may display a dialog confirming that you want to remove the information from your MacBook Air.

6 Click **Delete from Mac** if you are sure you want to remove the information.

7 Repeat steps **4** to **6** until you have configured all the items available for syncing.

8 Click **Close** (⊗) or press ⌘ + Q to close the System Preferences application.

Repeat steps **1** to **7** on each Mac that you want to keep in sync.

Note: You can only sync information from one iCloud account under each user account on your MacBook Air. Each user account can — and normally should — use a different iCloud account.

TIP

How do I keep information synced on my iOS devices?

To use the same information on an iPhone, iPad, or iPod touch, configure your iCloud account on each of those devices. Press the **Home** button to display the Home screen, then tap **Settings** to open the Settings app. Tap **iCloud**, and enter your account information. Once your information is verified, set the status switch for each type of information you want to keep in sync, such as Mail, Contacts, and so on, to On (▭). This causes the data on the device to sync with iCloud, which in turn syncs with your Macs.

Using iCloud Photo Stream

Photo Stream provides online storage for your photos and other images, making it easy to have your photos available on all your devices. For example, with Photo Stream enabled, each photo you take with an iPhone is automatically uploaded to your Photo Stream. Your MacBook Air and your iPad, configured to use Photo Stream, then automatically download the photo, so you can view and edit it on any of your devices. Photo Stream also provides a temporary backup for your photos. If you lose your iPhone, the photos you took with its camera and uploaded to Photo Stream are still available to download.

Using iCloud Photo Stream

Set Up Photo Stream in OS X

1. Click **Apple** (🍎).

2. Click **System Preferences**.

   The System Preferences window opens.

3. Click **iCloud**.

   The iCloud pane opens.

4. Select the **Photos** check box (☐ changes to ☑).

5. Click **Options**.

   The iCloud Photos dialog opens.

6. Select the **My Photo Stream** check box (☐ changes to ☑).

7. Select the **Photo Sharing** check box (☐ changes to ☑) if you want to share your photos with others.

8. Click **OK**.

   The iCloud Photos dialog closes.

9. Click **Close** (⊗) or press ⌘ + Q.

   The System Preferences window closes.

Set Up Photo Stream in iPhoto

1 Click the **iPhoto** icon () on the Dock.

2 Click **iPhoto**.

3 Click **Preferences**.

4 Click **iCloud**.

5 Select **My Photo Stream** (☐ changes to ☑).

6 Select **Automatic Import** (☐ changes to ☑) if you want iPhoto to add your My Photo Stream photos to its list of Events, Photos, Faces, and Places.

7 Select the **Automatic Upload** check box (☐ changes to ☑) if you also want photos or other images you add to iPhoto to be uploaded to your Photo Stream.

8 Select the **Photo Sharing** check box (☐ changes to ☑) if you want to create photo streams that you share with others.

9 Click **Close** (⊗).

Any photos uploaded to your Photo Stream automatically download into iPhoto. If you selected the Automatic Upload check box in step **7**, any photos or other images that you add to iPhoto automatically upload to your Photo Stream. From there, they automatically download to other devices accessing your Photo Stream.

TIP

How can I remove photos from my Photo Stream?

In iPhoto, click **iCloud** in the Sidebar. In the My Photo Stream view, Control+click the photo you want to delete, then click **Delete from My Photo Stream** on the contextual menu that appears.

Using iCloud to Store Documents Online

In addition to information, you can store documents in iCloud. The same documents are available on each device, so you can create a document on your MacBook Air, edit it on your iPhone, and then finalize it on your iPad. Only those applications designed to use iCloud can store documents in iCloud. Currently, TextEdit, Preview, and the three iWork applications — Pages, Numbers, and Keynote — are among the Apple applications that support iCloud documents.

Using iCloud to Store Documents Online

Set Up Online Documents in OS X

1 Control+click **System Preferences** (🌀) on the Dock.

2 Click **iCloud**.

3 Select the **Documents & Data** check box (☐ changes to ☑).

4 Click **Options**.

The Documents & Data Options dialog opens.

5 Select a check box (☐ changes to ☑) to enable an application to store documents and data in iCloud.

6 Deselect a check box (☑ changes to ☐) to disable an application from storing documents and data in iCloud.

7 Click **Done**.

The Documents & Data Options dialog closes.

8 Click **Close** (⊗).

The System Preferences window closes.

Work with Online Documents in Pages

1. Click **Launchpad** (🚀) on the Dock.

2. Click **Pages**.

   The Pages dialog opens.

3. Click **iCloud**.

A The list of Pages documents stored in your iCloud account appears.

4. Click the document you want to work with.

5. Click **Open**.

B The document downloads to your MacBook Air and opens.

6. Change the document.

7. When you finish working with the document, click **Close** (⊗).

   The document closes.

   OS X saves the updated version of the document in iCloud. You can open it from any device that can access your Pages documents, including other Macs, iPads, and iPhones.

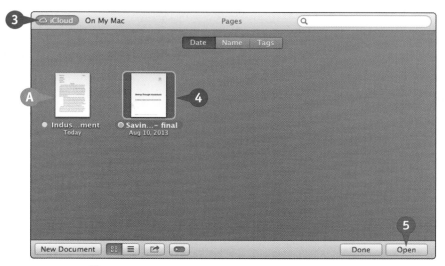

Saving Through Investment

TIP

How do I access my documents on an iPad or iPhone?
Press the **Home** button to display the Home screen, then tap **Settings** to open the Settings app. Tap **iCloud**, and then tap **Documents & Data**. Set the Documents & Data switch to On ( ). If you want documents to be synced even when you are using a cellular connection, set the Use Cellular Data switch to On ( ). Open an iCloud-enabled app on the device. Tap **Use iCloud**. You see the documents associated with that application stored on the cloud. Tap a document to work with it. Any documents you change or create are stored on the cloud from where they are synced onto other devices.

Secure Your Passwords with iCloud Keychain

iCloud Keychain gives you an easy way to store your passwords and credit card information securely on your Macs and iOS devices. Instead of having to remember the password for each website, or look at a credit card when you need to enter its details, you can have iCloud Keychain automatically provide the details. To use iCloud Keychain, you first set it up in the iCloud pane of System Preferences on your MacBook Air. Once you have done this, you can access the information in your iCloud Keychain from browsers such as Safari.

Secure Your Passwords with iCloud Keychain

1 Click **Apple** (🍎).

The Apple menu opens.

2 Click **System Preferences**.

The System Preferences window opens.

3 Click **iCloud**.

The iCloud pane opens.

4 Select the **Keychain** check box (☐ changes to ☑).

The Enter your Apple ID password to set up iCloud Keychain dialog opens.

5 Type your Apple ID password.

6 Click **OK**.

The Create an iCloud Security Code dialog opens.

7 Type the code you want to use.

8 Click **Next**.

9 Reenter the code when prompted.

10 Click **Next**.

The Enter a Phone Number That Can Receive SMS Messages dialog opens.

11 Click the **Country** pop-up menu (⬍) and select your country.

12 Type your phone number.

Note: Use a phone number that can receive text messages, not a landline.

13 Click **Done**.

OS X enables the iCloud Keychain feature.

14 Click **Close** (⊗) or press ⌘+Q.

The System Preferences window closes.

TIP

How can I make sure my iCloud Keychain information is secure?

You can secure your iCloud Keychain with a complex code instead of a four-digit numeric code. In the Create an iCloud Security Code dialog, click **Advanced,** and then click **Use a Complex Security Code** (◯ changes to ◉). Click **Next** and type the security code, and then click **Next** again and type the code once more to confirm it. By making the code longer and including numbers and symbols as well as upper- and lowercase letters, you can secure your iCloud Keychain more tightly.

Explore Safari

Safari is the web browser that comes with OS X. Safari is a powerful application, but it is easy to use. You can either keep Safari in its default configuration, which has preferences set to suit most users pretty well, or choose preferences to tailor the way Safari works for you.

Safari in Browse Mode

A Back and Forward

Click **Back** (◀) to move back to the previous page in the chain of pages displayed in this tab or window. Click **Forward** (▶) to move forward to the next page in the chain after moving back.

B Show iCloud Tabs

As you browse through iCloud, you can click **Show iCloud Tabs** (☁) to jump to Safari tabs open on other devices.

C Address and Search Bar

Shows the current web address (Uniform Resource Locator, or URL). You can also type information here to perform a search.

D Title

Shows the title of the web page being shown.

E Refresh or Stop Loading

Click **Refresh** (🗘) to make Safari load the current version of the page. Click **Stop Loading** (✖) to stop loading a page.

F Bookmarks Bar

The Bookmarks bar provides quick access to your favorite bookmarks.

G Top Sites

Click **Top Sites** (▦) to display a screen containing thumbnails of your most frequently visited web pages that you can click to visit.

H Web Page

Displays the contents of the web page you are visiting.

I Tab Bar

Each tab can show a different webpage; click a tab to display its page.

Safari in Bookmarks Mode

Ⓐ Bookmarks Editor

Click **Bookmarks** and **Show Bookmarks Editor** or press Option + ⌘ + B to switch to the Bookmarks Editor. Click **Bookmarks** and **Hide Bookmarks Editor** or press Option + ⌘ + B to switch back to the page you were on.

Ⓑ Show Sidebar Button

Click **Show Sidebar** (📖) to toggle the display of the sidebar.

Ⓒ Sidebar

Displays the contents of the Bookmarks folder or the Reading List folder.

Ⓓ Bookmarks Tab

Displays the Bookmarks pane in the Sidebar, hiding the Reading List pane.

Ⓔ Reading List Tab

Displays the Reading List pane in the Sidebar, hiding the Bookmarks pane.

Ⓕ Bookmark Folders in the Sidebar

Bookmark folders contain the bookmarks you have placed in them. Click a folder to reveal the list of bookmarks it contains. Click the folder again to collapse it.

Ⓖ Bookmarks in the Sidebar

Each bookmark contains the address of a web page. Click a bookmark to display the page.

Ⓗ Bookmark Folders in the Bookmark Editor

Bookmark folders contain the bookmarks you have placed in them. Double-click a folder to reveal its bookmarks. Double-click the folder again to collapse it.

Ⓘ Bookmarks in the Bookmark Editor

Each bookmark contains the address of a web page. Click a bookmark's name and then press Return to open the name for editing.

Ⓙ New Folder Button

Click **New Folder** to start creating a new folder.

Ⓚ Search Bookmarks Box

Enables you to search for bookmarks.

Navigate to Websites

The most basic task when you use the web is to move to the website you are interested in and then navigate within that site's pages. You can do this in a number of ways, and you will probably use all of them as you explore the web.

Moving to a website by entering its URL is the most flexible method, and is the one you can always use. For most sites that you use regularly, you need to type the URL only once. After that, you can move back to it with a bookmark or by using the Safari History menu.

Navigate to Websites

Navigate to a Website by Entering a URL

1 Click **Safari** (🧭) on the Dock.

2 Type the address of a website.

Safari automatically adds the http:// prefix or https:// prefix, so you do not need to type it. If the address begins with www, you do not need to type the www part, either. For example, to go to http://www.apple.com, you just need to type **apple.com**.

Note: You can also type search terms into the address box. See the section "Search the Web" for details.

A As you type in the address bar, Safari displays matches and suggestions.

3 When the address becomes the one you want or when you finish typing it, press **Return**.

Safari loads the web page, and you see its content.

Navigate to Websites with a Bookmark

1 To use a bookmark on the Bookmarks bar, click the bookmark.

B Bookmarks can be organized in folders on the Bookmarks bar. Click a folder to see the bookmarks it contains and then click the bookmark you want to use.

Note: Folders on the Bookmarks bar have a downward-pointing triangle.

2 To access a bookmark stored on the Bookmarks menu, click **Bookmarks**.

3 Highlight the bookmarks folder on the menu.

The folder's contents appear.

4 Click the bookmark you want to use.

That web page opens.

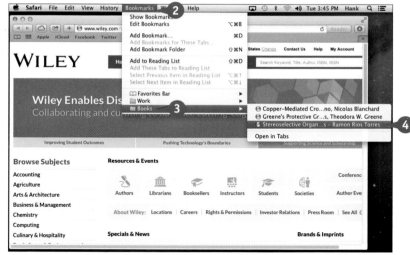

TIPS

How can I use the same bookmarks on all my devices?

If you use more than one Mac, you are likely to create different bookmarks as you surf the web on each computer. Fortunately, if you use iCloud, you can synchronize the bookmarks on each Mac you use so that whether you use your MacBook Air, a different Mac, or an iOS device, you always have the same set of bookmarks available to you.

How do I know specifically where a bookmark points?

Because you can name a bookmark anything you want, and you usually use an abbreviated name when you add a bookmark to the Bookmarks bar, you might not remember where a bookmark points. To see a bookmark's address, point to the bookmark on the Bookmarks bar without clicking it. After a second or two, the full address for the bookmark appears.

continued ▶ 193

As you navigate through web pages, you create a path of pages along which you can move backward and forward as needed. You can do this because Safari stores the address of each page you display. Safari also temporarily stores each page on your MacBook Air, a process called *caching*. You can also go to web pages from outside Safari by clicking hyperlinks in documents, such as e-mail and text documents. When you click a web link, OS X recognizes it as an address and opens it in your default web browser.

Navigate to Websites (continued)

5 Click **Show Sidebar** (▦).

The Sidebar opens on the left side of the Safari window.

6 Click **Bookmarks** (▦).

The Bookmarks pane appears.

7 Double-click a bookmarks folder to display its contents.

8 Click the bookmark for the page you want to view.

Safari loads the page.

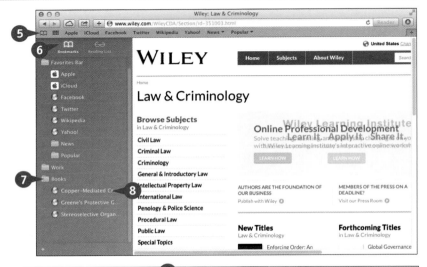

Navigate to Websites Using History

1 Click **History**.

The History menu opens.

The fourth section of the menu shows the web pages you have visited most recently.

2 If the page you want to return to is on the list, click it.

3 If the page is not on the list, click the folder for the time period in which you visited it.

4 Click the page you want to visit on the resulting menu.

Safari opens the page you chose.

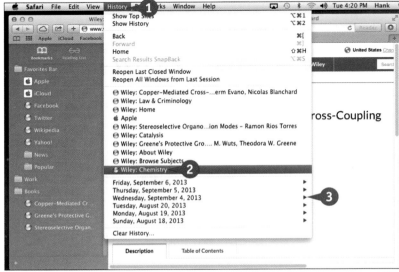

Navigate to Web Pages Using a Link

1 Click a link in the Contacts application, in an e-mail message, or in another application or document.

Note: In various other applications, you can open a web address by selecting it, Control+clicking in the selection, and then clicking **Open URL** on the contextual menu.

Safari opens and displays the web page.

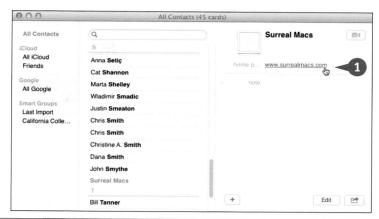

Move Through Web Pages

1 Click a link to display the web page to which it links.

2 Click **Back** (◀) to display the previous page.

3 Click **Forward** (▶) to display a later page in the current path of pages you have been browsing.

Note: To go back or forward along the path by several pages, click and hold **Back** (◀) or **Forward** (▶), and then select the appropriate page on the pop-up menu that appears.

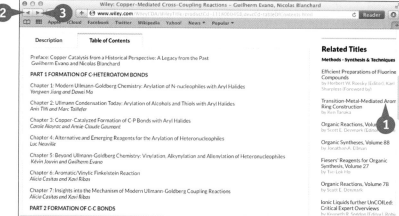

What does the http that Safari adds to the front of URLs stand for?
The http prefix stands for Hypertext Transfer Protocol, and is the basic *protocol*, or language, that web browsers employ. The https prefix stands for Hypertext Transfer Protocol Secure, a protocol used with information that needs to be protected, such as bank accounts. You can access other protocols with Safari, such as the File Transfer Protocol, or FTP, in which case the URL starts with ftp: instead of http:. The vast majority of sites that you will visit with Safari use http, and so Safari assumes that this is the kind of site you want. To go to a different kind of site, add that prefix at the beginning of the URL, such as ftp://.

Search the Web

One of the most useful things to do on the web is to search for information, and one of the best search engines is Google. Google searching is by default built into Safari to make web searches fast and easy.

You can perform a Google search by using the Search tool built into Safari. If you want to use a different search engine temporarily, you can type its URL into the address bar and press **Return**. If you want to use a different search engine by default, you can change the Default Search Engine preference in the Safari Preferences window.

Search the Web

1 Type the information you want to search for in the address bar.

A When you type something other than a web address, Safari goes into search mode and you see the type of search you are doing in the address bar.

B As you type, Safari presents a list showing you suggested searches and your previous searches.

2 To search on the term you entered, press **Return** or click the search term you want to use on the list.

Safari performs the search and displays the results.

3 Click a link to visit one of the search results.

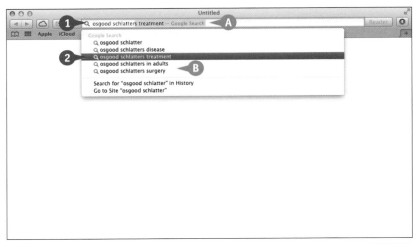

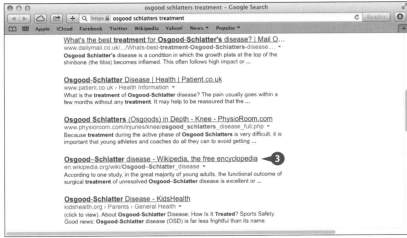

That web page appears.

4 View and use the web page.

5 Click **History**.

The History menu opens.

6 Click **Search Results SnapBack**.

Note: You can also press Option + ⌘ + S to return to your search results.

The search results appear again.

7 Scroll the page to explore other results.

Note: When you get to the bottom of a search results page, you see how many pages are in the results. Click **Next** to move to the next page of results, or click a page's number to jump to it.

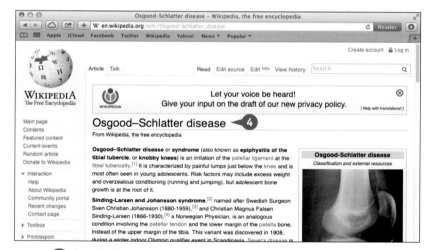

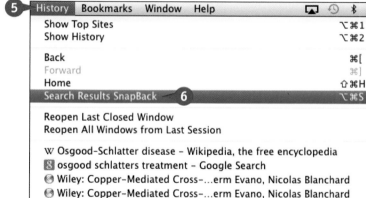

How can I repeat a previous search?
Safari remembers the most recent searches you have performed. Start to repeat the search by typing the same text you did the first time. When the suggestions appear, look in the Bookmarks and History sections, and then click the search you want to repeat.

Can I use any search page with Safari, or do I have to use Google?
You can use any search page by going to its URL. For example, to search with Yahoo!, type **yahoo.com**. The search page appears and you can use its tool to search the web. By default, when you search using the Safari address bar, you search using Google. You can change this to use Bing or Yahoo! instead by setting a preference covered later in this chapter.

Download Files

You can download a vast number of different kinds of files from the web. These include images, PDF documents, music files, applications, and video files, among many other file types.

After you download a file, how you use it depends on the kind of file it is. Most applications are provided in a disk image file, which has the filename extension .dmg, and which OS X usually mounts automatically in the file system. Some files, such as PDF documents, are downloaded as they are. Other files are compressed so that you need to decompress them before you use them.

Download Files

Download Files from the Web

1. Locate a file that you want to download.

2. Click the file's download link or button.

The file begins to download.

3. Click **Downloads** (📥) to open the Downloads window if you want to monitor the progress of the download.

Note: You do not really have to monitor a file download because it downloads in the background. You can continue to do other things as files download.

When the download is complete, the file is ready for you to use.

Use Disk Images You Have Downloaded

1 Open a Finder window.

Note: Many disk images are self-mounting, in which case you click the mounted disk image instead of double-clicking it in step **2**.

2 Click or double-click the disk image that you downloaded.

3 Run the application installer, or install it with drag-and-drop, as explained in Chapter 5.

Use Document Files You Have Downloaded

1 Click the **Downloads** stack on the Dock.

2 Click the downloaded document you want to use.

Note: To open the Downloads folder in a Finder window, click **Open in Finder** or *X* **More in Finder**.

The file opens using the application associated with it.

Note: When you download a group of files that have been compressed using the Zip format, OS X decompresses them for you automatically. Instead of a single file, you see a folder with the Zip file's name. Open that folder to see the files it contains.

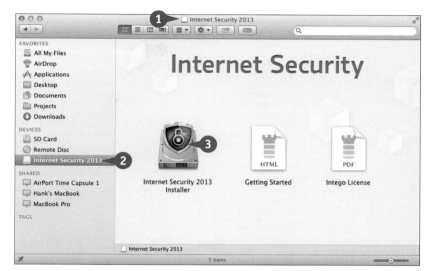

TIP

What about FTP?

Some sites use File Transfer Protocol, FTP, to provide files for you to download. Such sites' URLs start with ftp:// instead of http://. FTP usually transfers files faster than through HTTP, so it is good for transferring large files or many files. You can access FTP sites in Safari, or you can use an FTP application, such as FileZilla or ForkLift. Most FTP sites require you to have a username and password to download files.

Browse the Web with Tabs

Tabs in Safari enable you to open as many web pages at a time as you want, while keeping all those pages in one window so that you do not clutter up your desktop. To display a page, you simply click its tab.

Browse the Web with Tabs

Configure Safari's Tabs

1. In Safari, press ⌘+,.

2. Click **Tabs**.

3. Click the **Open pages in tabs instead of windows** pop-up menu (⬍) and select how new pages open.

4. Select the top check box (☐ changes to ☑) if you want to be able to open a web page in a new tab by ⌘+clicking its link.

5. Select the second check box (☐ changes to ☑) if you want to immediately display new tabs and windows you open.

6. Review the keyboard shortcuts.

7. Click **Close** (⬤) to close the Preferences window.

Open and Use Tabs

1. Open a Safari window and move to a web page.

2. Press ⌘+T.

   Ⓐ A new tab appears.

3. Open a web page in the new tab using any of the techniques described earlier in this chapter.

   The web page fills the tab.

4. To open a link in a new tab, ⌘+click the link.

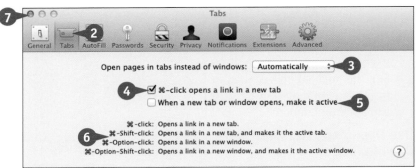

B A new tab opens and displays the linked page.

Note: If you did not enable the preference to make new tabs active, click the new tab to make it active.

C You can click another tab to make it active.

D You can point to the left side of a tab and click **Close** (☒) to close a tab.

Note: If you want to close all the other tabs except one, point to the left side of the tab you want to keep open, and then Option +click **Close** (☒).

5 Click **Show All Tabs** (▭).

Safari shrinks the tabs into a list you can scroll horizontally.

Note: You can also pinch inward with four fingers on the trackpad to display the tab list.

6 Scroll left or right until you reach the tab you want.

7 Click the tab.

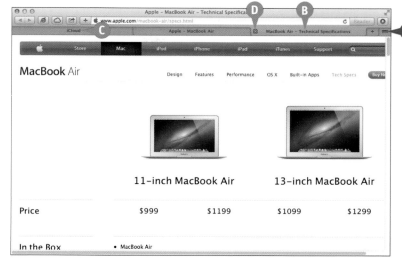

How can I move through open tabs with the keyboard?

Press Control + Tab to move to the next tab, or press Shift + Control + Tab to move to the previous tab.

When should I open more windows instead of tabs?

Open multiple windows when you need to see two or more pages at the same time. To open a new window, click **File** and then click **New Window** or press ⌘ + N. You can convert a tab into a window in two ways: either drag the tab out of the Safari window; or display the tab and click **Window**, and then click **Move Tab to New Window**. You can also drag a tab from one Safari window to another, or click **Window** and then click **Merge All Windows** to put all your tabs into a single window.

Set and Organize Bookmarks

ookmarks make returning to sites you previously visited much faster and easier than typing URL addresses. By default, Safari includes a number of bookmarks that you can use, but you can create as many other bookmarks as you need. So anytime you find a site you want to be able to return to, create a bookmark for it. Because you are likely to end up with many bookmarks, you need tools to keep them organized. Safari also helps with that. You can organize your bookmarks either as you create them or afterward, whichever you find most convenient.

Set and Organize Bookmarks

Create Bookmarks

1 Go to a web page that you want to bookmark.

2 Click **Bookmarks**.

The Bookmarks menu opens.

3 Click **Add Bookmark**.

The Bookmark sheet opens.

Note: You can also press ⌘ + D to open the Bookmark sheet.

4 Click the **Add this page to** pop-up menu (⬍) and select the location in which you want to store the bookmark.

A The location you selected appears in the pop-up menu.

5 Type a name for the bookmark.

Note: You can leave the default name as is, edit it, or replace it with something completely different.

6 Click **Add**.

Safari creates the bookmark in the location you selected. You can return to the page at any time by clicking the new bookmark.

Organize Your Bookmarks in the Sidebar

1 Click **Show Sidebar** (📖).

The Sidebar opens.

2 Click **Bookmarks** (📖) if the Reading List pane appears at first.

The Bookmarks pane appears in the Sidebar.

Note: You can also click **View** and then click **Show Bookmarks Sidebar** or press **Control** + **⌘** + **1**.

3 Double-click a folder to expand it or collapse it.

4 To create a new bookmarks folder for bookmarks, click **Create a Bookmarks Folder** (⊞).

A new untitled folder appears.

5 Type the name for the folder and press **Return**.

6 Drag a bookmark from one folder to another to rearrange your bookmarks.

Note: You can also drag your folders into a different order.

7 Click **Show Sidebar** (📖).

The Sidebar closes.

TIPS

How do I store bookmarks on the Favorites bar?

The Favorites bar is a convenient way to store and access bookmarks. You can move to a bookmark just by clicking its button on the bar. To add a bookmark to the bar, choose **Favorites Bar** on the pop-up menu on the New Bookmark sheet. Adding the bookmark places it on the left edge of the bar, becoming the first bookmark on the bar.

How do I change the location of a bookmark on the Favorites bar?

Click the bookmark's button and drag it along the Favorites bar to where you want it.

continued ▶

Set and Organize Bookmarks (continued)

Bookmarks not only give you an easy way to open web pages, but also reduce the chance for errors when you type a URL, so you will likely create many bookmarks. To navigate your bookmarks easily, organize them as explained here.

Place the bookmarks you use most often on the Favorites bar or on the Bookmarks menu so that you can get to them easily. Use folders to create sets of bookmarks related to specific topics or purposes, such as finance or news.

Set and Organize Bookmarks (continued)

Organize Bookmarks with the Bookmark Editor

1 Click **Bookmarks**.

The Bookmarks menu opens.

2 Click **Edit Bookmarks**.

Note: You can also press
Option + ⌘ + B to open the
Bookmarks Editor.

The Bookmarks Editor opens, taking up the entire Safari window.

3 Double-click a folder to expand it, showing the bookmarks it contains. or collapse it, hiding its contents.

Note: You can also click the reveal disclosure triangle (▶) to expand a folder. Click the collapse disclosure triangle (▼) to contract the folder.

4 Click the folder in which you want to create a new folder.

5 Click **New Folder**.

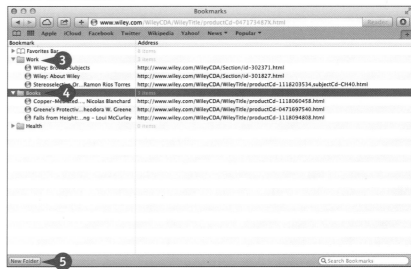

Safari creates a new folder called Untitled Folder and displays an edit box around the name.

6 Type the name for the folder and press Return.

The folder appears in the list of folders.

7 Drag your bookmarks to rearrange them.

Note: You can also drag a subfolder from one folder to another.

Note: To delete a bookmark or a folder, click it and then press Delete.

8 When you finish editing bookmarks, press Option + ⌘ + B or click **Bookmarks**, and then click **Hide Bookmarks Editor**.

Safari hides the Bookmarks Editor and displays the page you were viewing before you opened the Bookmarks Editor.

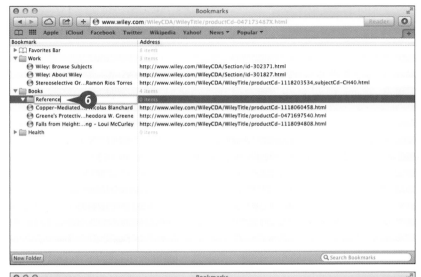

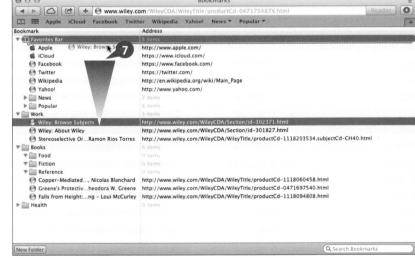

When should I bookmark a page?
Bookmark a page whenever you want to be able to return to it easily. You can keep the bookmark as long as you find it useful. But when you no longer need the bookmark, delete it so that you can navigate your other bookmarks more easily.

Can I change the order in which folders are shown in the Bookmarks window?
Yes. To reorder folders in the Bookmarks section of the Source pane, drag them up or down into the order you want.

Using and Setting Top Sites

Safari's Top Sites feature displays thumbnails of your most-used websites. You can click a thumbnail to quickly access a site. As you browse the web, Safari tracks the sites you visit and automatically adds those you visit most to your Top Sites page. Because of this, the contents of your Top Sites page normally change over time. You can also manually add pages to your Top Sites page and pin them to the page so they stay there. You can also choose how many sites appear on the page.

Using and Setting Top Sites

Use Top Sites

1. Click **Top Sites** (▦) on the Favorites bar.

A. Your Top Sites page appears. A thumbnail represents each web page.

2. Click the thumbnail for the site you want to display.

Safari opens the default page for the site.

Add a Web Page to Your Top Sites

1. Open the web page you want to add.

2. Drag the icon located to the left of the web page's address to the Top Sites (▦) button.

Safari adds the page to your Top Sites list.

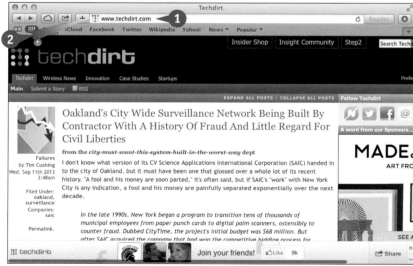

Organize Your Top Sites

1 Click **Top Sites** (▦).

The Top Sites page opens.

2 Move the mouse pointer (▶) over the thumbnail you want to change.

3 Click **Never Include as Top Site** (✕) to remove the site from the Top Sites screen and prevent it from returning.

4 Click **Mark as Permanent Top Site** (✈ changes to ✈) if you want to keep the site on the Top Sites screen.

5 Drag the sites into your preferred order.

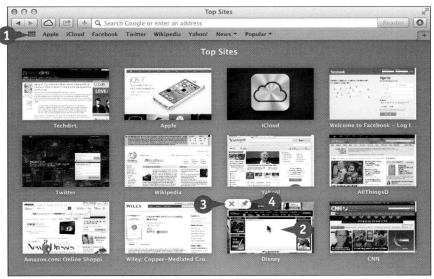

How do I change the number of thumbnails on the Top Sites page?

Click **Safari** and then click **Preferences** to open the Safari Preferences window. Click **General** to display the General pane. Click the **Top Sites Shows** pop-up menu (⬍) and select **6 sites**, **12 sites**, or **24 sites**, as appropriate. Click **Close** (⊗) to close the Safari Preferences window.

What are other ways to add pages to my Top Sites page?

You can drag a link from any document, such as an e-mail message, and drop it onto the Top Sites page to add it to your Top Sites. You can also open a new document, such as a text document, type a URL, and drag it from the document to your Top Sites page.

Using AutoFill to Quickly Complete Web Forms

When you complete web forms, such as when you register for an account, you often need to fill in the same basic set of information, such as your name, address, and telephone number. With the Safari AutoFill feature, you can complete this basic information using a single click to access data from a designated card in the Contacts application. AutoFill integrates with iCloud Keychain, enabling you to share your AutoFill data with your other iCloud devices, such as your iPhone.

Using AutoFill to Quickly Complete Web Forms

Specify Your Contact Card in Contacts

1. Click **Contacts** (▣) on the Dock.

   The Contacts application opens.

2. Click the card that contains the contact information you want to use.

3. Click **Card**.

4. Click **Make This My Card**.

5. Click **Close** (⊗).

Set Up AutoFill in Safari

1. With Safari open and active, click **Safari**.

2. Click **Preferences**.

3. Click **AutoFill**.

4. Select the **Using info from my Contacts card** check box (☐ changes to ☑).

5. Select the **User names and passwords** check box (☐ changes to ☑) to have Safari remember usernames and passwords for websites.

6. Select the **Credit cards** check box (☐ changes to ☑) if you want to store credit card details.

7. Click **Edit**.

8 Click **Add**.

A new credit card entry appears.

9 Fill in the details of your credit card.

10 Click **Done**.

The Credit Card sheet closes.

11 Select the **Other forms** check box (☐ changes to ☑) to store other form data.

12 Click **Close** (⊗).

The Safari Preferences window closes.

Your AutoFill data is ready to use.

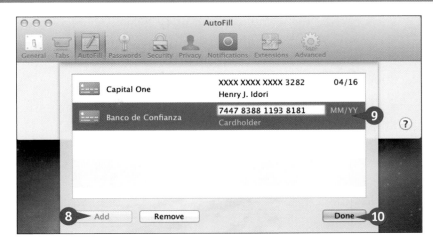

Is it safe to use AutoFill?
AutoFill uses encryption to store your data, so it is pretty safe as long as you prevent others from using your OS X account. For security, make sure the contact card you use for AutoFill contains only information you want to use on web forms. Create a separate contact card for AutoFill instead of using your main card that contains other personal information.

How do I fill in a form using AutoFill?
Go to a website that contains a form. Start to fill in your information. When the AutoFill prompt appears, click it, and then click **AutoFill** in the dialog that opens. After AutoFill enters your information, you will need to complete any remaining fields manually.

Save or Share Web Pages

As you explore the web, you will probably find web pages that you want to view again. Because the web is always changing, there is no guarantee that a page you are viewing now will be there when you return. To make sure you can view a page again in the future, you can save it on your MacBook Air; alternatively, you can add it to Reading List.

Some pages that you encounter are worth sharing. You can easily share pages; for example, you can send links to web pages to others or share a web page via the Messages application.

Save or Share Web Pages

Save Web Pages

1 Open a web page you want to save.

2 Click **File**.

The File menu opens.

3 Click **Save As**.

Ⓐ The Save As sheet appears.

4 Edit the default name for the web page as needed.

5 Apply any tags that will help you identify the file.

6 Choose the location in which you want to save it.

7 Click the **Format** pop-up menu (⬍) and select **Web Archive**.

8 Click **Save**.

Safari saves the page in the location you specified.

Note: A page that you save is a copy of what it was at the time you viewed it. To see the current version, you need to return to it on the web.

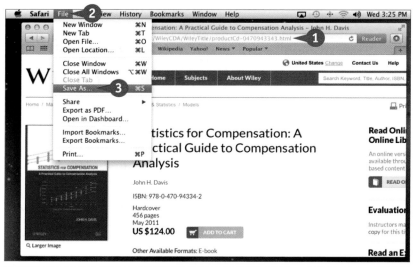

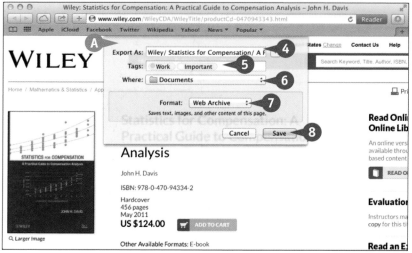

E-mail a Web Page or a Link

1 Go to a web page you want to share.

2 Click **Share** (⬆).

The Share pop-up menu opens.

3 Click **Email this Page**.

Safari creates a new e-mail message in Mail with the title of the page as its subject.

4 Add recipients.

5 Click the **Send Web Content As** pop-up menu (◆) and select **Reader**, **Web Page**, **PDF**, or **Link Only**, as needed. See the tip in this section for details.

Note: When you send a link, the recipient opens the current version of the page, which may have changed since you sent the link. If you send a Reader, web page, or PDF version, the recipient gets the version of the page as it is when you send it.

6 Edit the subject line if you want.

7 Type any explanatory text in the body of the message.

Note: Do not change the link that was pasted into the e-mail message or it might not work.

8 Click **Send** (📧).

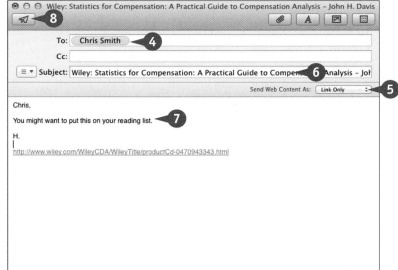

TIP

What are the different ways to share a web page via Mail?
Click **Reader** on the Send Web Content As pop-up menu to send the web page formatted for easy reading. Click **Web Page** to send the web page as it normally appears in Safari. Click **PDF** to create a PDF file containing the web page's contents. Click **Link Only** to send only a link. When the recipient receives the message, she can click the link to view the page — assuming it is still there.

Using the Reading List

The Reading List enables you to save a list of pages to read at a later time. When that time comes, you open the Reading List and see the pages you have added there. The Reading List is useful for storing pages that you do not necessarily want to bookmark because you will use them only temporarily. To be able to read any content linked to from a page on your Reading List, you have to be connected to the Internet to read the linked content; you can read the pages on your Reading List without being connected.

Using the Reading List

Add Pages to Reading List

1. Open a web page you want to add to your Reading List.

2. Click **Bookmarks**.

   The Bookmarks menu opens.

3. Click **Add to Reading List**.

   Alternatively, you can press **Shift** + **⌘** + **D** to add the page to your Reading List.

   Safari adds the page to your Reading List.

Note: If you want to add all of the tabs you are viewing to your Reading List, click **Bookmarks** and then **Add These Tabs to Reading List**.

4. Repeat steps **1** to **3** to add more pages to your Reading List.

Read Pages on the Reading List

1. Click **Show Sidebar** (📖).

   The Sidebar opens.

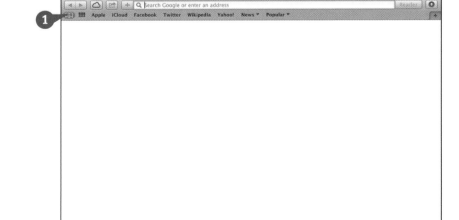

2 Click **Reading List** (⬚).

The Reading List pane opens.

3 Click the page you want to read.

A You can remove a page from the Reading List by moving the mouse 🔺 over it and then clicking **Delete** (⊠).

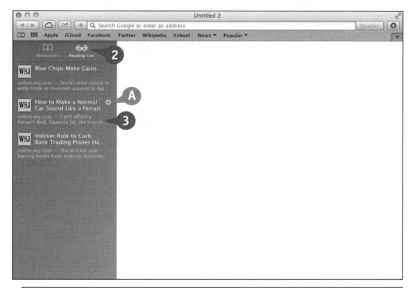

The page appears in the right part of the window.

4 Read the page.

5 When you are done with your Reading List, click **Show Sidebar** (▦).

The Sidebar closes.

TIP

How do I delete all pages from the Reading List?

1 Control+click in the Reading List pane in the Sidebar.

2 Click **Clear All Items**.

3 Click **Clear** in the confirmation dialog that opens.

Are you sure you want to clear your **Reading List?**

All items in your Reading List will be removed.

Cancel   Clear

Set Safari Preferences

Safari includes many preferences that you can set to change the way it looks and works. You set other Safari preferences similarly to the Tab and AutoFill preferences. For more information, see the sections "Using AutoFill to Quickly Complete Web Forms" and "Browse the Web with Tabs."

Set Safari Preferences

1 Press ⌘ + [,], or click **Safari** and then click **Preferences**.

2 Click **General**.

3 Click the **Default search engine** pop-up menu (⬍), and select the search engine you want to use.

4 Click the **Safari opens with** pop-up menu (⬍), and then click **A new window** or **All windows from last session**.

5 Click the **New windows open with** pop-up menu (⬍), and select the page (if any) you want to open automatically.

6 Click the **New tabs open with** pop-up menu (⬍), and select the page (if any) you want to open automatically.

7 Type or paste the URL for the home page you want to use. Leave the box blank to display a blank page instead.

Ⓐ You can click **Set to Current Page** to use the current page.

8 Use these settings to specify how Safari handles history items, downloads, and links.

9 Deselect the **Open "safe" files after downloading** check box (☑ changes to ☐) if you do not want Safari to open supposedly safe file types automatically after downloading them.

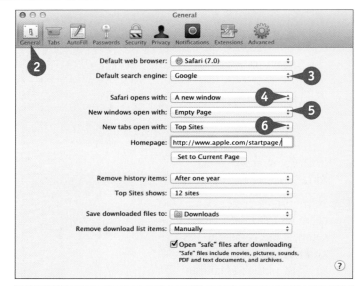

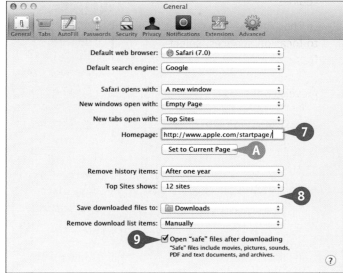

10 Click **Security**.

11 Select the **Warn when visiting a fraudulent website** check box (☐ changes to ☑) if you want to be warned when you try to open a page on a site with reported problems.

12 Use the Web content check boxes to enable plug-ins and JavaScript, or to block pop-ups.

13 Click **Privacy**.

14 To remove web information stored on your computer, click **Remove All Website Data**.

15 In the Block cookies and other website data area, select **From third parties and advertisers** (◯ changes to ◉) to block unhelpful cookies.

16 In the Limit website access to location services, select **Deny without prompting** (◯ changes to ◉) to prevent websites from identifying the location of your MacBook Air.

17 Select the **Ask websites not to track me** check box (☐ changes to ☑). This is a request that sites may not honor.

18 Click **Close** (⊗).

The Safari Preferences window closes.

TIPS

What are Notifications preferences?
Some websites can provide information to you through OS X's notifications feature. The Notifications tab shows you the websites that have requested permission to notify you. Click a website and click **Remove** to stop it from sending notifications to you.

What are the other preferences?
The Extensions preferences help you manage software that works with Safari. You can enable or disable this software, update it, and so on. The Advanced preferences enable you to set universal access features, such as minimum font size and enabling web page navigation with Tab. You can also choose a default style sheet and configure a proxy server if you use one.

Explore Mail

E-mail is a vital means of communication for most people today. Once you have connected your MacBook Air to the Internet, you can use the Mail application included with OS X to send and receive e-mail. Mail is easy to get started with and to use, but it is also a powerful e-mail application that provides the features and capabilities you need to work efficiently and effectively with e-mail.

Ⓐ Mail Icon

Click the Mail icon on the Dock to launch the Mail application. When Mail is running, the Dock icon also shows you how many new messages you have.

Ⓐ Toolbar

Contains tools you can use to work with e-mail.

Ⓑ Inbox

Contains mailboxes for each e-mail account.

Ⓒ Account Mailboxes

Contain e-mail for the accounts you have configured in Mail.

Ⓓ Account Mailbox Folders

Organize e-mail in different states, such as Sent or Drafts, for each account.

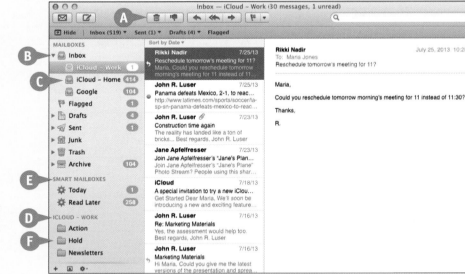

Ⓔ Smart Mailboxes

Automatically organize e-mail based on criteria you define.

Ⓕ Mailboxes

Folders in which you can store and organize e-mail.

A Selected Source

The source of e-mails you want to work with, such as those you have received in a specific account.

B Message Pane

Shows the messages in the selected source.

C Sort Criteria

Shows how the list of messages is sorted, such as by Date.

D Read/Unread

A blue dot indicates a message that you have not read.

E From

The name of the person who sent the message to you.

F Date Received

The date or time you received the message. The time appears for the current day. The date appears for older messages.

G Subject

The subject of the message.

H Selected Message

The message pane shows the selected messages highlighted in blue.

A Reading Pane

Displays the selected message.

B Message Details

Who the message is from, the subject of the message, when it was sent, and who the other recipients are.

C Sender's Image

Shows the image, if any, associated with the sender in Contacts.

D Body

The message's text.

E Attachments

Shows files attached to the message and enables you to save or view them. Image files may appear within the body of the message.

Set Up E-Mail Accounts

Before you can work with e-mail, you must obtain one or more e-mail accounts and configure Mail to access them. The details of configuring an e-mail account vary depending on the type of account. But for all types of accounts, you can set up the account by entering the configuration details in the appropriate fields in Mail. You can also use the Internet Accounts pane of the System Preferences application to set up accounts to use in Mail. See Chapter 6.

Set Up E-Mail Accounts

1 Click **Mail** (⬛) on the Dock.

The Mail application opens.

2 Press ⌘+⬚ or click **Mail** and then click **Preferences**.

The Mail Preferences window opens.

3 Click **Accounts**.

The Accounts pane appears.

4 Click **Add** (➕).

The Choose a mail account to add sheet appears.

5 Click the account type. This example uses Google.

6 Click **Continue**.

A sheet for entering the account details opens.

7 Type your name the way it to appear in your outgoing messages.

8 Type the e-mail address for the account.

9 Type the password for the account.

10 Click **Set Up**.

Note: If the Set Up button does not appear, click **Continue** and work through the following screens to specify additional details for the account.

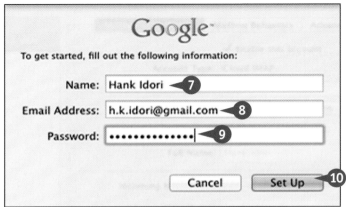

Mail sets up the account.

11 Select the **Contacts**, **Calendar**, **Messages**, and **Notes** check boxes, as needed (☐ changes to ☑).

12 Click **Done**.

13 Click **Mailbox Behaviors**.

14 To store draft messages online so you can access them from other computers, select the **Drafts** check box (☐ changes to ☑).

15 To store sent messages online, select the **Store sent messages on the server** check box (☐ changes to ☑). Click the **Delete sent message when** pop-up menu (⬍) and select when to delete the messages.

16 To store apparent spam messages online, select the **Store junk messages** check box (☐ changes to ☑). Click the **Delete junk messages when** pop-up menu (⬍) and select when to delete the messages.

17 Use the **Trash** check boxes and pop-up menu to determine how Mail deals with messages you delete.

18 Click **Close** (⊗) and save your changes at the prompt.

The account is ready to use.

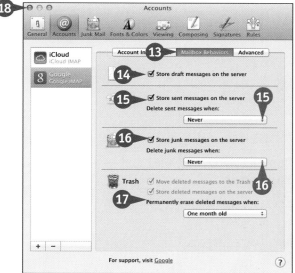

TIPS

An iCloud e-mail account was already set up when I launched Mail. How did that happen?
When you configure an iCloud account, either during the initial MacBook Air setup or on the iCloud pane of the System Preferences application, OS X automatically sets up the iCloud e-mail account in Mail. See Chapter 10 for more information about iCloud online services.

Where can I get free e-mail accounts?
You can obtain a Gmail account at www.google.com. You can also get a free e-mail account at www.yahoo.com. Having at least two e-mail accounts is a good idea so that you can use one for activities more likely to draw spam. For more information, see the section "Reduce Spam."

Read and Reply to E-Mail

When you receive e-mail messages, you will probably want to read them. With Mail, you can read e-mail in the reading pane, as described in the following steps, or you can double-click a message to open it in its own window. You can also easily reply to e-mail that you receive to start or continue an e-mail conversation, also called a *thread*.

Read and Reply to E-Mail

Read E-Mail

1. Click the Inbox.

2. Click the message you want to read.

   The message appears in the reading pane.

3. Read the message.

   If the message has images attached, they may appear in the message's body.

Note: After you have viewed a message in the reading pane, its blue dot disappears to indicate that you have read it.

4. If the message is too long to fit into the current window, press Spacebar to scroll down in the message.

5. To open a message in its own window, double-click it.

   The message appears in a separate window.

6. Read the message and look at the images it contains.

7. When you finish with the message, click **Close** (⊗).

   The message window closes.

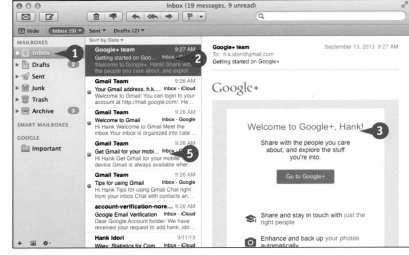

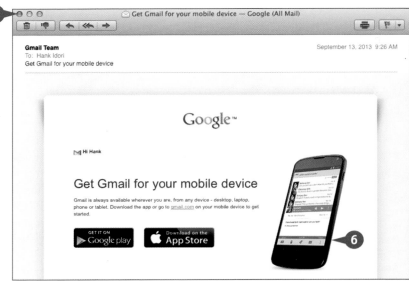

Reply to E-Mail

1 Click a message in the message list.

2 Click **Reply** (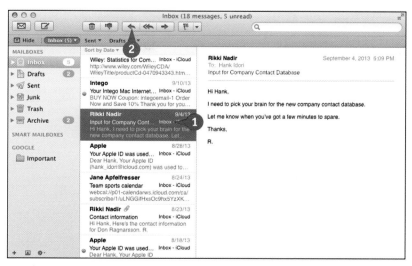).

Note: If more than one person is listed in the From or Cc field and you want to reply to everyone listed, click **Reply All** (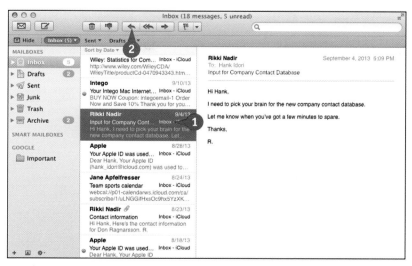) instead.

A A new message appears, addressed to the sender of the message. If you clicked **Reply All**, the message is addressed to all recipients except for any in the Bcc field, whose addresses you do not see.

B Mail adds "Re:" to the beginning of the subject to show that the message is a reply.

C Mail places the contents of the original message in the body in blue and marks it with a vertical line to indicate it is quoted text.

D Optionally, add other recipients to the To or Cc field.

3 Type your reply.

4 Click **Send** (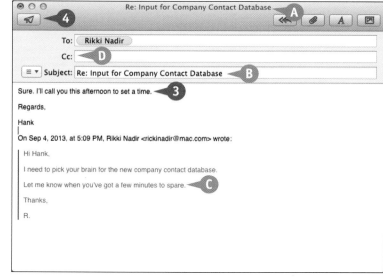).

The window closes.

Mail sends the message, and you hear the sent mail sound effect.

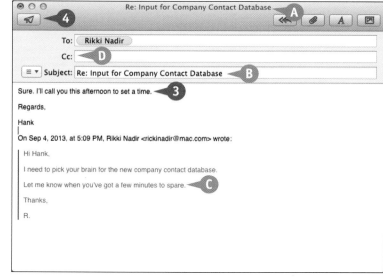

TIP

How do I reply using a different e-mail account?

In the reply window, click **Choose Fields** (☰▾), and then click **Customize** on the pop-up menu. The window displays all the fields you can add to the message, including Bcc, Reply To, Account, and Priority. Select the **Account** check box (☐ changes to ☑), which shows the account name, and then click **OK**. You can then click the **Account** pop-up menu and select the account from which to send the reply.

Send E-Mail

In addition to reading and replying to e-mail messages that you receive, you will want to create and send your own messages. When you want to e-mail someone, you create a new message, address it, add the contents, and then send it. You can add addressees in three ways: To, Cc, and Bcc. You put the primary recipients in the To field and any secondary recipients in the Cc field. If you need to send the message to yet other people but hide the fact from the To and Cc recipients, you put them in the Bcc field.

Send E-Mail

1 Click **Compose New Message** (☑).

2 Type the name or e-mail address of the first recipient in the To field.

As you type, Mail attempts to match a previously used e-mail address or an address in Contacts to what you type. Select an e-mail address to insert it.

3 Press Tab.

Note: When it can, Mail replaces an e-mail address with the person's name.

4 Type another e-mail address.

5 Click in the Cc field or press Tab to move there, and type e-mail addresses of people who should receive a copy of the message.

6 Type the subject of the message in the Subject field.

A The subject appears in the title bar.

7 If you have displayed the Account pop-up menu, click the **Account** pop-up menu and select the account to use.

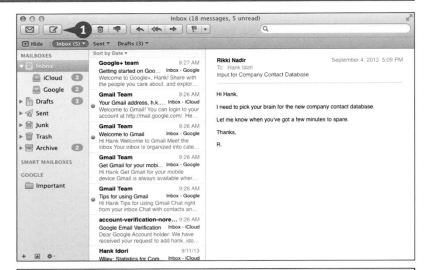

8 Type the message in the body.

Note: You can use **Show Format Bar** (A) to display the Format toolbar. You can use the tools on this toolbar to format new messages.

As you type, Mail checks your spelling. Mail underlines misspelled and unrecognized words in red.

9 To correct a misspelled word, Control+click it.

10 Click the correct spelling on the list.

Note: If the word is spelled correctly and you want to add it to the dictionary so that Mail does not flag it as a mistake in the future, click **Learn Spelling**.

11 Review your message and make sure it is ready for sending.

12 Click **Send** (✈).

The window closes.

Mail sends the message, and you hear the sent message sound effect.

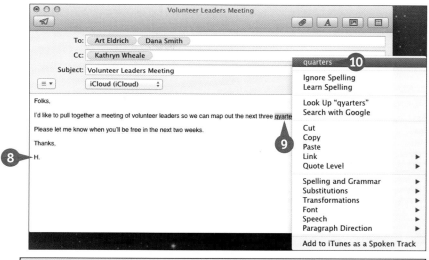

How do I avoid having to type e-mail addresses?
You can store e-mail addresses in Contacts so that you can type an e-mail address by typing a person's name, which is usually much easier to remember. As you type an e-mail address, Mail searches e-mail that you have sent, e-mail that you have received, and cards in Contacts to identify e-mail addresses for you. You can select one of these to easily address a message.

From where else can I start a new e-mail message?
When you are using an OS X application, such as Contacts, and you see an e-mail address, you can almost always start an e-mail message to that address by Control+clicking it and clicking **Send Email** on the contextual menu. Mail creates a new message to that address, and you can then complete and send it.

Work with Files Attached to E-Mail

In addition to communicating information, e-mail is a great way to send files to other people, and for people to send files to you. You can send most types of files, such as documents, photos, or even applications, but you must make sure the file size is not too large, because many e-mail servers reject huge messages. The limits vary, but 5 to 10MB is typical. Mail can display some file attachments, such as photos and PDF files, within an e-mail message. In all cases, you can save attachments on your MacBook Air for your use. After saving attachments, you can click **Message** and **Remove Attachments** to remove them from the message so your mailbox does not grow too large.

Work with Files Attached to E-Mail

1 Click a message containing attachments.

2 Move the mouse pointer (🔺) into the top of the reading pane.

Ⓐ The floating toolbar appears just above the body of the message.

3 Click the **Save** pop-up menu (⬚).

Ⓑ To preview the attachments, click **Quick Look**.

Ⓒ You can also work with the attachments by Control+clicking their icons in the body of the message and then using the commands on the contextual menu. Alternatively, you can drag an attachment to a Finder window or to the Desktop.

4 Click **Save All** to save all the attachments, or click a specific attachment to save it.

5 Click the location in which you want to save the attachments.

6 Click **Save**.

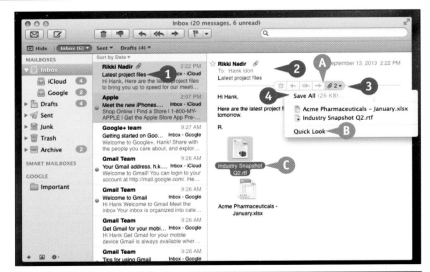

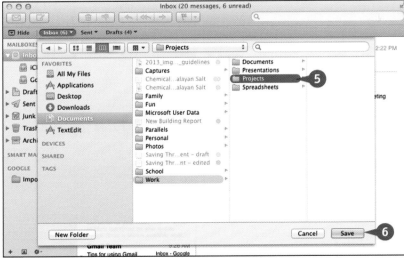

Attach Files to E-Mail

Y ou can attach files to e-mail messages you send to share those files with other people. As long as the recipient has a compatible application, she can use the files you send.

Attaching files increases the size of the message by the size of those files plus some overhead for encoding the file. If you attach only one or two small files, you can attach them as is. But to attach many or large files, you should compress them and send the compressed file as an attachment instead. See Chapter 4 for instructions on compressing files.

Attach Files to E-Mail

1 Click **Compose New Message** (![icon]) on the Mail toolbar.

A New Message window opens.

2 Address the message.

3 Type the subject.

4 Type any body text needed.

5 Click **Attach** (![icon]).

Note: You can also attach files to a message by dragging them from the desktop or a Finder window into the New Message window.

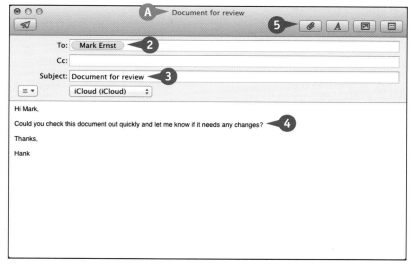

The Attach File sheet opens.

6 Navigate to and select the files you want to attach.

Note: You can select multiple files to attach by clicking the first, and then holding down ⌘ while you click each of the others.

7 Click **Choose File**.

8 Click **Send** (![icon]).

When the recipients receive the message, they can work with the attachments you included.

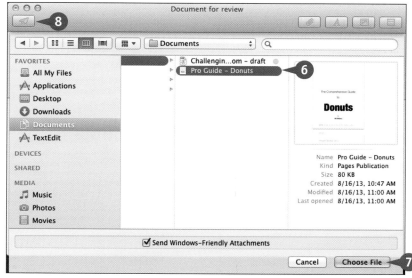

Organize E-Mail

As you use Mail, you are likely to end up with a lot of e-mail messages. Mail provides two powerful tools to keep your e-mail organized: Mailboxes and Smart Mailboxes. Mailboxes are like folders in the Finder. Smart Mailboxes automatically collect aliases to e-mail messages based on rules that you create.

To keep your e-mail organized, delete any message you no longer need. The fewer messages you keep, the fewer you have to organize, and the less storage space your e-mail requires. You should delete messages both from your MacBook Air and from the mail server.

Organize E-Mail

Organize E-Mail in Mailboxes

1. To create a new mailbox, click **New** (➕).

2. Click **New Mailbox**.

3. Click the **Location** pop-up menu (🔅), and select **On My Mac**.

   This setting stores the folder on MacBook Air instead of on the mail server.

Note: If you want the messages you store in the mailbox to be available from other devices, choose a location accessible over the Internet, such as a folder in your iCloud account.

4. Type the name for the mailbox.

5. Click **OK**.

   The New Mailbox sheet closes.

Ⓐ The mailbox appears in the On My Mac section of the mailbox list.

6. Drag a message from the Messages pane onto the new mailbox.

   Mail moves the message to the mailbox.

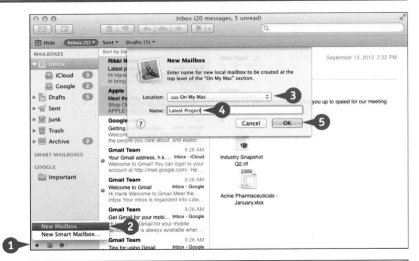

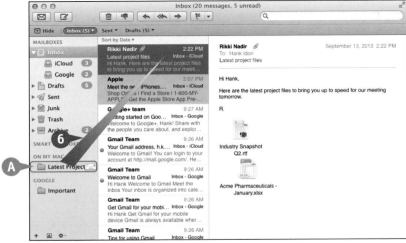

Organize E-Mail with Smart Mailboxes

1 click **New** (⊞).

2 Click **New Smart Mailbox**.

3 Type the name for the new Smart Mailbox.

4 Click the **Contains messages that match** pop-up menu (⬍), and select **any**.

5 Use the first line of pop-up menus and fields to create the first condition.

6 To add another condition, click **Add** (⊞).

7 Use the pop-up menus and fields to configure the condition.

8 Repeat steps **6** and **7** until you have added all the conditions you want.

Note: To remove a condition, click **Remove** (⊟).

9 Select the **Include messages from Trash** check box (☐ changes to ☑) if you want to include messages in the Trash.

10 Select the **Include messages from Sent** check box (☐ changes to ☑) if you want to include messages in the Sent folder.

11 Click **OK**.

Mail creates the Smart Mailbox.

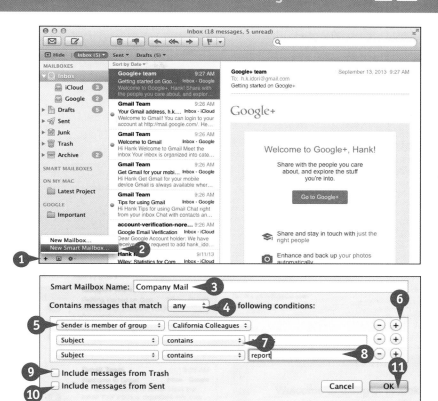

TIP

How do I change how the Messages list sorts messages?
Click the **Sort by** menu and choose how you want the list sorted. For example, click **From** to sort messages by the sender. To change the order of how the list is sorted, open the menu and click **Ascending Order**. You can also drag the right edge of columns to change their width.

Search E-Mail

You can use the Mail Search box to quickly find important messages. If the messages are stored on the server, you will need an Internet connection to search; if the messages are on your MacBook Air, you can search even when offline.

Search E-Mail

1 Type the information for which you want to search in the Search bar.

A As you type, Mail presents search options that relate to your search. For example, when you search for a name, it may suggest messages containing the name or people with that name.

2 Click the search option you want to use.

B Mail displays the messages that meet your criteria.

3 To read a message, click it.

C The message opens in the reading pane on the right side of the window.

Note: By default, Mail searches the currently selected mailbox, which is highlighted in blue. You can change the search location or just click the mailbox you want to search before you search.

4 To search in all mailboxes, click **All**, or to search in the Sent folder, click **Sent**.

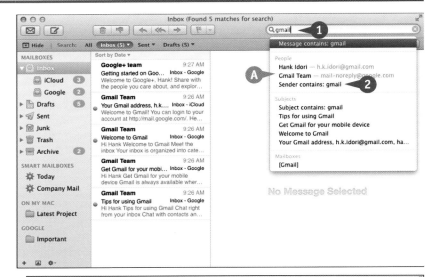

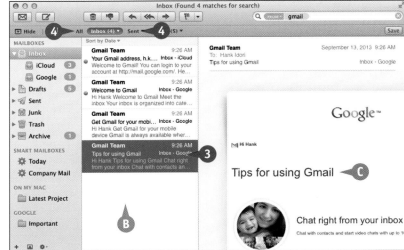

5 Click the menu that appears next to your search term to indicate what part of the messages you want to search.

For example, click **To** if you want to search for messages by recipient.

The results are refined, based on the choices you made.

Note: When you click **Entire Message**, Mail searches all parts of the messages.

6 To save a search as a Smart Mailbox so that you can run it again, click **Save**.

7 Type the name for the Smart Mailbox.

8 Click **OK**.

You can repeat the search at any time by selecting its folder in the Smart Mailboxes section of the Mailboxes pane.

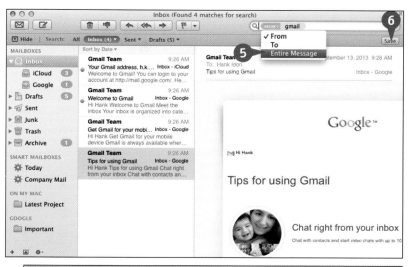

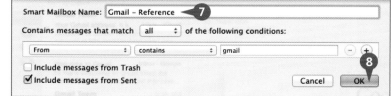

TIPS

Do I have to be using Mail to search e-mail?
The OS X Spotlight feature enables you to search for information on your MacBook Air no matter where that information is found, including files, folders, and e-mail. If you are sure the information you need is in an e-mail message, search in Mail. If not, use Spotlight instead, but be aware that Spotlight does not search e-mail messages stored on mail servers instead of on your MacBook Air. To learn how to use Spotlight, see Chapter 4.

Can I have the same message in more than one mailbox?
A message can exist in only one mailbox in the same location, such as the mailboxes stored on MacBook Air, unless you copy the message and place the copies in different locations. Because Smart Mailboxes contain aliases to messages rather than the actual messages, the same message can appear in multiple Smart Folders as well as the folder that actually contains it.

Reduce Spam

One of the perils of receiving e-mail is spam. Spam is annoying at best, with messages that stream into your Inbox with advertising in which you have no interest. At worst, spam contains offensive or dangerous messages that promise all kinds of rewards for just a few simple actions, but usually attempt to steal your data or your identity. By using tools built into OS X, you can reduce the amount of spam you see. Sadly, it is not possible to eliminate spam or prevent it altogether.

Reduce Spam

① In Mail, press ⌘+🔲.

The Mail Preferences window appears.

② Click **Junk Mail**.

③ Select the **Enable junk mail filtering** check box (🔲 changes to ✓).

④ Select **Mark as junk mail, but leave it in my Inbox** (🔘 changes to ⦿) if you want Mail to highlight junk e-mail, but not do anything else with it.

⑤ Select **Move it to the Junk mailbox** (🔘 changes to ⦿) if you want Mail to move spam to the Junk mailbox.

⑥ Select **Perform custom actions (Click Advanced to configure)** (🔘 changes to ⦿) if you want to define what Mail does using a mail rule.

⑦ Select the check boxes (🔲 changes to ✓) to specify e-mails that are exempt from junk mail filtering.

⑧ If you selected **Perform custom actions (Click Advanced to configure)** (⦿), click **Advanced**. Otherwise, go to step **12**.

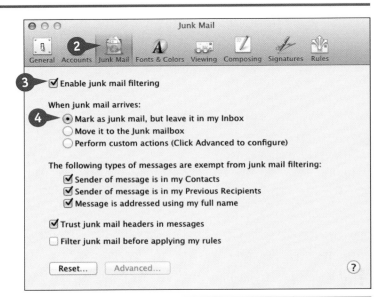

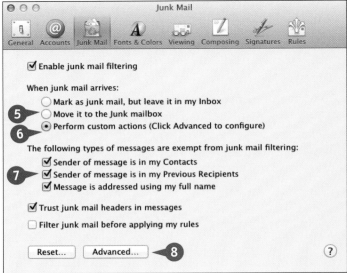

9 Adjust the existing conditions as needed.

Note: The Junk folder is a special Smart Folder. To adjust the conditions for the Junk folder, use the techniques explained in the section "Organize E-Mail."

10 Click **OK**.

11 Click **Close** (⊗).

12 Click the **Junk** folder.

A The contents of the Junk folder appear.

13 Select and review each message.

14 If a message is junk, do nothing; the message stays in your Junk folder.

Note: By default, Mail does not load any images in junk mail, because spammers can use them to determine when and where you read a message.

15 If a message is not junk, click **Not Junk**.

Any images in the message appear, and you can move the message to a different folder if you want to keep it.

16 Click **Delete** (🗑) to delete junk messages.

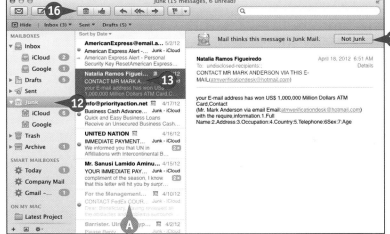

TIP

I have received a message saying I need to update my account. What should I do?
One effective technique that criminals use is to model their spam e-mails to look like e-mail from legitimate companies. They usually mention that your account is out of date or compromised, and that you need to provide information to correct the situation. If in doubt about whether a message is spam, point to a link in it *without clicking* to make the URL pop up. If the first part of the URL shows a site that has nothing to do with the real company, you know the message is not legitimate.

Create and Use E-Mail Signatures

An e-mail signature is canned text that Mail can insert automatically in new messages or you can insert manually. A signature normally provides relevant information, such as your phone number or website address, a quote or thought, or advertising. You can configure Mail to make adding signatures easier and faster. You can create many different signatures and easily use the most appropriate one for a specific e-mail message that you send. You can also associate different signatures with different e-mail accounts and have Mail insert a signature into new messages automatically.

Create and Use E-Mail Signatures

Create Signatures

1 In Mail, press ⌘+☐.

2 Click **Signatures**.

3 Click **All Signatures**.

4 Click **Add** (➕).

5 Type a name for the signature and press Return.

6 Type the content of the signature in the right column.

7 If you use a default font for your messages, select the **Always match my default message font** check box (☐ changes to ☑) so that the signature uses that font.

8 If you use default quoting, select the **Place signature above quoted text** check box (☐ changes to ☑).

9 Repeat steps **4** to **7** to create as many signatures as you want.

10 Drag signatures from the center column onto the e-mail accounts with which you want to use them in the left column.

11 Click an e-mail account.

12 Click the **Choose Signature** pop-up menu (⬍) and select the default signature for the account.

Whenever you send an e-mail from the account, Mail inserts the default signature automatically.

13 Click **Close** (⬤).

The Mail Preferences window closes.

Use Signatures

1 Create a new message.

Ⓐ The default signature for the e-mail account, if you configured one, is pasted in the new message.

2 To change the signature, click the **Signature** pop-up menu (⬍) and select the signature.

TIPS

What are the other choices on the Choose Signature pop-up menu on the Signatures tab?

If you choose **At Random** on the **Choose Signature** pop-up menu, Mail selects a signature randomly each time you create a message. If you choose **In Sequential Order**, Mail selects the first signature on the list for the first message, the next one for the second message, and so on.

Can I put images or links in my signature?

Yes. To add an image to a signature, drag the image file from the desktop onto the right pane of the Signatures tab. You can also add links to a signature by typing the URL in the signature block or by copying and pasting it in. Internet etiquette recommends that you keep signatures short — up to about four lines maximum — and that you not include images. If the recipient uses a plain-text e-mail client, any image comes as an attachment instead of in the message.

Create E-Mail Rules

If you find you perform the same tasks with certain kinds of e-mail, you can probably configure Mail to do those tasks for you automatically by configuring rules. *Rules* are automatic actions that Mail performs for you. To create a rule, you set up conditions for identifying suitable messages and then specify the action or actions to perform on them. The following steps describe how to create a rule to automatically file e-mails from specific people in a folder and to alert you that they have arrived. You can configure other rules similarly.

Create E-Mail Rules

1 Press ⌘+. .

2 Click **Rules**.

Ⓐ Mail includes the News from Apple rule by default.

3 Click **Add Rule**.

4 Type the name for the rule.

5 Click the **If** pop-up menu (⬍) and select **any** if only one condition has to be true for the rule to apply. Select **all** if all of the conditions have to be true for the rule to apply.

6 Click the left pop-up menu (⬍) and select the attribute for the first condition.

7 Click the center pop-up menu (⬍) and select the operand for the condition, such as **contains**.

8 Type the condition value.

9 Click **Add** (⊞).

10 Repeat steps **6** to **8** to set up the new condition.

Note: To remove a condition, click **Remove** (⊟).

11 Repeat steps **9** and **10** to add other conditions.

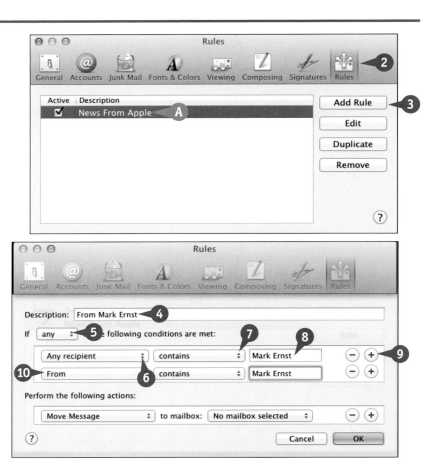

⑫ In the Perform the following actions area, click the top-left pop-up menu (⬍) and select the action.

⑬ Click the top right pop-up menu in the Perform the following actions area, and select the result of the action, such as a location or a sound.

⑭ To add another action, click **Add** (⊞).

⑮ Repeat steps **12** and **13** to configure the new action.

⑯ Repeat steps **14** and **15** to add and configure more actions.

⑰ Click **OK**.

Ⓑ The rule appears on the list of rules on the Rules pane.

⑱ Click **Close** (⬤).

When messages arrive that meet the rule's conditions, Mail performs the rule's actions automatically.

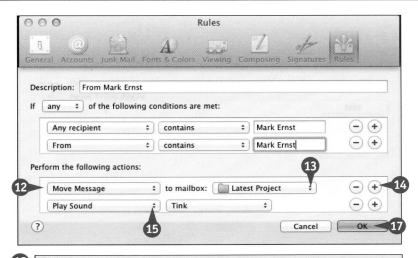

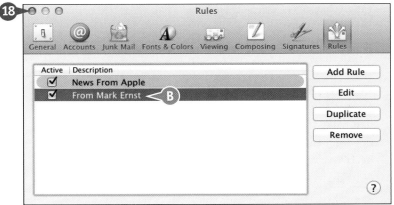

What are some examples of useful actions available for rules?

Move Message moves e-mail messages to specific locations, such as mailboxes that you have created on your MacBook Air or even the Trash. Forward Message can be useful when you always want to forward messages to another address in specific situations. If you usually reply to a specific person's e-mail, Reply to Message can be useful.

How do I know a rule is working?

Click a message to which the rule should apply, click the **Message** menu, and then click **Apply Rules**. If the actions you expect happen, then the rule is working. You should also select a message to which the rule should not apply and do the same thing. If the rule's actions occur, then the rule is not configured correctly.

Set Mail Preferences

M ail's preferences include General, Fonts & Colors, Viewing, and Composing. You use the General tab to set general Mail preferences, such as sound effects and where attachments are stored.

Set Mail Preferences

Set General Preferences

1. Press ⌘+, to open the Preferences window.

2. Click **General**.

3. Choose how often to check for new messages.

4. Choose the sound to play when new messages arrive.

5. To mute sounds for other actions, deselect the **Play sounds for other mail actions** check box (☑ changes to ☐).

6. Choose the mailboxes for which to display the number of unread messages on the Mail icon in the Dock.

7. Choose the default folder for attachments.

8. Choose what you want Mail to do with attachments that you have not changed when you delete the associated message.

9. Select the check boxes (☐ changes to ☑) to specify which items searches should include.

Set Fonts & Colors Preferences

1. Click **Fonts & Colors**.

2. Click the **Select** button next to the fonts you want to format and use the resulting Fonts panel to configure that font.

3. If you want a fixed-width font for plain text messages, select the **Use fixed-width font for plain text messages** check box (☐ changes to ☑).

4. Select the **Color quoted text** check box (☐ changes to ☑) and the pop-up menus to set the color for quoted text.

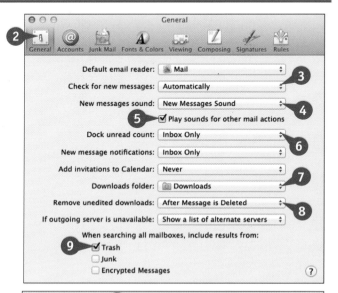

Set Viewing Preferences

1 Click **Viewing**.

2 Choose the level of information at the top of e-mail messages.

3 To show unread messages in bold, select this check box (☐ changes to ☑).

4 To suppress images not embedded in messages, deselect this check box (☑ changes to ☐).

5 If you prefer to see e-mail addresses and names, deselect this check box (☑ changes to ☐).

6 Select this check box (☐ changes to ☑) to set how Mail indicates that messages are part of the same conversation.

Set Composing Preferences

1 Click **Composing**.

2 Click the **Message Format** pop-up menu (⬍), and select **Rich Text** or **Plain Text**.

3 Click the **Check spelling** pop-up menu (⬍) and select **as I type**, **when I click Send**, or **never**.

4 To see the individuals in a group when you address a message to the group, select this check box (☐ changes to ☑).

5 If you have more than one e-mail address, click the **Send new messages from** pop-up menu (⬍), and select the default account for new messages.

6 To use the same format as the original message, select this check box (☐ changes to ☑).

7 To select the text to be quoted when you reply to a message, select this option (◯ changes to ◉).

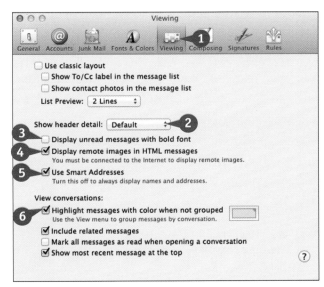

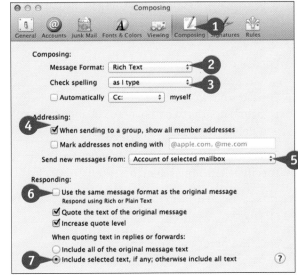

TIP

How else can I use threading?
Threading is a way to identify and group messages on the same topic (that have the same subject line), which is called a *conversation* in Mail. Click the **View** menu, and select **Organize by Conversation** to show these messages in groups that you can collapse or expand. When you click the parent message in a thread, you see a summary of all the messages that thread contains.

Chat with FaceTime

FaceTime is a great way to communicate because you can chat either via audio only or audio and video. You can use FaceTime to have a video chat with anyone who uses current versions of Macs, iPhones, iPod touches, or iPads.

Before you can start having FaceTime chats, you need to set up FaceTime with your Apple ID. Once that is in place, conducting FaceTime chats is easy.

Chat with FaceTime

Configure FaceTime

1 Click **FaceTime** (🔲) on the Dock.

The FaceTime window opens.

2 Click the **FaceTime** switch to move it to the On position.

The first time you turn on FaceTime, it prompts you to type your iCloud password.

3 Type your password.

4 Select the **Remember this password in my keychain** check box (☐ changes to ☑) if you want to store the password.

5 Click **Log In**.

6 Confirm or update your e-mail address.

Note: People use your e-mail address to request a FaceTime session.

7 Click **Next**.

FaceTime verifies the address you used, and then displays the Contacts pane.

Conduct a FaceTime Chat

1 Click **Contacts**.

You see the contacts in your Contacts.

2 Click the contact with whom you want to have a FaceTime session.

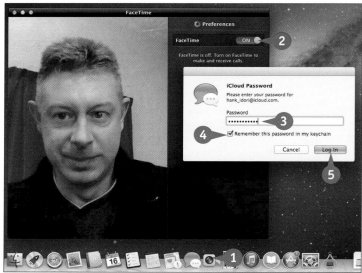

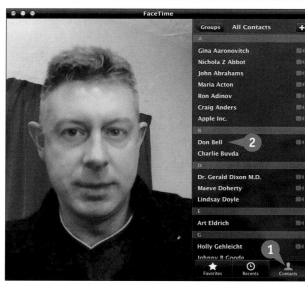

The contact's details appear.

3 Click **FaceTime**.

Note: To use a phone number, the person with whom you want to have a FaceTime session must have an iPhone 4 or later.

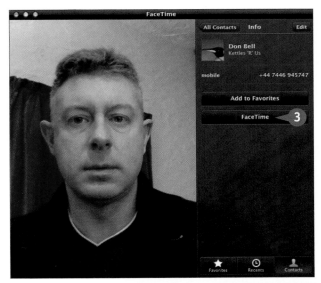

FaceTime notifies the contact and requests a session.

If the contact accepts your request, the FaceTime session starts and you can hear and see your contact. If the contact declines, is not available, or does not have a FaceTime capable device, you see a "not available" message.

A You can drag the preview window that the other person is seeing to change its location.

Note: If you do not see the buttons on the screen, move the pointer over the window and they appear.

4 Mute the audio and darken the video by clicking **Mute** (🎤).

5 Click **Full Screen** (▣) to have a full screen FaceTime window.

6 Click **End** to end the FaceTime session.

TIP

Are there easier ways to find someone to have a FaceTime chat with?
Yes. Click the **Recents** tab at the bottom of the Contacts pane to display a list of the people with whom you have had a FaceTime chat recently. You can request a FaceTime session by clicking one of the recent FaceTime chats. You can also save a contact as a favorite by viewing the contact and clicking **Add to Favorites**; you can then request a chat from the contact by double-clicking the favorite on the Favorites tab.

Explore Messages

The Messages application packs all the features that you need for text, audio, and video chats. After you configure Messages, you can use it to communicate with people in any format you choose. Messages can even help when you have computer problems, because you can use it to share the desktop of your MacBook Air with someone else over the Internet or over a local network.

Ⓐ Messages Window

Text conversations appear in the Messages window.

Ⓑ Person You Are Texting

At the top of the window, you see the person with whom you are texting.

Ⓒ Other Person's Last Text

On the left side of the window, you see the last text from the other person involved in the conversation.

Ⓓ Your Recent Comments

On the right side of the window, you see your most recent contributions to the conversation.

Ⓔ Text Box

When you want to add to the conversation, you can type text in the text box.

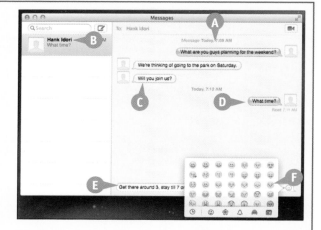

Ⓕ Emoticon Menu

You can add emoticons to a conversation by selecting them from the menu.

Ⓐ Audio Chat Window

When you audio chat with people, you see a visual representation of the sounds you hear.

Ⓑ Person Involved or Number of People

At the top of the window, you see the name of the person you are chatting with. If you are chatting with multiple people, you see the number of people.

Ⓒ Each Person Participating

Participants in the conversation have their own sound bar so that you can see when they speak.

Ⓓ Your Volume Level

The bottom bar represents how loud your speech is.

Ⓔ Add Button

You can click **Add** (⊞) to add more people to the conversation.

Ⓕ Mute Button

You can click **Mute** (▦) to mute your sound.

Ⓖ Volume Slider

You can use this slider to set the volume level of a conversation.

A Video Chat Window

This window shows each of the people with whom you are having a video conference.

B Participant Windows

Each participant gets her own window for the chat.

C Your Window

During a video chat, you see yourself as the other participants see you.

D Effects

You can use the Effects tools to apply a variety of interesting effects to the video.

E Add

You can add up to three other people in a video conference.

F Mute

You can click **Mute** (🎤) to block sound from your end.

G Full Screen

When you click **Full Screen** (🖵), the video conference fills the desktop.

A Shared Screen

You can use Messages to view and control another person's computer.

B Your Computer

When you are sharing a desktop, you see a preview of your desktop; you can click it to move back to your computer.

C Shared Applications

When someone shares a screen with you, you can work with applications and documents on her computer just as if you were seated in front of it.

Configure Messages Accounts

Before you start chatting, you need to configure the accounts you are going to use to chat. With an iCloud account, you can have text chats. With an America Online Instant Messenger, or AIM, account, you can also have audio and video chats. You can also chat with the Jabber instant message service and with Google Talk. To set up chat accounts, you use the Messages Preferences window. The type of account you use determines which features you can use in Messages.

Configure Messages Accounts

Create Accounts

1 Click **Messages** (📷) on the Dock.

The Messages application opens.

Note: The first time you start up Messages, the Setup Assistant walks you through creating an account.

2 Click **Messages**.

The Messages menu opens.

3 Click **Preferences**.

The Preferences window opens.

4 Click **Accounts**.

5 Click **Add** (➕).

The Choose a messages account to add dialog opens.

6 Select the account type (⭕ changes to ◉). This example uses **Google**.

7 Click **Continue**.

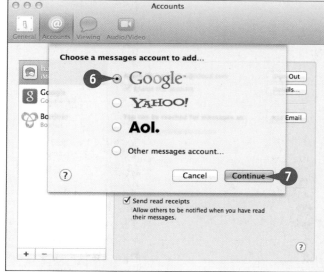

A dialog for entering the account information opens.

⑧ Type your name the way you want it to appear.

⑨ Type your e-mail address.

⑩ Type your password.

⑪ Click **Set Up**.

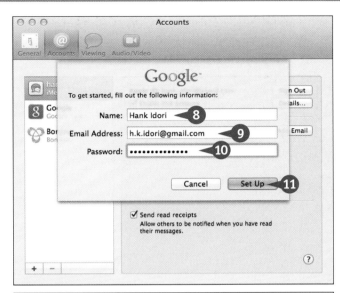

A dialog opens, showing controls for choosing which applications to use with the account.

⑫ Select the check box (☐ changes to ☑) for each application you want to use.

⑬ Click **Done**.

The account appears in the Accounts pane in the Preferences window.

TIPS

How do I disable a chat account I am not using?
Click **Messages** and then click **Preferences** to open the Preferences window. Click **Accounts** in the upper tab bar to display the Accounts pane. Click **Account Information** in the lower tab bar to display the Account Information pane. Deselect the **Enable this account** check box (☑ changes to ☐).

How do I change the format of my text messages?
Click **Messages** and then click **Preferences** to open the Preferences window. Click **Viewing** to display the Viewing pane. Here, you can change the fonts and colors used during text chats along with the background colors.

Chat with Text

Text chatting is a great way to have real-time conversations with other people while not consuming all of your and their attention throughout the conversation. With Messages, you can also include photos and documents in your chats.

The easy way to start chats with your contacts is to set them up as buddies in Messages. You can then quickly access your buddies from the Buddies list.

Chat with Text

Add a Buddy

1 In the Messages application, press ⌘ + 1.

The Buddies window opens.

Note: You can also click **Window** on the menu bar and then click **Buddies** to open the Buddies window.

2 At the bottom of the Buddies list, click **Add** (➕).

3 Click **Add Buddy**.

4 Type the buddy's account name.

5 Select the group in which you want to place the buddy.

6 Type the buddy's first name.

7 Type the buddy's last name.

8 Click **Add**.

Messages adds the person to your Buddies list.

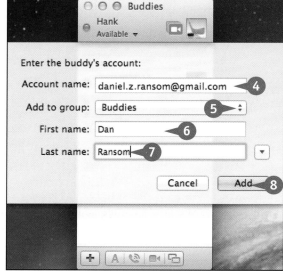

Start a Text Chat

1 Press ⌘ + **1**.

The Buddies window opens.

2 Double-click the buddy with whom you want to chat.

A The Messages window becomes active.

B An entry appears in the left column for the buddy with whom you plan to chat.

3 Type your message.

4 Press Return.

Messages sends your message and adds it to the message log at the top of the window next to your icon.

5 Read the reply.

C You can view images included in the chat.

6 Type your response.

7 To add an emoticon, click the pop-up menu and select the appropriate icon.

8 Press Return.

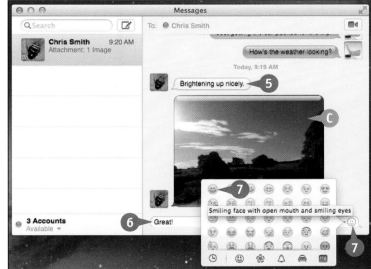

TIPS

How do I respond when someone wants to chat with me?

When someone wants to chat with you, a new message appears in the Message list along the left side of the Messages window and you hear the new message sound. Click the message and read its content. You can then reply to the message.

How can I send a photo in a text chat?

Drag the photo's file from a Finder window or the desktop and drop it into the conversation. Messages adds it as a button in the text field. If you want to send text along with the photo, type the text. Press Return. Messages sends the text and photo to the person with whom you are chatting. When that person accepts the file transfer, the photo appears in the Messages window.

Chat with Audio

Text chatting is great, but being able to talk to someone can be even better. Using the Messages audio chat feature, you can have conversations with one or more people at the same time at no cost to you. Before you start talking, take a moment to set up your MacBook Air microphone; you can use the built-in microphone or you can use an external microphone, such as a USB or Bluetooth headset.

Chat with Audio

Check the Microphone

1 Control+click **System Preferences** (image) on the Dock.

2 Click **Sound**.

3 Click **Input**.

4 Click the microphone to use.

A As you speak, the input level indicator shows the relative input volume.

5 Drag the input volume slider to set the input volume.

6 Select the **Use ambient noise reduction** check box (☐ changes to ☑) to reduce background noise.

7 Click **Close** (image).

Audio Chat

1 Click **Messages** (image) on the Dock.

2 Press ⌘+1 to open the Buddies window if it is not open already.

3 Click the buddy with whom you want to chat.

4 Click **Start an Audio Chat** (image).

Note: If the Start an Audio Chat icon (image) is unavailable, the buddy is not capable of audio chatting with you.

246

The Audio Chat window opens and Messages attempts to connect to the buddy you selected. If the person is available and accepts your chat request, the audio chat begins.

5 Speak to the person and listen as you would on a telephone.

6 To change the volume, drag the slider to the left to decrease the volume level, or to the right to increase it.

7 To add another person to the chat, click **Add** (➕).

8 Click the buddy you want to add.

After the second person accepts, all three of you are able to hear each other.

Note: You can add further people by repeating steps **7** and **8**.

9 When you are done, click **Close** (⊗).

The chat window closes.

TIPS

How do I avoid chat requests?
To prevent any chat requests from popping up, you need to quit Messages. If you want to show your status to others, open the **Status** pop-up menu just below your name at the top of the Buddies window. Choose the status you want them to see on their Buddy lists. Select **Offline** if you do not want to chat. To chat again, select **Available** from the menu.

How do I respond to an audio chat request?
When someone wants to have an audio chat, a prompt appears and you hear the invite tone. Click the prompt. Click **Accept** to start the chat, click **Decline** to avoid it, or click **Text Reply** to reply with text. If you decline, the person who requested the chat sees a message saying that you have declined.

Chat with Video

Earlier, you saw how easy it is to use FaceTime to video chat with someone. You can also use Messages to video chat. Messages has some benefits over FaceTime. One is that you can chat with more than one person at the same time. Another benefit is that the people with whom you chat only need a video chat-capable application, instead of requiring FaceTime. Conducting a video chat is similar to an audio chat. First, make sure your video and audio are set up correctly. Second, start a chat.

Chat with Video

Check the Camera

1 Click **Camera** (⬚) next to your name at the top of the Buddies or Bonjour list.

The My FaceTime HD Camera window opens.

2 Move your MacBook Air or yourself until the image is what you want others to see.

3 When you are satisfied with the view, click **Close** (⊗).

The My FaceTime HD Camera window closes.

Video Chat

1 Press ⌘+1 to open the Buddies window if it is not open already.

2 Click **Camera** (⬚) to the right of the buddy.

Note: If the Camera button does not appear, the buddy is not able to video chat with you.

The Video Chat window opens and Messages attempts to connect to the buddy you selected. If the person is available and accepts your chat request, the video chat begins.

Ⓐ You see the buddy's image in the window.

Ⓑ The inset preview window shows you what the other person is seeing in his chat window.

③ Drag the preview window to where you want it to be on the screen.

Note: See the section "Add Effects and Backgrounds to Video Chats" to apply interesting effects during your chats.

④ To mute your end of the conversation, click **Mute** (🔇); click it again to resume your conversation.

Ⓒ To make the window fill the desktop, you can click **Full Screen** (🔲).

⑤ To add another person to the conversation, click **Add** (➕).

The Add pop-up menu opens.

⑥ Click the buddy you want to add.

When the person accepts your invitation, a third video window appears and you see the second person.

You can see and talk to the other people, and they can see and talk to each other.

⑦ When you are done, click **Close** (🗙).

The Video Chat window closes.

How many people can I have in a video or audio conference at the same time?
You can have up to four participants, including yourself, in a single video conference. You can have up to ten people, including yourself, in an audio conference at the same time.

Add Effects and Backgrounds to Video Chats

To enliven your video chats, you can apply special effects to the images being shown during a video chat, and you can apply background images or movies to video chats to make them more interesting. With a motion background, it appears as if you are in front of or in whatever the background is; this is like the green screen technique used during weather broadcasts, movies, and so on. A static image as a background can also make it appear that you are somewhere you are not.

Add Effects and Backgrounds to Video Chats

1 Start a video chat.

Note: You can apply an effect after placing a call and before your buddy answers.

2 Click **Effects**.

The Video Effects palette opens.

A You can click **Next** (➡) and **Previous** (➡) to move through the various Effects screens.

3 Click the effect, image, or video that you want to apply.

B Messages applies the effect to your image.

4 Click **Next** (➡) until you see the video backgrounds.

5 Click a video background.

6 Move out of the camera view at the prompt.

7 When the prompt disappears, move back into the picture.

C Messages applies the background to your video.

8 Click **Original** in the middle of the Video Effects palette to remove the effect.

Share Documents via Messages

Chatting via Messages is a great way to collaborate on work as well as to catch up with friends. Whether you are using Messages for work or for play, you might want to transfer files back and forth. For example, if you are discussing a work project, you might want to share a document or a spreadsheet.

You can send and receive files easily, either directly from Messages or by dragging in the files from a Finder window. The recipient gets to decide whether to accept the file.

Share Documents via Messages

1 Start a chat.

This example shows a text chat, but you can share files during an audio chat or a video chat as well.

2 Click **Buddies**.

The Buddies menu opens.

3 Click **Send File**.

The Send File sheet opens.

4 Navigate to the file and click it.

5 Click **Send**.

Messages adds a button for the file to the text box.

6 Type any explanatory text needed.

7 Press Return.

Note: You can also send a file to a buddy by Control+clicking the buddy's icon in the Buddies list and then clicking **Send File**. In the sheet that opens, click the file, and then click **Send** to send it.

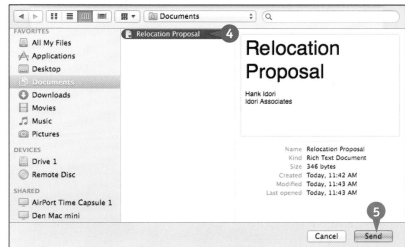

Share Desktops with Others

You can share your desktop so that the people with whom you are chatting can see and control what happens on your computer. When you share someone else's screen, you can see and control his computer. Sharing screens is a great way to collaborate on projects, to share information, or to troubleshoot Mac problems.

Share Desktops with Others

Share Your Desktop

① Press ⌘+1 to open the Buddies window if it is not open already.

② Click the buddy.

③ Click **Start Screen Sharing** (🖥).

④ Click **Share My Screen with *buddy***, where *buddy* is the name of the buddy you selected.

Ⓐ When the buddy accepts your invitation, he can control your MacBook Air and see what you do on the desktop. You can chat to discuss what you are doing.

While screens are being shared, you can audio chat. It is good practice for the person controlling the computer to explain what she is doing as she does it.

Ⓑ The Screen Sharing menu icon appears and alternates between 🖵 and 🖥.

⑤ To end screen sharing, click **Screen Sharing** (🖵 or 🖥) on the menu bar.

The Screen Sharing menu opens.

⑥ Click **End Screen Sharing**.

The sharing connection ends.

Share a Desktop Belonging to Someone Else

1 Press ⌘ + 1 to open the Buddies window.

2 Click the buddy.

3 Click **Start Screen Sharing** (🖥).

4 Click **Ask to Share** *buddy's* **Screen**.

Messages sends a share request to the buddy. When he accepts, screen sharing begins.

C Your buddy's desktop appears on your screen, either full screen or in a large window.

D Your desktop appears in a small window labeled My Computer.

Note: You can move the My Computer window around the screen if it blocks the part of the shared desktop that you want to see.

5 You can work with the buddy's computer just as if you were sitting in front of it.

6 To move back to your desktop, click the My Computer window.

The two windows flip-flop so that your desktop now appears full screen.

7 To end screen sharing, click **Screen Sharing** (🖥 or 🖥) on the menu bar.

8 Click **End Screen Sharing**.

The sharing connection ends.

TIP

How do I know when someone wants to share his screen with me?
You receive a screen-sharing invitation in Messages. When you click the invitation, you have the following options: **Accept** to start screen sharing, **Decline** to prevent it, or **Text Reply** to send back a text message. If you choose to share the person's screen, you are able to see and control that person's computer.

Communicate with Twitter

Twitter is a popular way to communicate in very short messages called *tweets*. Each tweet can be up to 140 characters long. You can follow someone on Twitter, which means you can see any messages she posts to her Twitter account. You can respond to tweets on someone's account. You can also post messages on your account, and people who follow you can read them. To use Twitter, you need a Twitter account; you can then tweet either using an application or the Twitter website, which you can access in Safari or another browser. A Twitter account is free, as are many Twitter applications.

Communicate with Twitter

Set Up Your Twitter Account

Note: To obtain a Twitter account, visit http://twitter.com.

1 Click **Apple** ( ).

The Apple menu opens.

2 Click **System Preferences**.

The System Preferences window opens.

3 Click **Internet Accounts**.

The Internet Accounts pane opens.

4 Click **Twitter**.

The Twitter dialog opens.

5 Type your user name.

6 Type your password.

7 Click **Next**.

Another Twitter dialog opens.

8 Click **Sign In**.

OS X signs you into Twitter.

Your Twitter account appears in the Internet Accounts pane.

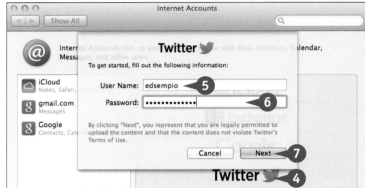

Send and Read Twitter Messages

1 Open your Twitter application and sign in to your Twitter account if required.

Note: You can also use Twitter by visiting `http://twitter.com`.

A You see the messages from people you are following.

2 Scroll the window to read all the tweets.

3 To tweet a message to your followers, click **Tweet** (📝).

4 Type your tweet.

5 Click **Tweet**.

Anyone who follows you can see the message in his Twitter feed.

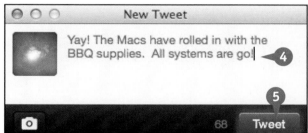

How do I find and install a Twitter application?
Open the App Store application. In the Search box, type **Twitter**. There are a number of Twitter applications. Click the **Install** button for the application you want to use. OS X downloads the application and installs it. You can then run the application from Launchpad.

How else can I use Twitter?
You can share photos and other content on Twitter. To do so, select the item you want to send via Twitter, click the **Share** button, and click **Twitter**. The item you selected is sent in a tweet.

PART IV

Taking MacBook Air Further

Your MacBook Air can help you get things done, such as printing documents and managing your contacts and calendars. To keep it working well, you should know how to maintain it and troubleshoot problems. You can use iTunes to enjoy audio and video and to sync your iOS devices with your MacBook Air.

⬤ ⬤ ⬤		Add	
Default	Fax	IP	Windows		Search

Name	▲ Kind
Officejet Pro 8000 A809 [2DEF02]	Bonjour

Name: Officejet Pro 8000 A809 [2DEF02]

Location: Kitchen Nook

Use: Officejet Pro 8000 A809

The selected printer software is available from Apple. Click Add to download it and add this printer.

Add

Understanding Printers

Although we live in an electronic world, you will likely need to print documents from your MacBook Air. The two most common types of printers are inkjet printers and laser printers. You can connect a printer to your MacBook Air in several ways. You can make a direct connection using either a USB cable or an Ethernet cable and an adapter. You can print wirelessly over a network to a printer connected to a device such as an Apple AirPort. Or you can print directly between the computer and a wireless printer.

Inkjet Printers

Inkjet printers create text and graphics by spraying droplets of ink on paper in various combinations. Inkjet printers produce high-quality output, especially when using the appropriate paper. These printers are inexpensive and many offer features such as scanning and faxing. Inkjet printers are usually less expensive than laser printers initially, but they consume large amounts of ink, which is expensive. You can expect to pay a significant portion of the purchase price of the printer each time you replace one or more ink cartridges; in some cases, you may pay more for new cartridges than you do for a new printer. Still, for many people, inkjet printers make a lot of sense.

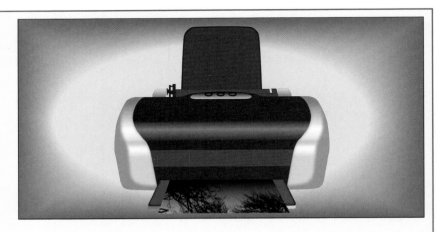

Laser Printers

Laser printers use a laser, mirrors, and an imaging drum to apply toner to paper. Laser printers produce very high quality output and are fast relative to inkjet printers. Although a laser printer is typically more expensive than an inkjet printer, the cost per page of a laser printer can actually be significantly less than that of an inkjet printer. Like inkjet printers, many laser printers print in color. With some careful shopping, you can often get a color laser printer for not much more than an inkjet printer.

Printer Connections

You can connect a MacBook Air to a printer in three ways. First, some printers use USB to communicate. Second, networkable printers have an Ethernet port that you use to connect the printer to the network your MacBook Air is on. Third, and most convenient, you can connect wirelessly. Some printers support wireless connections directly; however, you can connect a printer to an AirPort Extreme, AirPort Express, or AirPort Time Capsule by using an Ethernet port or its USB port to print to it wirelessly.

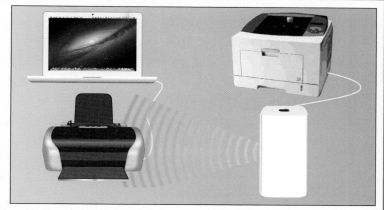

Printer Sharing

If you have more than one computer, you can share the same printer with all the computers over a wired or wireless network. You can connect the shared printer directly to a Mac through USB or Ethernet, but it is usually better to connect the printer to an AirPort, which makes the printer available on the network even when the Mac is not running. See Chapter 7 for information about setting up a wireless network.

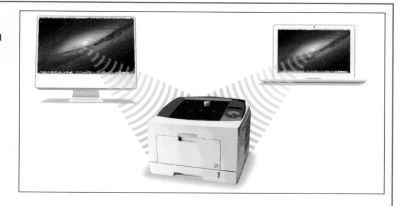

PDF

Adobe invented the Portable Document Format — PDF — as a means to share and print documents that do not depend on the specific applications or fonts installed on a computer. PDF is the standard format for electronic documents, no matter how they are distributed. You can read PDF documents using the Preview application, and you can print any document to the PDF format so that you can easily share it with others through e-mail or over the web.

Install and Configure a USB Printer

Connecting a USB printer directly to a MacBook Air is simple. After you have connected the printer to your MacBook Air, you need to configure your computer to use it. To print to a specific printer, your MacBook Air must have that printer's driver software installed on it. In most cases, OS X downloads the printer's current software and installs the appropriate software automatically as soon as you add the printer to your computer. If not, you can download the printer's software from the manufacturer's website, install the software, and then install the printer.

Install and Configure a USB Printer

1 Connect the printer to a power source and turn it on.

2 Connect the printer to the MacBook Air using a USB cable.

3 Click **Apple** (🍎).

The Apple menu opens.

4 Click **System Preferences**.

The System Preferences window opens.

5 Click **Printers & Scanners**.

The Printers & Scanners pane opens.

6 Click **Add** (➕).

7 Click **Add Printer or Scanner**.

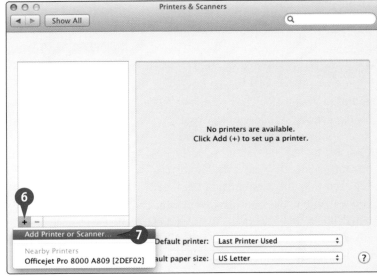

The Add dialog opens.

8 Click the printer you connected with the USB cable.

Note: If you are prompted to download and install software, you can click **Install** to do so now or click **Not Now** and the software will be installed after step **11**.

9 Optionally, change the printer's default name to a descriptive name. For example, you might type **Monochrome Printer** or **Main Color Printer**.

10 Optionally, type a description of the printer's location. For example, type **MacBook Air**.

11 Click **Add**.

Your MacBook Air downloads and installs any necessary software.

A The printer appears in the Printers & Scanners pane.

12 If you want the printer to be the default, click the **Default printer** pop-up menu (🔹) and select the printer.

13 Click the **Default paper size** pop-up menu (🔹) and select the default paper size to use.

14 Click **Close** (🔘).

The System Preferences window closes.

The printer is ready to use.

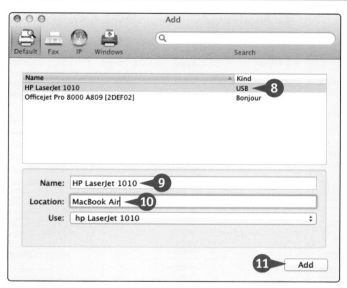

Can I use any printer with a MacBook Air?
Not quite, but you can use any printer that has OS X–compatible drivers. Most printers do have such drivers available, and OS X either includes them or downloads them for you automatically. The printer must also offer a connection your MacBook Air can use, such as USB, Wi-Fi, or Ethernet; most printers offer one or more of these, so you can usually connect easily enough.

Install and Configure a Network Printer

Your MacBook Air is wireless, so you do not have to use a cable to print. Fortunately, many printers are designed to connect to a network so that any computer that can connect to that network can use the printer. This is especially useful when a switch or router provides a wireless network.

One way to connect a printer to your network is by using Ethernet. This provides fast and trouble-free connections. The only downside is that the printer has to be within cable range of a switch or router, such as an AirPort Extreme or an Ethernet switch, on the network.

Install and Configure a Network Printer

1 Connect the printer to a power source and turn it on.

2 Connect the printer to a switch or router using an Ethernet cable.

3 Connect the MacBook Air to the same network using Wi-Fi or an Ethernet adapter and Ethernet cable.

4 Control+click **System Preferences** (⬚) on the Dock.

The System Preferences contextual menu opens.

5 Click **Printers & Scanners**.

Note: If System Preferences does not appear on the dock, click **Apple** (⬚) and **System Preferences**. In the System Preferences window, click **Printers & Scanners**.

The Printers & Scanners pane appears.

6 Click **Add** (⊞).

7 Select the printer you want to use.

Ⓐ OS X downloads and installs the software for the printer, if necessary.

Note: If your printer has configurable options, a dialog opens. Choose settings and then click **OK**.

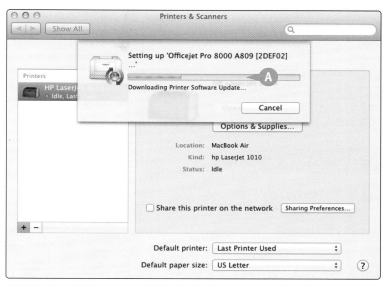

Ⓑ The printer appears in the Printers & Scanners pane.

❽ If you want the printer to be the default, click the **Default printer** pop-up menu (⬍) and select the printer.

❾ Click the **Default paper size** pop-up menu (⬍) and select the default paper size to use.

❿ Click **Close** (⬤).

The System Preferences window closes.

The printer is ready to use.

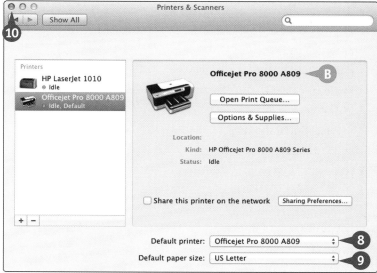

TIPS

What is Bonjour?
Bonjour is the OS X network discovery technology. When a device can use Bonjour, it broadcasts its identity on the network. When you connect your MacBook Air to that network to search for a device, such as a printer, it discovers Bonjour devices automatically.

Should I buy an inkjet printer or a laser printer?
If you print relatively few pages or you mostly print photos, an inkjet printer is usually your best option. But if you print a lot or print mostly text documents, a laser printer will save you money over the long run. For the ultimate in printing, get a color laser printer.

Print to Paper

With at least one printer connected to your MacBook Air, you are ready to print. The steps to start the print process are the same, regardless of what type of printer you are using. However, each printer offers its own set of options, so the configuration for your print job will depend on your type of printer. After you print to a printer the first time, you will often use the same settings, so you can just skip the configuration of options.

Print to Paper

1 With a document open, click **File** and select **Print**.

A The Print sheet appears and displays a preview.

2 Select the printer you want to use from the **Printer** menu.

3 Set the number of copies.

4 Click the **Pages** pop-up menu (⬍) and select the number of pages you want to print.

5 If you are ready to print, click **Print** and skip the rest of these steps.

6 To select more printing options, click **Show Details**.

7 To preview the document, click **Forward** (▶) or **Back** (◀).

8 To print specific pages, select **From** (◯ changes to ◉) and type the starting and ending pages in the boxes.

9 Click the pop-up menu (⬍) and select **Cover Page**.

10 Configure the cover page options.

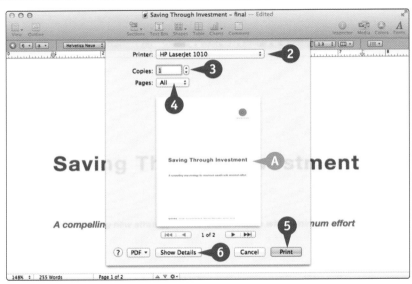

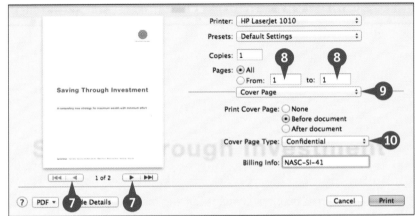

264

11 Click the pop-up menu (⬍) and select **Paper Handling**.

12 Configure the paper handling options. For example, you might want to print only odd pages or only even pages, or reverse the page order.

Note: The details and options you see depend on the specific printer you are using. Explore the menus and options for your printer to see your choices.

13 Click the pop-up menu (⬍) and select **Layout**.

14 Configure the layout options. For example, you might need to change the number of document pages printed on each sheet of paper and specify the direction in which to lay them out.

15 Click **Print**.

The Print sheet closes.

The document prints to the selected printer using the options you chose.

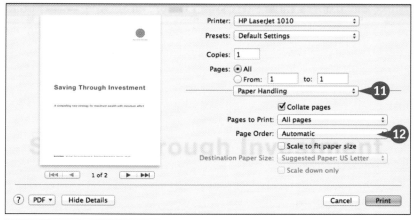

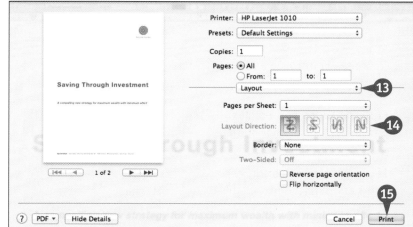

Print to PDF

The Portable Document Format, or PDF, is a great way to distribute documents you create to other people. This is because PDF files appear correctly on any computer equipped with a PDF reader application, regardless of the fonts installed on it, and people cannot easily change PDF documents you create. Support for creating PDF documents is built into OS X so that you can create a PDF file from any file you work with. The filename extension for PDFs is *.pdf*. It is added automatically, so you just need to make sure you do not change it.

Print to PDF

1. Open the document from which you want to create a PDF file.

2. Press ⌘ + P or click **File** and select **Print**.

3. Click **PDF**.

4. Select **Save as PDF**.

5. Type a name for the PDF file you are creating.

6. Click **Tags** and then click each tag you want to apply to the PDF.

7. Click the **Where** pop-up menu (⬦) and then click the location in which you want to save the PDF file.

8. Type a title for the PDF file.

9. Type the author's name.

10. Type an additional subject in the Subject field.

11. Type keywords used during Spotlight and other searches in the Keywords field using commas to separate the keywords.

12. To set passwords for the PDF file, click **Security Options**.

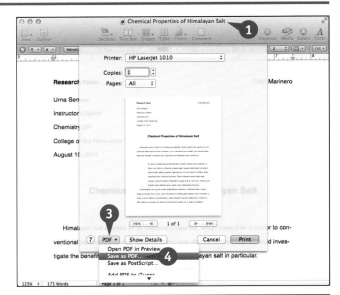

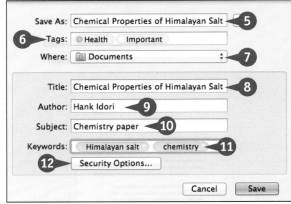

The PDF Security Options dialog opens.

13 To require a password to open the PDF file, select the **Require password to open document** check box (☐ changes to ☑) and type the password in the Password and Verify fields.

14 To require a password to copy content from the document, select the **Require password to copy text, images and other content** check box (☐ changes to ☑) and type the password in the Password and Verify fields.

15 To require a password to print a document, select the **Require password to print document** check box (☐ changes to ☑) and type the password in the Password and Verify fields.

16 Click **OK**.

The PDF Security Options dialog closes, and the Save As PDF dialog reappears.

17 Click **Save**.

The application creates the PDF file.

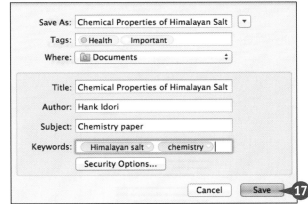

What applications can open a PDF document?

By default, PDF documents open in the OS X Preview application, which provides the basic set of tools you need to view and print them. A number of other applications can open PDF files as well, most notably the free Adobe Reader application, available at http://get.adobe.com/reader/. Reader offers many features for viewing and working with PDF documents.

Explore the Contacts Window

The Contacts application is both a powerful and easy to use contact information manager. You can quickly assemble your contact information and then use that information in many ways.

You can open Contacts by clicking its Dock icon, which is a book with the @ symbol on its cover, or by double-clicking its icon in the Applications folder. Before you start using Contacts, check out a few important concepts that will help you navigate and manage your contacts quickly and easily.

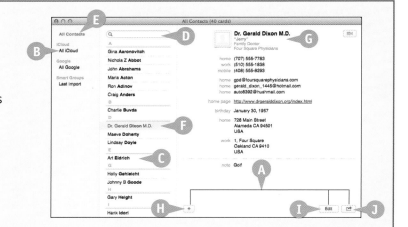

Ⓐ Toolbar

Provides the Add Card button, Edit button, and Share button.

Ⓑ Groups

Shows the groups in which your contacts are organized.

Ⓒ List

Shows the contacts in the group you are currently browsing.

Ⓓ Search Bar

Enables you to search for contacts.

Ⓔ Selected Group

You can select a group to browse the contacts it contains.

Ⓕ Selected Card

The highlight shows the card selected on the List.

Ⓖ Card

Shows the detailed contact information for the card selected on the List.

Ⓗ Add Card

Use this button to add cards for new contacts.

Ⓘ Edit

Use this button to change the information on the card being shown.

Ⓙ Share

Use this button to send the current card to someone via Mail, Messages, or AirDrop.

Cards

Each contact is represented by a card. Unlike physical cards, Contacts cards are virtual cards, or *vCards*, making them flexible because you can store a variety of information on each card. You can also store different pieces of information for your various contacts.

Hank Idori
Idori Associates

Contact Information

Each card in Contacts can hold many physical addresses, phone numbers, e-mail addresses, URL addresses, and so on. Because vCards are flexible, you do not have to include each category of information; you include only the information appropriate for each contact. Contacts displays only fields that have data in them so that cards are not cluttered with empty fields.

home	(707) 555-7783
work	(510) 555-1838
mobile	(408) 555-8293
home	gpd@foursquarephysicians.com
home	gerald_dixon_1445@hotmail.com
home	auto8392@hushmail.com
home page	http://www.drgeralddixon.org/index.html
birthday	January 30, 1957
home	728 Main Street Alameda CA 94501 USA

Groups

Groups are collections of cards. They are useful because you can do something once with a group and the action affects all the cards in that group. For example, you can create a group containing family members whom you regularly e-mail. Then you can address a message to the one group instead of addressing each person individually.

All Contacts

iCloud
All iCloud

Google
All Google

Smart Groups

Smart Groups are also collections of cards for which you define criteria and cards are added to the group automatically. For example, suppose you want to be able to contact your colleagues in the same state. You can simply create a Smart

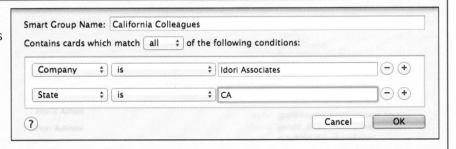

Smart Group Name: California Colleagues

Contains cards which match [all ⇕] of the following conditions:

[Company ⇕] [is ⇕] [Idori Associates] ⊖ ⊕

[State ⇕] [is ⇕] [CA] ⊖ ⊕

(?) [Cancel] [OK]

Group with suitable criteria, and Contacts adds all the matching contacts to the group automatically.

Contacts Actions

In addition to using information stored on cards indirectly — for example, looking at a phone number to dial it — you can use some data to perform an action by clicking the information's label and choosing an action. Some of the most useful actions are sending e-mails, visiting websites, and looking up an

Send Email
FaceTime
Send Message
Send My Card
Search with Spotlight

address on a map. You can also access extra actions by Control+clicking an item to display its contextual menu.

Add a Contact Manually

Before you can work with contacts, you need to create a card for each contact you want to manage. One way to do this is to create a card manually and add the contact information it needs. You can add new fields to cards as needed, so you can store almost any amount of information on a card. In many cases, you start a new card from another application, such as Mail, and add information to it by editing the card, which works similarly to creating a new card.

Add a Contact Manually

1 In the Contacts application, click **Add** (⊞).

Note: You can also create a new contact card by pressing ⌘+N.

2 Click **New Contact**.

A new, empty card appears in the Card pane.

3 Type the contact's first name in the First field, which is highlighted.

4 Press Return.

5 Type the contact's last name in the Last field.

Note: Press Return or Tab to move the highlight to the next field. Press Shift+Tab to move to the previous field.

6 Press Return.

7 Type the contact's company or organization in the Company field.

8 Press Return.

9 Click the pop-up menu (⬍) next to the first field. By default, this field is Mobile.

10 Click the type of phone number you want to enter. For example, click **iPhone**.

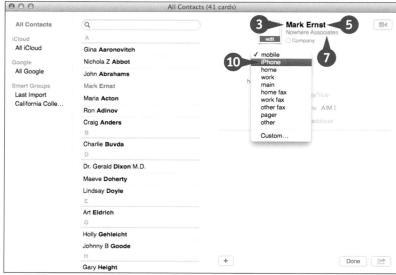

11 Type the phone number.

12 Repeat steps **8** to **11** to enter information into each relevant field.

13 To remove a field from the card, click **Delete** (⊟).

14 To add another field of the same type to a card, use the new field that appears when you have filled in all the existing fields of that type.

15 To add an image to the card, drag it from the desktop and drop it onto the image well.

16 Drag the slider to the left to make the image smaller, or to the right to make it larger.

17 Drag the image so that the part you want on the card appears within the box.

18 Click **Done**.

The image is saved, the sheet closes, and you return to the card.

19 Click **Done**.

Contacts saves the card and displays it, showing only the fields that contain information.

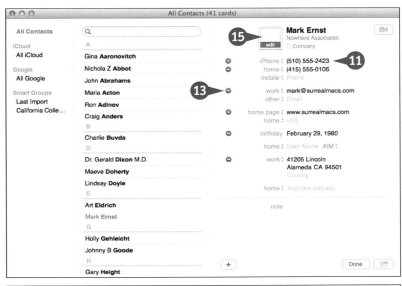

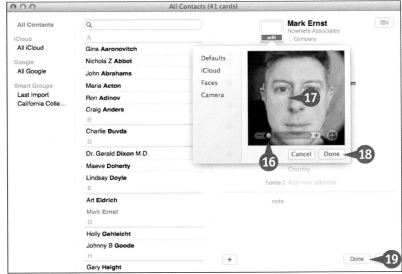

What if the information I want to enter is not on a pop-up menu?
Click the menu arrow and select **Custom**. In the Add Custom Label dialog, type the label for the field you want to add, and then click **OK**. Enter the information for that field.

How can I configure the default information on new cards?
Open the **Contacts** menu and choose **Preferences**. Click **Template**. Remove fields you do not want to appear by default by clicking **Delete** (⊟). Add more fields of an existing type by clicking **Add** (⊕) next to that type. Add fields that do not appear at all by clicking **Add Field** and then choosing the field you want to add to the template. Close the Preferences dialog.

Work with vCards

M any applications, including Contacts, use vCards to store contact information. One of the most common ways to receive vCards is as attachments to e-mail messages. vCard files have .vcf as their filename extension.

You can add contact information to Contacts using vCards other people send to you. You can also create a vCard for yourself to send to others so they can easily add your data to their contact information.

Add Contacts with vCards

1 In the Mail app, Control+click the vCard file attached to a message.

The contextual menu opens.

2 Click or highlight **Open With**.

The Open With submenu appears.

3 Click **Contacts**.

Note: If Contacts is the default application for vCard files on your MacBook Air, you can also double-click a vCard file to open it in Contacts.

The Contacts app becomes active.

A sheet appears, confirming that you want to add the card to your contacts.

4 Click **Add**.

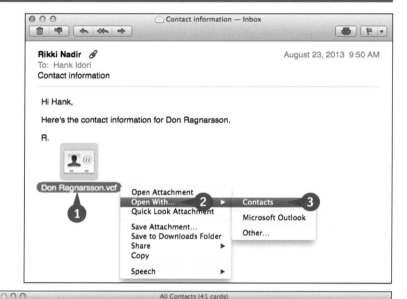

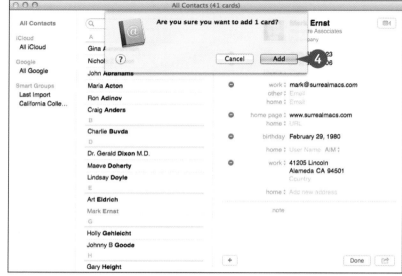

(A) Contacts adds the vCard. You can work with it just like cards you create within Contacts.

Share a vCard File Containing a Contact Record

1 Click the card you want to share.

Note: To quickly find your card, open the **Card** menu and choose **Go to My Card**. Your card, which is marked with a silhouette icon, appears in the Card pane.

2 Click **Share** (🖼).

The Share pop-up menu opens.

3 Click the means of sharing you want to use. For example, click **Email Card** to send the card via your default e-mail application, such as Mail.

Note: To share several contact cards in a single vCard file, select the cards, and then drag them out of the Contacts window onto the desktop or into a Finder window. Finder creates a vCard file containing all the contacts.

TIP

How can I add contact information to Contacts from e-mail when a vCard is not attached?
When you receive an e-mail in Mail, you can add the sender's name and e-mail address to Contacts. Position the pointer over an address and when the address becomes highlighted, click it to open the action menu. Choose **Add to Contacts**. A new card is created with as much information as Contacts can extract, usually the first and last name along with an e-mail address. Using Contacts, you can add other information to the card as needed.

Find Contact Information

Contacts makes it simple to quickly find information either by browsing your contacts or by searching for specific information. Browsing is most useful when you do not have many contacts or if you have them organized into groups containing a relatively small number of contacts that you can easily browse. Searching is usually the fastest way to find a contact among many contacts.

Find Contact Information

Browse for a Contact

1. If the Groups pane is not displayed on the left side of the Contacts window, press ⌘+1 or click **View** and **Groups** to display the Groups pane.

2. Select the group that you want to browse.

   Ⓐ To browse all your contacts, click **All Contacts**.

   Ⓑ The cards in the selected group appear on the List.

3. Scroll up and down to browse the list of names.

4. Click the card containing the contact information you want to view or to use.

5. To focus on this card, double-click it.

   Ⓒ The card opens in a separate window.

6. When you finish using the card, click **Close** (⊗).

   The card window closes.

Note: Opening cards in a separate window enables you to compare the contents of two or more contact records easily.

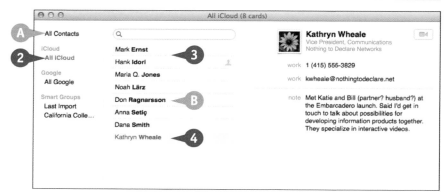

Search for a Contact

1 Select the group that you want to search.

Note: You can search with the Groups list displayed or with it hidden. When the Groups list is displayed, you search the selected group. When the Groups list is hidden, you search the All Contacts group.

All the cards in the selected group appear in the Name pane.

2 Type search text in the Search bar.

Note: Contacts searches all the fields at the same time, so you do not need to define what you are searching for, such as a name instead of an address.

D As you type, Contacts reduces the cards shown to only those that match your search.

3 Continue typing in the Search bar until the card you want appears in the Name pane.

4 Click the card to view its information.

E The part of the card that matches your search is highlighted in gray.

5 Clear the Search bar by clicking **Clear** (⊗).

All the cards in the selected group appear again.

TIP

Can I search for contact information by phone number or e-mail address?

When you perform a search, Contacts searches all the fields on all cards simultaneously. If it finds a match in any of these fields, a card is included in the search results shown in the Name pane. For example, if you enter text, it looks for matches in any fields that include text. Likewise, if you type numbers, Contacts searches any fields containing numbers.

Create a Group of Contacts

A contact group is useful because it enables you to store many cards within it. Then you can take an action on the group to affect all the cards included in the group. Groups make working with multiple cards at the same time easier and faster.

For example, when you want to send an e-mail to everyone in a group, you can do so by sending one message to the group rather than adding each person's e-mail address individually. You can also create a group for contacts that you use frequently to make finding contacts by browsing faster.

Create a Group of Contacts

1 In the Groups list, point to the account in which you want to store the new group. For example, to create the group in iCloud, move the mouse pointer ( ) over the iCloud group.

The Add button ( ) appears.

2 Click **Add** ( ).

A new group appears in the Group pane with its name ready to be edited.

3 Type a name for the group.

4 Press Return.

The group is created and is ready for you to add cards to it.

5 Click **All Contacts**.

All the cards in Contacts appear in the Name pane.

6 Select one or more cards you want to add to the group.

Note: To select multiple cards, click the first card, and then hold down ⌘ while you click additional cards.

7 Drag the card or cards onto the group. Drop the card or cards when the group is highlighted.

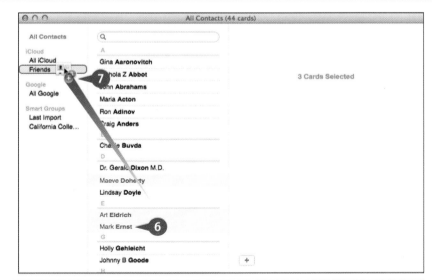

8 Select the group to which you added cards.

A The cards included in the group appear.

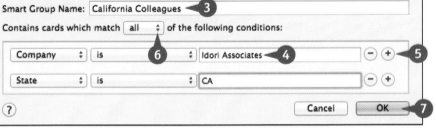

TIP

How do I create a Smart Group?

1 Click **File**.

2 Click **New Smart Group**.

3 Type the name for the Smart Group.

4 Use the pop-up menus and other controls to specify the first criterion.

5 Click **Add** (⊞) to add another criterion.

6 Click ⊞ and then click **all** or **any**, as needed.

7 When you finish adding criteria, click **OK**.

Using Contact Cards and Groups

After you have added all your contact information, Contacts helps you use your contacts in many ways. For example, you can quickly create and address a new e-mail message using a contact's card. Or you can see a physical address on a map and visit a website with just a couple of clicks on a contact's card. Unlike with physical contact information, such as Rolodex cards, you can use contacts in the Contacts application directly to perform tasks. Check out the following tricks you can perform with Contacts. While these are not all you can do with contacts, they will get you started.

Using Contact Cards and Groups

Address E-Mail

1 Click the card for the person you want to e-mail.

2 Click the label for the e-mail address. For example, click **home** to send an e-mail message to the home e-mail address.

The pop-up menu appears.

3 Click **Send Email**.

Your default e-mail application opens and creates a new message to the address you selected in step **2**.

Visit a Website

1 Click a card that contains the URL for the web page.

2 Click the label next to the URL you want to visit.

The pop-up menu opens.

Note: If the URL is in blue, you can click it to go to the website.

3 Click **Open URL**.

Your default web application opens the URL you clicked.

View the Map for a Physical Address

1 Click the card that contains the address you want to map.

2 Click the label of the address you want to see.

3 Click **Open in Maps**.

The Maps application opens and displays the map for the address.

Print an Envelope or Mailing Label in Another Application

1 Click the card containing the address.

2 Click the label of the address you want to place on an envelope or label.

3 Choose **Copy Address**.

4 Open or switch to the application you use to print envelopes or labels.

5 In the application, create an envelope.

6 Click **Edit**.

7 Click **Paste**.

8 Use the application's printing feature to print the envelope or label.

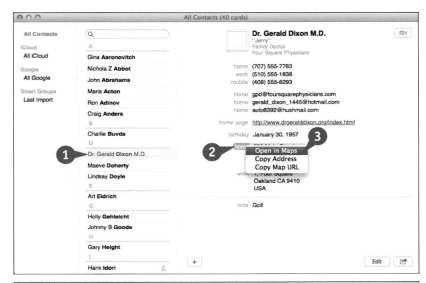

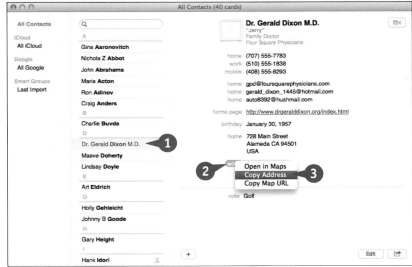

What other actions can I take with contacts using the pop-up menus?

You can take various actions from the pop-up menus, including the following:

Phone number. Send a message or start a FaceTime call.

E-mail address. Start a FaceTime call, send a message, send your contact card, or search using Spotlight.

Address. Copy the map URL so you can look up the address in a mapping application such as Google Maps.

Change or Delete Contact Cards or Groups

Over time, you will need to update your contacts by adding new information, changing existing information, or removing information you no longer need. The Contacts application makes all these tasks easy. You can change information for existing cards or groups. You can add new information to a card using the same techniques you use to create a new card manually. You can also remove information for a card or change existing information. You can delete a card or group you no longer need. When you delete a group, the cards it contained remain in the Contacts application.

Change or Delete Contact Cards or Groups

Change Address Cards

1 Click the card you want to change.

2 Click **Edit**.

Existing fields become editable and Delete buttons (🔲) appear.

3 Click the information you want to change.

4 Make changes to that information.

Note: You move between fields on a card by pressing `Return` or `Tab`.

5 Choose a label for a field from the pop-up menu.

6 To delete information from the card, click 🔲.

The field clears; after you exit Edit mode, that field no longer appears on the card.

7 To add information to the card, enter it in an existing field, or if all the current fields are full, enter it in the add new field section for the type of information you want to add.

280

8 Type information into the field.

9 After you have made all the changes to the card, click **Done**.

The Contacts application saves the changes you made to the card.

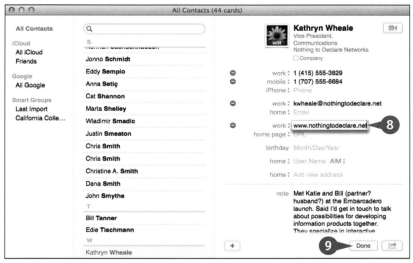

Delete Cards from Contact Groups

1 Click the group that contains the card you want to delete.

2 Click the card you want to remove from the group.

3 Press Delete.

A warning dialog appears.

4 Click **Remove from Group**.

The Contacts application removes the card from the group but leaves it in your contacts.

TIPS

How do I delete a card I do not need anymore?
Select the card you want to remove and press
Delete. Click **Delete** in the confirmation dialog.
The card is removed from Contacts.

How do I delete a group I do not need?
Select the group you want to delete and press
Delete. Click **Delete** in the confirmation dialog.
The group is removed from Contacts, but the cards
that were in that group remain in Contacts.

Print Envelopes and Contact Lists

Contacts enables you to print your contact information a number of ways, including mailing labels, envelopes, contact lists, and a pocket address book. Printing envelopes takes the tedium out of addressing envelopes and makes envelopes look better. Contact lists are a good way to carry contact information with you when you do not have your MacBook Air handy.

Print Envelopes and Contact Lists

Print Envelopes

1. Select the cards for which you want to print envelopes.

2. Click **File**.

3. Click **Print**.

Note: Click the **Show Details** button if it appears.

4. Click the **Style** pop-up menu (⬍) and select **Envelopes**.

5. Click the **Label** tab.

6. Select the **Print my address** check box (☐ changes to ☑).

7. Click the **Print my address** pop-up menu (⬍), and then click the return address.

8. Click the **Addresses** pop-up menu (⬍), and then click the address to use — for example, **work**.

9. Click the **Print in** pop-up menu (⬍), and select the print order.

10. Select the check boxes (☐ changes to ☑) to include additional information on the envelope.

11. Click **Color** and select the color to print the text.

12. Click **Print**.

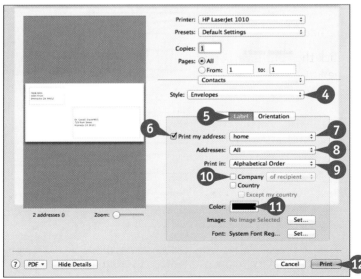

Print Contact Lists

1 Select the cards you want to include on the list. To include everyone in a group, click the group.

2 Click **File**.

The File menu opens.

3 Click **Print**.

The Print dialog opens.

4 Click the **Style** pop-up menu (⬦) and select **Lists**.

5 Click the **Orientation** buttons to set the orientation of the list to portrait or landscape.

6 Select the **Attributes** check boxes (☐ changes to ☑) to choose which information to include.

7 Click the **Font Size** pop-up menu (⬦), and select the font size to use for the list.

8 Click **Print**.

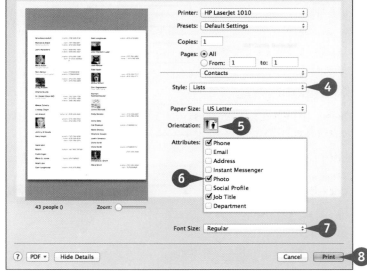

TIPS

What is a pocket address book?

A pocket address book is a smaller version of a contact list designed to be carried more easily than a list. You can print a pocket address book in a couple of formats, including Index, which shows contacts in alphabetical order, or Compact, which uses a compressed format.

How can I print addresses on standard mailing labels, such as those produced by Avery?

On the **Style** pop-up menu, select **Mailing Labels**. Click the **Layout** tab. On the **Page** pop-up menu, select the brand of labels you use, and then select the specific type on the related pop-up menu. This creates a format for the addresses that will fit onto the selected label when you print.

Explore Calendar

Calendar is OS X's calendar application. You can use it to track your calendar events, such as appointments, meetings, and dates. Calendar can remind you of upcoming events to help ensure you do not miss any unintentionally.

Calendar enables you to share your calendars on the web so other people can work with them. By subscribing to other people's calendars, you can see their commitments, which makes coordinating events among a group of people much easier. You can also use Calendar to directly coordinate events with other people, such as inviting people to a meeting you are hosting.

Ⓐ Back and Forward Buttons

Click these buttons to move back or forward in the calendar; these work when you are viewing the calendar by day, week, month, or year.

Ⓑ View Selection Buttons

Use these buttons to determine whether you view the calendar by day, week, month, or year.

Ⓒ Search Box

Enables you to search events on your calendars.

Ⓓ Calendars

Enables you to manage the calendars with which you are working.

Ⓔ Create Quick Event

Enables you to create an event with basic information.

Ⓕ Events

Colored blocks represent events; the color indicates the calendar on which those events are stored.

Ⓖ All-Day Events

At the top of each day, you see the events that are scheduled across the entire day.

Ⓗ Accounts

Calendars are associated with specific accounts, such as iCloud, Exchange, and so on.

Create a Calendar

In Calendar, you store events and reminders on a calendar. You can have as many calendars as you want. For example, you might want one calendar for work information and another for family events. You can configure a calendar so its events appear in the Calendar window or are hidden. In addition, each calendar can have its own color so that you can see what events and reminders are associated with it. You can create calendars for online accounts, such as iCloud or Exchange. This is useful because you can then access your calendars from other devices, such as an iPhone.

Create a Calendar

1 Launch Calendar by clicking its icon (📅) on the Dock.

2 Click **File**.

The File menu opens.

3 Click or highlight **New Calendar**.

4 Click the account in which to store the calendar.

5 Type the name of the calendar and press Return.

6 Perform a secondary click on the new calendar.

7 Select **Get Info**.

8 Type a description in the Description field.

9 If you want alarms on the calendar to be ignored, select the **Ignore alerts** check box (☐ changes to ☑).

10 Click the color pop-up menu (🔽) and select the color to use for the calendar.

11 Click **OK**.

The sheet closes and the new calendar is ready to use.

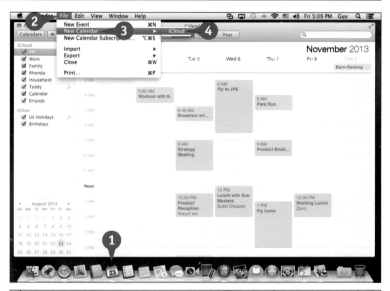

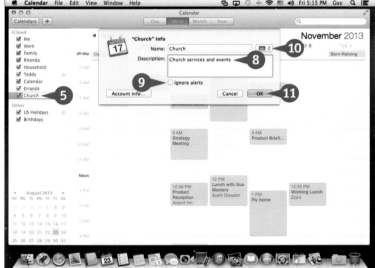

Add an Event to a Calendar

An event in Calendar is a period for which you want to plan, such as a meeting, recurring activity, or vacation. Each event is assigned to a specific time period on a calendar within Calendar. An event can also have lots of other information, including file attachments and web addresses.

You can create an event on a calendar and then set its details, such as the time, date, and alarms. You can drag to create events when viewing the calendar by Day or Week. You can double-click a date in Day, Week, or Month view to create an event.

Add an Event to a Calendar

1 Move to the calendar and to the date on which you want to create an event.

2 Drag over the time period for the event.

Note: You can drag across multiple days if the event extends beyond one day.

3 Release the trackpad when you reach the end of the event.

Note: You can create a new event quickly by clicking **Create Quick Event** (⊞) and then working on the sheet that pops up.

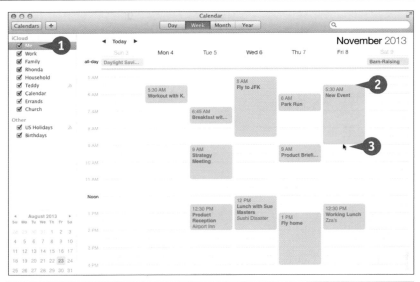

The new event is created.

The event summary window appears.

4 Type the name of the event.

A Click the color pop-up menu (▼) if you want to change the calendar to which the event is assigned.

5 Click **Location** and type the location for the event.

6 Click the date and time for the event.

7 If needed, change the event's date and times.

8 If the event repeats, select the frequency of the event on the **repeat** pop-up menu (⬚). Set the last date on which the event should be scheduled on the **end** pop-up menu.

Note: You can set a custom repeat schedule by clicking the **repeat** pop-up menu (⬚), clicking **Custom**, and working in the dialog that appears.

9 If the event requires travel, click the **travel time** pop-up menu (⬚) and select the time needed. Click **Custom** to set a custom time.

10 To set alerts for the event, select the kind of alert on the **alert** pop-up menu (⬚), and then configure it using the controls that appear.

Note: After setting one alert, you can click **Add** (⬚) to set up another alert — for example, for a vital appointment.

11 Click **Add Notes** and type any notes needed.

12 To store a file on the event, click **Add Attachment** and select the file you want to attach.

13 To include a URL with the event, type it in the **Add URL** field.

14 Click outside the Info window to close the window.

Calendar saves the event.

Note: To delete an event, select it and press Delete .

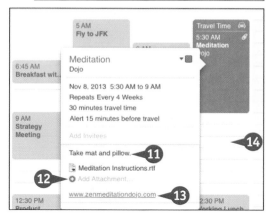

TIP

How can I be alerted to an event?

You can associate alerts with your events; an event can have multiple alerts. Alert options include Message that displays a message about the event; Message with Sound that displays a message and plays a sound; Email that sends an e-mail about the event; and Open file that causes a file to open. If you do not want to be alerted about an event, select **None**.

Schedule and Manage Events with Other People

Many of the events you manage in Calendar involve other people, such as meetings you want to have, group activities you are planning, and so on. You can include other people in events by inviting them.

Each invitee receives an e-mail containing information about the event with a calendar item as an attachment. If the invitees also use Calendar or another compatible calendar application and mail application, they can accept or decline your invitation. When you open the event's Info window, you see the status of each invitation, such as a question mark if the invitee has not responded.

Schedule and Manage Events with Other People

Schedule an Event with Other People

1 Create an event as described in the previous task.

2 Click **Add Invitees**.

3 Enter the e-mail address of the first invitee.

Note: If possible, Calendar replaces the e-mail address with the person's name.

4 Press `Tab`.

Note: If Calendar presents the address you want to use, click it or select it and press `Return`.

5 Repeat steps **3** and **4** until you have entered addresses for all the invitees.

6 Click **Send**.

Each person you invited receives a notification about the event. He can accept the event to add it to his calendar or he can decline.

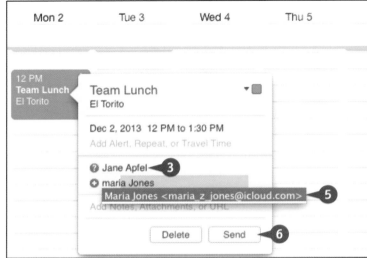

Accept or Decline Invitations

1 When you see the invitation badge on the Calendar icon or when a number appears in the Invitation button ( ), click it.

Note: To see the event on the calendar, click the event information box. The calendar scrolls so that you can see the event you are potentially adding to your calendar.

2 To add the event to your calendar, click **Accept**; to decline it, click **Decline**; or to indicate you are considering it, click **Maybe**.

The person who invited you to the event receives a notification about your decision.

Manage Events that Involve Other People

1 Open an event to which you have invited others.

A The icon next to each name indicates the status of the person's attendance. For example, if the person has accepted the event, the icon is a check mark in a green circle ( ).

2 When you finish viewing the status information, click outside the information window.

The information window closes.

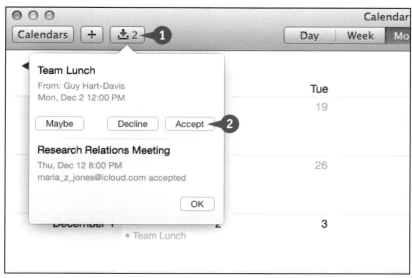

TIP

How do I invite someone to an existing event?
Open the event, click **Add Invitees**, and enter the e-mail address of the person you want to add to the event. Click **Update**. Calendar sends an invitation to the person you added.

Share Calendars with Other People

The Calendar app enables you to share your calendars with other people. You can share a calendar with specific people and choose whether each person can edit the calendar or only view it. Calendar invites the people via e-mail messages.

You can also publish a calendar to the web so that anybody can view it using a web browser. When you publish a calendar like this, only the people whom you have individually granted permission can edit the calendar; everybody else can only view it but not edit it.

Share Calendars with Other People

Share a Calendar

1 In the Calendars pane, move the mouse ![cursor] over the calendar you want to share.

Note: If the Calendars pane is not displayed at the left side of the Calendar window, click **Calendars** to display the pane.

2 Click **Share** (![icon]).

3 If you want to make this calendar public, select the **Public Calendar** check box (☐ changes to ☑).

Ⓐ The Share button (![icon]) appears.

4 Type the e-mail address of the first person you want to share the calendar with.

5 Press Tab.

The person's name or e-mail address appears as a button.

6 Repeat steps **4** and **5** to add each other person with whom you want to share the calendar.

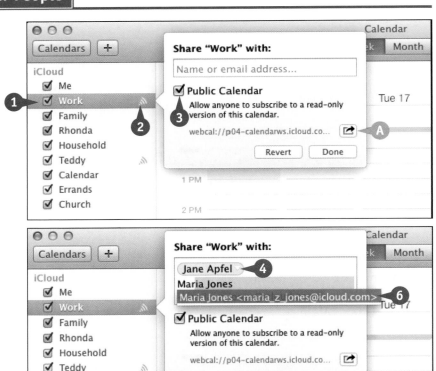

7 Click a person's button.

The pop-up menu opens.

8 Click **View & Edit** if you want the person to be able to edit the calendar. Otherwise, click **View Only** to allow only viewing.

9 Click **Done**.

The dialog closes.

Calendar e-mails invitations to the people you specified.

Accept or Decline an Invitation to a Shared Calendar

B If you see a notification inviting you to join a calendar, click **Join** or **Close**, as appropriate.

1 In the Calendar app, click **Invitations** (📥2).

The Invitations dialog opens.

2 Click **Join Calendar** or **Decline**, as appropriate.

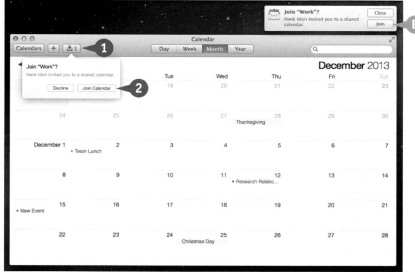

TIPS

How do I stop publishing or sharing a calendar?

Control+click the shared or published calendar in the Calendars pane, then select **Stop Sharing**. Click **Stop Sharing** again at the prompt. The calendar is no longer available to others.

How can I tell if someone has accepted my calendar?

When someone accepts your calendar, you see a notification informing you about it. You can also Control+click the calendar in the Calendars pane and then select **Sharing Settings** to display the Share dialog. You see the accepted icon (☑) next to people who have accepted the calendar.

Work with Shared Calendars

Other people who use Calendar can publish their calendars as easily as you can publish yours. When someone sends his calendar information to you, you can subscribe to the calendar or visit it on the web. If you subscribe to the calendar, you can only view its information.

When you subscribe to a calendar, the Calendar application adds it to your list of calendars, and you can view it in the same way you use to view your own calendars. When you visit a calendar on the web, you view it using a web browser, such as Safari.

Work with Shared Calendars

Subscribe to Calendars

1 Open an e-mail message containing calendar subscription information.

2 Click the link in the message.

Calendar becomes active and the subscribe sheet appears.

3 Click **Subscribe**.

Calendar downloads the calendar information, and you see the calendar's Info sheet.

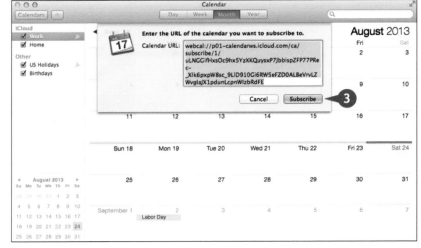

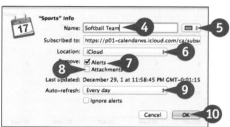

4 If you want to change the name of the calendar that appears in your Calendar application, edit the name in the Name field.

5 Click the color pop-up menu (⬦) and then select the color.

6 Click the **Location** pop-up menu (⬦) and then select the location.

7 Select **Alerts** (☑ changes to ☐) if you do not want to remove alerts from the calendar.

8 Select **Attachments** (☑ changes to ☐) if you do not want to remove attachments.

9 Click the **Auto-refresh** pop-up menu (⬦) and select the interval for updating the calendar.

10 Click **OK**.

Calendar adds the calendar to your list, and its events appear.

View or Share the Location of a Shared Calendar

1 Click the calendar in the Calendars pane.

2 Click **Share** (⬀).

3 Select the means of sharing you want to use. For example, select **Messages** to start creating an instant message containing the calendar's URL.

TIPS

How do I know when people have changed a shared calendar?

When changes are made to a shared calendar, you receive notifications informing you about the change.

What are the Birthdays calendar and the Holidays calendar?

The Birthdays calendar automatically creates events for the birthdays you have stored in your contact records in the Contacts app. The Holidays calendar contains national holidays for your region. If you do not want to use the Birthdays calendar or the Holidays calendar, disable them as explained in the next task.

Configure Calendar Preferences

You can customize the way Calendar works by changing its preferences. For example, on the General tab, you can determine whether weeks are five or seven days long and when days start. You can also configure the start and end time for the "working" part of the day. On the Advanced tab, you can determine how reminders are managed and control alarms for all Calendar events and reminders.

Configure Calendar Preferences

① In the Calendar app, click **Calendar** and **Preferences** or press ⌘+.

② Click **General**.

③ Click the **Days per week** pop-up menu (⬍) and select **5** if you want weeks to be shown as the five workdays. Select **7** if you want to see all seven days.

④ Click the **Start week on** pop-up menu (⬍) and select the first day of the week.

⑤ Click the **Scroll in week view by** pop-up menu (⬍) and select **Week** or **Day** to control how the calendar scrolls in this view.

⑥ Click the **Day starts at** pop-up menu (⬍) and select the time when the work day begins.

⑦ Click the **Day ends at** pop-up menu (⬍) and select the time when the work day ends.

⑧ Click the **Show** pop-up menu (⬍) and select the number of hours to show.

⑨ Click the **Default Calendar** pop-up menu (⬍) and select the calendar to use as the default for new events.

⑩ Deselect the **Show Birthdays calendar** check box (☑ changes to ☐) if you want to hide the Birthdays calendar.

⑪ Deselect the **Show Holidays calendar** check box (☑ changes to ☐) if you want to hide the Holidays calendar.

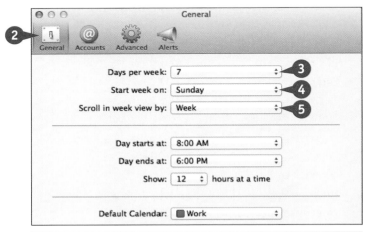

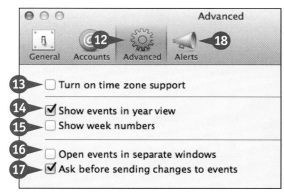

12 Click **Advanced**.

13 Select the **Turn on time zone support** check box (☐changes to ☑) if you want to be able to manage events in different time zones.

14 Select the **Show events in year view** check box (☐ changes to ☑) if you want to display events in Year view.

15 Select the **Show week numbers** check box (☐ changes to ☑) if you want to display week numbers.

16 Select the **Open events in separate windows** check box (☐ changes to ☑) if you want to open events in separate windows instead of using the floating window.

17 Deselect the **Ask before sending changes to events** check box (☑ changes to ☐) if you do not want Calendar to prompt you before sending events to invitees.

18 Click **Alerts**.

The Alerts pane appears.

19 Click the **Account** pop-up menu (⬍) and select the account you want to affect.

20 Click the pop-up menus ⬍ and select the alert timing to use for each option.

21 Select **Use these default alerts on only this computer** (☐ changes to ☑) if you want to use these defaults only on this computer.

22 Click **Close** (⊗).

TIP

How does time zone support work?

When you enable time zone support, Calendar can help you manage events across multiple time zones. When you create an event, you can associate it with a specific time zone. When viewing your calendars, you can set the current Calendar time zone using the Time Zone pop-up menu located in the upper-right corner of the Calendar window. When you set this, all events are shifted according to the relationship between their specific time zones and Calendar's so that you see all events according to the current time zone.

Print Calendars

Although using an electronic calendar is convenient and more powerful than a paper-based calendar, sometimes you might want to carry a paper calendar with you when you do not have your MacBook or iOS device. You can use Calendar to print calendars in various formats and with specific options. Printed calendars can mimic Calendar's Day, Week, or Month view, or you can print a calendar list, which is an efficient way to print information for many events.

Print Calendars

Print Day, Week, or Month View

1. Click **File**.

2. Click **Print**.

3. Click the **View** pop-up menu (⬍) and select **Day**, **Week**, or **Month**.

   Ⓐ The preview of the calendar in the left pane changes to reflect your selection.

4. Use the controls in the Time range section to determine how much calendar time the printed version covers.

5. Select the check box (☐ changes to ☑) for each calendar you want included on the printed version.

6. Deselect the check box (☑ changes to ☐) for each calendar you want to omit.

7. Select or deselect the **Option** check boxes to control what the calendar contains and how it appears.

8. Click the **Text size** pop-up menu (⬍) and select the relative font size to use.

9. Click **Continue**.

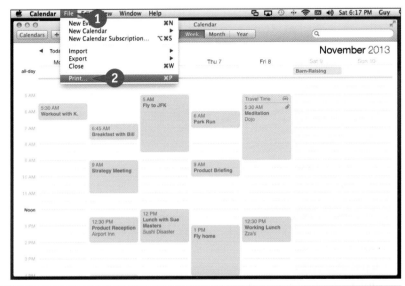

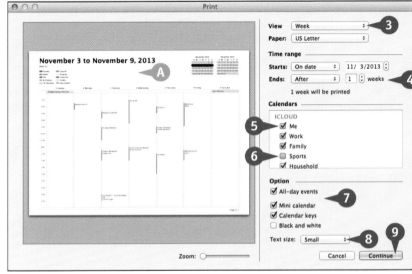

The Print dialog displays printer options.

Note: If the Show Details button appears, click it to display the full set of printer options.

10 Use the printer's options to configure the print job. These options vary depending on the printer you have.

11 Click **Print**.

The calendar prints using the settings you chose.

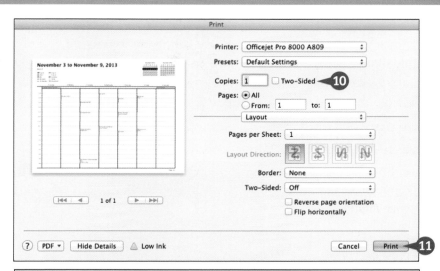

Print a Calendar List

1 Press ⌘+P or click **File** and **Print**.

The Print dialog appears.

2 Click the **View** pop-up menu (⟂) and select **List**.

B The Calendar events and reminders appear in a list format, which makes them more compact than a calendar view.

3 Use the Time range controls to set the number of days included on the printed list.

4 Use the other controls to set various options for the printed list, such as what calendars are included and whether timed events are included.

5 Click **Continue**.

6 Use the Print dialog to configure and print the list.

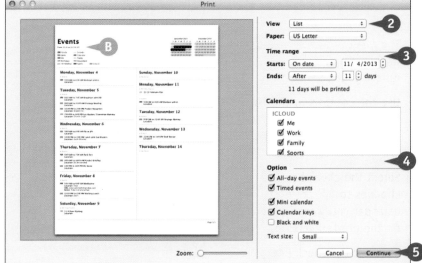

TIP

How can I access my calendars when I am away from my MacBook Air?

When you use a calendar stored on an online account, such as iCloud, Google, or Exchange, you can access that calendar from any device that has web browser access by logging in to your iCloud website and using its Calendar application. You can also set up your accounts on your iPhone, iPod touch, or iPad so that your calendars are available on those devices too.

Explore Reminders

The Reminders application gives you an easy way to create and maintain a list of reminders for things you need to do. You can use Reminders to remind you of anything that you want to be reminded of, such as items you have to do, things you want to pick up at the store, and so on. You can associate an alert with a reminder so your MacBook or your iOS device can prompt you to perform an action at a particular time or place.

Ⓐ Reminder Lists

You can create and manage multiple lists of reminders, such as one for work and one for a hobby.

Ⓑ Current List

When you select a list, you see the reminders it contains.

Ⓒ Complete Reminders

When you mark a reminder as complete, it disappears from the list, but is still available by clicking the Completed link.

Ⓓ Priority

You can associate an importance level with your reminders; this is indicated by the exclamation marks.

Ⓔ Due Dates

You can assign a due date to reminders, or you can leave them without a date.

Ⓕ Complete Check Box

Select a reminder's check box to mark it as complete.

Ⓖ Show Calendar

When you click this, a mini-calendar appears in the lower-left corner of the Reminders window.

Ⓗ Add List

Click this and select a location in which to create a new list.

Create a Reminder

Whereas events are periods of time for which you want to plan and that you want to manage, reminders are specific actions that you want to perform or are something you want to remember. Reminders can contain basic information about something, such as a description, along with information to associate it with a date or a location. You can configure reminders with alerts, a priority, and related information.

Create a Reminder

1 Select the list to which you want to add a reminder.

2 Click **Add** (➕).

3 Type the text for the reminder.

4 Move the mouse ▲ to the right side of the window and click the **Info** button (ⓘ).

5 To set an alert for the reminder, select the **On a Day** check box (☐ changes to ☑).

Note: You can also link a reminder to a location. Select the **At a Location** check box (☐ changes to ☑), type the location or pick it from the menu that appears, and then click **Leaving** or **Arriving** (◯ changes to ◉).

6 Use the date and time controls to set when you want to be alerted.

7 Click the **priority** pop-up menu (⬍) and select the priority for the reminder.

8 Enter notes about the reminder.

9 Click **Done**.

The reminder appears on the selected list.

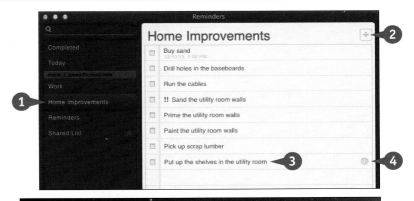

Keep App Store Software Current

Software developers regularly update their applications to improve them and to solve bugs. Apple not only issues updates to its applications, but more important, to OS X and the other system software that makes a MacBook Air work.

To keep your MacBook Air running well and to reduce security risks, keep your applications and system software current. You can use the Updates feature in the App Store application to keep your software up-to-date, and you can set the App Store preferences in the System Preferences application to check for updates automatically.

Keep App Store Software Current

Update App Store Software Manually

1 Click **Apple** (🍎).

2 Click **Software Update**.

The App Store application opens and automatically checks for updates to OS X and all software you have downloaded from the store. Any available updates appear in the Updates pane.

Note: If there are no updates, your software is current and you can click **App Store** and then click **Quit** to quit the App Store application.

3 Click **Update** for the application you want to update, or click **Update All** to apply all updates.

Your MacBook Air downloads and installs the update.

Note: Some updates require you to restart your MacBook Air. In this case, click **Restart** at the prompt.

Set Your MacBook Air to Update Apple Software Automatically

1 Click **Apple** (🍎).

2 Click **System Preferences**.

3 Click **App Store**.

4 Select the **Automatically check for updates** check box (☐ changes to ☑).

5 Select the **Download newly available updates in the background** check box (☐ changes to ☑).

6 Select the **Install system data files and security updates** check box (☐ changes to ☑).

7 If you have more than one Mac and want all the apps you download on your other Macs to be downloaded to your MacBook Air, select the **Automatically download apps purchased on other Macs** check box (☐ changes to ☑).

Ⓐ If updates are currently available, you can click **Show Updates** to display them in the App Store application.

8 Click **Close** (⊗).

The System Preferences window closes.

OS X automatically checks for updates and notifies you when they are available. It also downloads and installs important system and security files automatically.

TIP

What if I do not want to install the updates right now?
If you want to postpone the updates, click the **Update All** pop-up menu button (▣), and select **Try in an Hour**, **Try Tonight**, or **Remind Me Tomorrow**. This pop-up menu also contains the Install Now command. You can also simply quit the App Store application without installing the updates and without setting a reminder.

Maintain and Update Applications Not from the App Store

You should also keep current any applications you have installed from sources other than the App Store. Most applications support manual and automatic updates. Typically, you will find a Check for Updates command on the *Application* menu, where *Application* is the name of the application you are using, or on the Help menu. Most applications also support automatic checks for updates.

Maintain and Update Applications Not from the App Store

Manually Update Apps

1 Open the application.

2 Click **Help**.

3 Click **Check for Updates**.

If updates are available, the application prompts you to download and install them; follow the onscreen instructions. If updates are not available, you see a message saying so.

Automatically Update Apps

1 Open the application.

2 Click **Application**. This example uses Firefox.

3 Click **Preferences**.

4 Locate the Update preferences.

5 Click the update option you want to use (☐ changes to ◉).

Each time you launch the application, it checks for newer versions. When it finds one, it prompts you to download and install the newer version. Follow the onscreen instructions to complete the update.

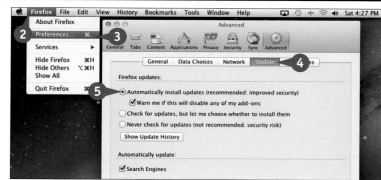

Profile Your MacBook Air

Each hardware and software component in your MacBook Air has a specific version and set of capabilities. Most of the time, you do not need to worry about these details. However, sometimes they can be very important, especially when you are trying to troubleshoot and solve problems.

Keeping a current profile of your MacBook Air is a good idea so that you have detailed information about it should you need to solve a problem or evaluate your MacBook Air's capabilities. You can use the System Information application.

Profile Your MacBook Air

1 Click **Apple** (🍎).

The Apple menu opens.

2 Click **About This Mac**.

The About This Mac window opens, showing information about the software version, processor, memory, and startup disk.

3 Click **More Info**.

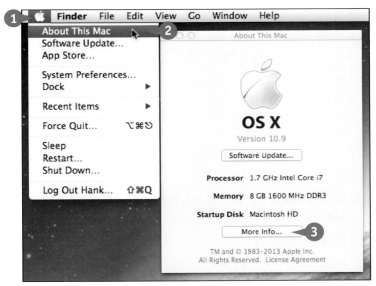

The System Information application appears.

Ⓐ At the top of the window, you see various categories of information about your MacBook Air, such as hardware components.

4 Click the tab of an area for which you want detailed information.

Ⓑ The details appear in the bottom pane of the window.

5 Continue to select other areas to get details about them.

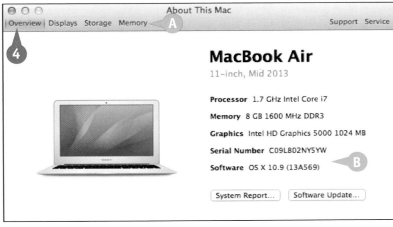

Monitor Your MacBook Air Activity

With the Activity Monitor application, you can examine the status of your MacBook Air in a very detailed way. For example, you can see how much processing time specific applications are using, which can often tell you when an application is having a problem.

Monitor Your MacBook Air Activity

1 Click **Launchpad** (⬚) on the Dock.

2 Type **act**.

3 Click **Activity Monitor** (▣).

The Activity Monitor application opens.

Note: If the Activity Monitor title bar shows *My Processes*, click **View**, and then click **All Processes** to display all processes.

4 Click **CPU**.

Ⓐ In the upper part of the window, you see a list of all the processes running on the MacBook Air.

Ⓑ At the bottom of the window, you see a graphical representation of the activity of various MacBook Air processes.

Ⓒ Click the **% CPU** column heading to sort the list of processes by the amount of processor time each process is using.

5 Click **Disk**.

The Disk pane appears.

Ⓓ At the bottom of the window, you see how data is being read from and written to the disk.

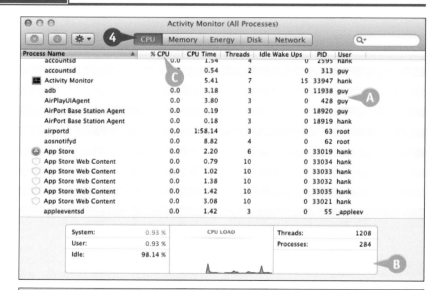

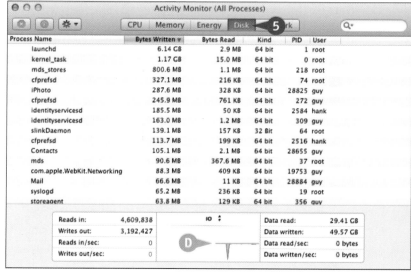

Note: You can limit the processes shown in the window to be just for applications, which can make the window's information easier to interpret.

6 Click **View** on the menu bar.

The View menu opens.

7 Click **Windowed Processes**.

E The list now includes only processes associated with applications that have windows open on the desktop.

8 Click **Bytes Written**.

Note: You can click the current column heading to reverse the sort order.

F Activity Monitor shows the processes listed by the amount of bytes they have written to disk.

9 Click **View** on the menu bar.

10 Click **All Processes**.

The full list of processes appears again.

11 Click **Memory**.

The Memory pane appears.

12 Click the **Memory** column heading.

G Activity Monitor shows the processes listed by the amount of memory they are taking.

H The Memory Pressure readout at the bottom of the window shows how light or heavy the memory pressure is.

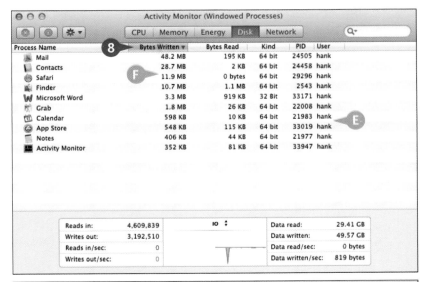

TIP

How do I deal with a process that is using a lot of CPU resources for a long period of time?

Switch to the application and try to quit it. If it does not quit, the application is hung, and you may need to force quit it, losing any unsaved data. Go back to Activity Monitor, select the process, and click **Force Quit** (▣). OS X forces the process to stop. Save your work in other open applications, and then restart your MacBook Air.

Maintain or Repair the Drive on Your MacBook Air

If the drive on your MacBook Air is not performing optimally, neither will your MacBook Air. To keep the drive in good condition, you should make sure it has as much free space as possible by removing unneeded files, as discussed in the tip at the end of this section.

When problems arise with the drive, you can repair them. To do so, you must start up your MacBook Air from the Recovery HD volume and then use the OS X Disk Utility application.

Maintain or Repair the Drive on Your MacBook Air

1 Shut down your MacBook Air.

2 Restart your MacBook Air while pressing and holding Option.

Ⓐ You see the startup drives available to you.

3 Click **Recovery HD**.

4 Click the arrow underneath the Recovery HD icon.

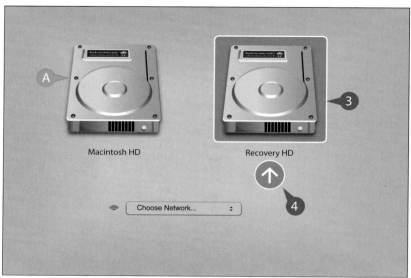

The MacBook Air starts up from the Recovery HD volume and the OS X Utilities window appears.

5 Click **Disk Utility**.

6 Click **Continue**.

Disk Utility opens.

7 Select the disk you want to maintain or repair, such as the internal disk on the MacBook Air.

8 Click **Repair Disk**.

B Disk Utility checks the drive for problems and repairs any that it finds. The progress appears at the bottom of the window.

Note: If Disk Utility finds and repairs any problems, your disk returns to good operating condition.

9 Click **Repair Disk Permissions**.

Disk Utility corrects problems associated with file and folder permissions on the disk. You can monitor the progress of the process in the bottom part of the window.

10 When repairs are complete, restart the MacBook Air.

The MacBook Air restarts from the internal drive automatically.

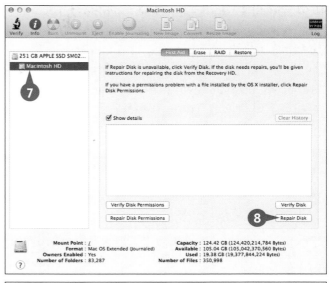
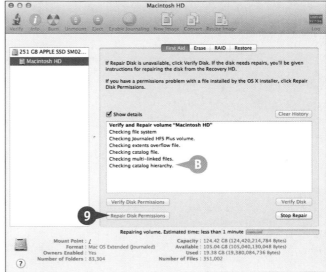

TIP

What other housekeeping practices can I use to optimize my MacBook Air?
When you are done with folders or files, move them off the internal drive. You can do this by deleting them if you are sure you will not need them again, or by archiving them by burning them onto a CD or DVD using an external SuperDrive and then deleting them from the hard drive. Try to keep your folders and files well organized so that you have a better idea of what you have stored on the hard drive. You should also make sure that you keep a good backup for all the important files on your internal drive.

Back Up with Time Machine and an External Hard Drive

If something really bad happens to your MacBook Air, you can lose all the files it contains. This includes data you create, such as your photos, movies, and documents. Much of this data simply cannot be replaced at any cost. To minimize this risk, back up your MacBook Air consistently using the Time Machine application built into OS X. You can back your file up easily to either an external hard drive, as explained in this section, or to an AirPort Time Capsule, as explained in the next section. Either way, you can easily recover files when you need them.

Back Up with Time Machine and an External Hard Drive

1 Connect an external hard drive to your MacBook Air.

Note: See Chapter 8 for information on connecting an external hard drive to your MacBook Air. You should use a hard drive with a large storage capacity for this purpose to provide the longest period of protection possible.

2 Click **Apple** ().

The Apple menu opens.

3 Click **System Preferences**.

The System Preferences window opens.

4 Click **Time Machine**.

The Time Machine pane opens.

5 Click the right side of the Time Machine switch to move it to the On position.

Time Machine activates.

The Select Backup Disk sheet appears.

6 Click the drive on which you want to store the backups.

A If you want the backed-up data encrypted, select the **Encrypt backups** check box (☐ changes to ☑). This prevents the data from being used without the encryption passcode.

Note: If you encrypt your backups, make sure you never lose the password.

7 Click **Use Disk**.

The sheet closes.

Note: If you chose to encrypt your backups, a sheet opens, prompting you to set your backup password. Type the password and a hint to help you remember it, and then click **Encrypt Disk**.

The Time Machine pane appears again.

B The drive you selected appears at the top of the pane along with status information about the backup process.

C You can select the **Show Time Machine in menu bar** check box (☐ changes to ☑) to display the Time Machine pop-up menu (🕐) in the menu bar for quick access to Time Machine.

8 Click **Options**.

TIP

Why would I exclude files from my backups?
The more and larger files you back up, the more room each backup consumes on your backup disk, resulting in fewer backups being stored. This reduces how far you can move "back in time" to restore files from the backup. By excluding files, you make your backups smaller, which means you can go farther back in time to restore files.

continued ▶

Time Machine makes it very easy to create a backup system, and after a few minutes of setup time, backing up is automatic. Unfortunately, many Mac users do not create a backup system. If you do not back up your files, you will eventually lose data. It is not a question of "if," but "when."

At some point, you will lose files that you either have to pay to get again or cannot re-create at all, such as your iPhoto collection. With a backup system in place, recovering these files is a simple exercise. Without one, it might be impossible.

Back Up with Time Machine and an External Hard Drive (continued)

The Exclude sheet appears, where you can exclude files from the backup process. This is useful because you can exclude files that do not need to be backed up to make your backups smaller.

9 To prevent backups when your MacBook Air is running on battery power, deselect the **Back up while on battery power** check box (☑ changes to ☐).

10 If you want OS X to notify you when it deletes old backups, select the **Notify after old backups are deleted** check box (☐ changes to ☑).

11 Click **Add** (⊞).

The Select sheet appears.

12 Navigate to and select the folders or files you want to exclude from the backup.

13 Click **Exclude**.

If you chose to exclude system files, the You've chosen to exclude the System folder dialog opens. Otherwise, go to step **15**.

14 Click **Exclude System Folder Only** to exclude only files in the System folder, or click **Exclude All System Files** to exclude system files no matter where they are stored.

Note: Exclude All System Files is usually the better option.

The Exclude sheet reappears, showing the list of folders you have excluded from the backup.

15 Click **Save**.

Time Machine starts to back up your files.

Time Machine automatically backs up your data every hour.

Note: After you disconnect the external hard drive so you can move the MacBook Air around, Time Machine makes the next backup the next time you reconnect the external hard drive. Connect the backup drive frequently to ensure your backups are current.

TIPS

How long is my data protected?
Time Machine backs up your data for as long as it can until the backup hard drive is full. It stores hourly backups for the past 24 hours. It stores daily backups for the past month. It stores monthly backups until the backup disk is full. To protect yourself as long as possible, use the largest hard drive you can afford, and exclude files that you do not need to back up.

How can I tell when the last backup was made?
At the top of the Time Machine pane, you see status information about your backups, such as the time and date of the most current backup.

Back Up Wirelessly with a Time Capsule

The AirPort Time Capsule device combines an AirPort Extreme with a hard drive. This makes wireless backups simple because the Time Capsule provides the wireless network you use, so that any computer on the network can also access the AirPort Time Capsule's hard drive to back up data.

To start backing up wirelessly, install an AirPort Time Capsule on your network. Then, configure Time Machine on your MacBook Air to back up to it.

Back Up Wirelessly with a Time Capsule

① Install an AirPort Time Capsule on your network.

Note: See Chapter 7 for details on AirPort Time Capsule.

② Click **Apple** (🍎).

The Apple menu opens.

③ Click **System Preferences**.

The System Preferences window opens.

④ Click **Time Machine**.

The Time Machine pane opens.

⑤ Click the right side of the Time Machine switch to move it to the On position.

The Select Backup Disk sheet appears.

CHAPTER 17

Maintaining a MacBook Air and Solving Problems

6 Select the Time Capsule.

A If you want the backed-up data encrypted, select the **Encrypt backups** check box (☐ changes to ☑). This prevents the data from being used without the encryption passcode.

7 Click **Use Disk**.

Note: If you chose to encrypt your backups, a sheet opens, prompting you to set your backup password. Type the password and a hint to help you remember it, and then click **Encrypt Disk**.

8 Type the password for the AirPort Time Capsule.

9 Click **Connect**.

The Time Machine pane appears again.

Time Machine starts to back up your files.

Time Machine automatically backs up your data every hour.

TIPS

How can I maximize the length of time my files are protected?
You should eliminate files that are protected in some other way, such as system files that you can always re-install. To do this, click the Time Capsule and then click Options. Use the resulting sheet to exclude files.

How can I further protect my files?
Online backup services, such as www.carbonite.com, are ideal for this because you can back up any time you are connected to the Internet. Your files are even safer because they are stored in a completely different location than your computer, providing extra protection.

Restore Files with Time Machine

You can use Time Machine to restore files that are included in your backups. You can restore files and folders from the Finder, and you can recover individual items from within some applications. For example, you can recover photos from within iPhoto.

Even if you have not actually lost files, you should try restoring files regularly to make sure your backup system is working correctly and to familiarize yourself with the process.

Restore Files with Time Machine

1 Click **Finder** (🖼️) on the Dock.

A Finder window opens to your default folder.

2 Navigate to the location or folder in which the files you want to recover were stored.

3 Click **Time Machine** (🕐).

4 Click **Enter Time Machine**.

The desktop disappears and the Time Machine window fills the entire space.

A The Finder window appears in the center of the screen. Behind it, you see all the versions of the window stored in your backup from the current version as far back in time as the backups go.

B Along the right side of the window, you see the timeline for your backups. Backups in magenta are stored on your backup drive, while those shown in gray are stored on your internal drive. You can restore files from either location.

5 Click the date and time on the timeline when the version of the files you need were available.

Note: If you chose not to display the Time Machine menu on the menu bar, launch Time Machine by clicking **Launchpad** () on the Dock, typing **t**, and then clicking **Time Machine** ().

⑥ When you reach the files or folders you want to restore, select them.

⑦ Click **Restore**.

If any of the files and folders currently exists in the folder, the Copy dialog opens.

⑧ Click **Replace** if you want to replace the current version of the file with the older version you are restoring. Click **Keep Original** if you want to keep the current version. Click **Keep Both** if you want to keep both versions; OS X appends *(original)* to the name of the current version.

OS X restores the files and folders you selected to their prior locations.

TIPS

How else can I move back using Time Machine?
In addition to using the timeline to move back in time, you can click the windows behind the front-most window; each time you click a window, it moves to the front and becomes the active window. You can also click the large backward and forward arrows in the lower-right corner of the Time Machine window to move back or forward in time, respectively.

How can I restore individual files for an application that supports Time Machine?
Some applications, such as iPhoto, support Time Machine directly. To restore files to such applications, open the application and move to the location where the file was previously stored. Launch Time Machine. Move back in time, select the files you want to restore, and click **Restore**.

Troubleshoot and Solve MacBook Air Problems

Your MacBook Air and OS X are designed to be reliable, but you may still run into problems. An application may hang, displaying the spinning color wheel icon but not responding to the trackpad or keyboard, it may quit unexpectedly, or you might not be able to get your MacBook Air to start up at all. The first step in solving any problem is understanding when and how it happens. Part of this is determining if the problem is general or related to a specific user account. Once you have some idea of how and when the problem occurs, you can try to solve it.

Troubleshoot and Solve MacBook Air Problems

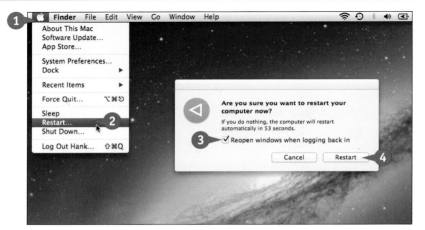

Restart and Find the Cause

1 Click **Apple** (🍎).

2 Click **Restart**.

3 Select the **Reopen windows when logging back in** check box (☐ changes to ☑) if you want to restore your current windows after restarting.

4 Click **Restart**.

The MacBook Air restarts.

5 Try to replicate the problem by doing the same things you did when it first occurred.

6 If you cannot cause the problem to happen again, assume it was solved by the restart and continue working.

7 If you can cause the problem to happen again, use Activity Monitor to see if any applications or processes appear to be consuming large amounts of resources. If they are, you have found a likely source of the problem.

8 In the Activity Monitor window, check if the MacBook Air is running out of memory.

9 To see if your problem might have to do with newly installed software, click the **System Report** button in the System Information application to get detailed information about your MacBook Air profile.

10 Click the **Applications** category.

11 Click the **Last Modified** down arrow (▼) to sort the window by the last modified date.

12 Look for any applications you installed just before you started having problems.

Determine if a Problem Is System-Wide or User-Specific

1 Log in to your troubleshooting user account.

2 Try to replicate the problem under the new account.

If you can repeat the problem, it is systemic instead of being specific to a user account. If you cannot repeat the problem, it is likely related to an issue with your user account. In most cases, the issue is related to a preference file that has been corrupted. The next steps explain how to remove preference files.

TIP

How can I check whether the drive on my MacBook Air is too full?
Click **Finder** (🗔) to open a Finder window. Click **Go** and click **Computer**, and then Control+click **Macintosh HD** and click **Get Info**. In the Info window, look at the Capacity readout and the Available readout. If less than 15 percent of the capacity is available, remove files to free up space on the drive.

continued ▶

O S X enables you to force an application to quit when it has stopped responding to the keyboard and trackpad. When you force an application to quit, you lose any unsaved changes in its open documents. So before you force an application to quit, give it two or three minutes to deal with whatever problem it has encountered. Similarly, if your MacBook Air stops responding to commands, you can force it to shut down by pressing and holding the Power button; press the Power button again to restart the computer. Shutting your MacBook Air down this way loses all unsaved data, so use this move only when you must.

Troubleshoot and Solve MacBook Air Problems (continued)

3 Click the desktop.

4 Click **Go**.

5 Press Option.

The Library item appears on the menu.

6 Click **Library**.

Your Library folder opens.

7 Click **Preferences**.

8 Delete the preference files for the application you are having trouble with. The application's name is part of the preference's filename.

9 Try to replicate the problem.

If you cannot repeat the problem, you have likely solved it.

Deal with a Hung Application

1 Identify the hung application by the spinning color wheel remaining on the screen for several minutes.

2 Press ⌘ + Option + Esc.

3 In the Force Quit Applications window, click the hung application.

4 Click **Force Quit**.

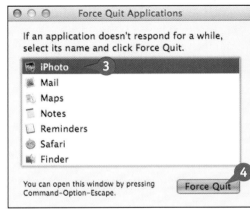

⑤ At the prompt, click **Force Quit**.

⑥ Restart your MacBook Air.

If the application works normally, the problem is solved. If the application continues to hang, you should update it.

Deal with a Startup Problem

① Make sure your MacBook Air is connected to power.

② Restart from the Recovery HD volume.

Ⓐ Your MacBook Air starts up from the Recovery HD and you see the OS X Utilities window.

If MacBook starts up, you know the problem is with the system software installed on the primary startup disk.

③ Try repairing the startup drive.

If the problem does not recur, you are done. If the problem does recur, you need to reinstall OS X.

④ Restart from the Recovery HD volume.

⑤ Launch the Reinstall OS X application.

⑥ Follow the on-screen steps to reinstall or repair the system software on the primary startup disk.

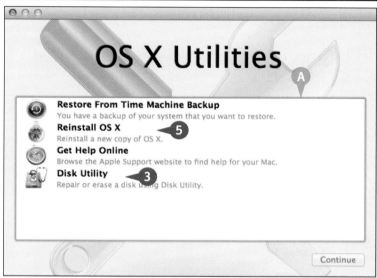

TIP

How can I limit damage resulting from MacBook Air problems?
First, back up your data consistently. You should always have current backups of your data because losing data is the most severe consequence of any MacBook Air problem you might encounter. Second, know how to start up from the recovery drive. If something happens to the system software on your MacBook Air, you can restart from this drive and hopefully solve the problem you are having. Third, keep a record of important usernames and passwords, such as your Apple ID, so that you will be able to recover content, such as applications, should you need to.

Explore iTunes

iTunes is a powerful application that enables you to easily manage your music and media libraries. Using iTunes, you can organize and enjoy music, video, books, and more on Macs, Windows PCs, iPods, iPads, or iPhones. iTunes is also the application you use to access the iTunes Store, from which you can add audio, video, books, and apps for mobile devices to your iTunes library whenever you want.

Ⓐ Playback Controls

Enable you to control the playback of music, move backward and forward among songs, and set the volume.

Ⓑ AirPlay Button

Enables you to play back music through connected speakers that use the AirPlay technology or through an AirPort Express or an Apple TV. You can also stream video to an Apple TV.

Ⓒ Display

Shows the details of the item you are currently playing. When iTunes is performing other actions, such as syncing an iPad or downloading an update, you can view the details on the display.

Ⓓ Search Box

Enables you to search through the content of your library.

Ⓔ Source Button

Enables you to switch quickly among different sources of content in iTunes. The Source button displays the current content source — for example, Music. The Source button and navigation bar appear by default instead of the sidebar that earlier versions of iTunes used for navigation. To display the sidebar, click **View** and then click **Show Sidebar**.

Ⓕ Navigation Bar

Provides buttons for navigating among the different areas of iTunes and for accessing the iTunes Store.

Ⓖ iTunes Store Button

Takes you to the iTunes Store, where you can browse, preview, and purchase music, movies, and other material.

Ⓗ Content Pane

Shows detailed information about the content of the selected source.

Ⓐ Songs Button

Displays your music library listed by songs.

Ⓑ Sidebar

Shows all the sources of content available to you. To display the sidebar, click **View** and select **Show Sidebar**; to hide it, click **View** and select **Hide Sidebar**. When you display the sidebar, iTunes hides the navigation bar in some views.

Ⓒ Column Browser

Enables you to browse the selected source quickly.

Ⓓ Song List

Shows the songs in the album you have selected.

Ⓔ Status Bar

Shows information about the selected source, including how long the content will play and how much disk space it consumes. To display the sidebar, click **View** and select **Show Status Bar**; to hide it, click **View** and select **Hide Status Bar**.

Ⓕ New Button

Enables you to create new playlists, Smart Playlists, and playlist folders.

Ⓖ Action Button

Enables you to take actions with the selected item.

Ⓐ Artists Button

Displays the list of artists on the left of the iTunes window.

Ⓑ Artist List

Enables you to navigate to an artist's albums.

Ⓒ Album List

Shows the list of albums and the songs they contain. You can start a song playing by double-clicking it.

Ⓓ Pop-Up Menu

Gives you quick access to useful commands for the song over which you hold the mouse pointer (▶).

For example, you can click **Show in iTunes Store** to display this item in the iTunes Store.

Explore the iTunes Store

The iTunes Store makes it easy to add music, movies, TV shows, books, and other content to your iTunes library. Because the iTunes Store is integrated within the iTunes application, moving between the store and your own content is seamless. You can browse for content by clicking any of the text or graphics. You can also search for specific content in the store and preview items of interest. When you are ready to download content, making the purchase takes only a couple of clicks.

Ⓐ iTunes Store Home Page

Links take you to specific content as well as to categories.

Ⓑ Albums

Album covers and titles are links to those albums.

Ⓒ Categories

These links take you to the home pages for categories of content, such as Movies or TV Shows.

Ⓓ Quick Links

These links take you to tools such as your account or your alerts.

Ⓔ Sign In Button

Click this button to sign in to the iTunes Store. After you sign in, your username appears on the button.

Ⓕ Library Button

Click this button to return to your iTunes library.

Ⓐ Content Page

This section displays information about a specific item.

Ⓑ Buy Button

Buy an item by clicking its **Buy** button.

Ⓒ Tracks

The contents of the current item are shown in the bottom of the window.

Ⓓ Preview

Click this button to hear or watch a preview.

Ⓔ Buy Button

Use a track's **Buy** button to buy only that track.

Ⓕ Artist Link

Click the artist name to see all content by that artist.

Obtain an iTunes Store Account

The iTunes Store provides a wide range of digital media files, including music, movies, TV shows, podcasts, and other e-books. You can browse the iTunes Store freely, preview items except for e-books, and purchase items you want. You can also rent some items, such as movies. To purchase or rent content from the iTunes Store, you need to have an iTunes account and be logged into it. You can create an account from within iTunes.

Obtain an iTunes Store Account

Note: If you already have an Apple ID, such as one you use to make purchases from the online Apple Store or your iCloud account, you can skip these steps.

1 Click **iTunes Store** on the navigation bar.

The iTunes Store home page appears.

2 Click **Sign In**.

The Sign In dialog appears.

3 Click **Create Apple ID**.

The Welcome to the iTunes Store screen appears.

4 Follow the on-screen instructions to create your account.

When you have created your account, you have an Apple ID and password. This enables you to log in to your account on the iTunes Store and purchase content from it.

Note: If you want to browse or buy e-books, use the iBooks application instead of accessing the iTunes Store through iTunes. The iBooks application enables you to download samples of e-books, which iTunes does not.

Understanding the iTunes Library

The iTunes library is where you store all of your content, including music, movies, TV shows, books, and ringtones. Before you can enjoy content in iTunes, it has to be available there; you can add content from many sources, including ripping music from CDs you already own and downloading content from the iTunes Store. Once you have added content to your iTunes library, you can use the features in iTunes to keep that content organized so that you can easily access it and enjoy it.

Categories

iTunes automatically organizes the content in your library by categories, including Music, Movies, TV Shows, and Books. To navigate among the categories, you click the **Source** button on the navigation bar and then click the category you want to see. If you have displayed the sidebar, you simply click the category. The category's content appears in the main part of the iTunes window, where you can browse it and search through it. When you find the content you want, you can listen to it, view it, create playlists, burn it to disc, and so on.

Devices

iTunes considers sources of content stored outside of its database to be *devices*. If you connect an iPhone, iPad, or iPod to your MacBook Air, it appears as a button at the right end of the navigation bar in iTunes. Devices also include audio CDs if you connect an optical drive or use

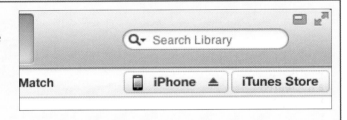

the Remote Disc feature. Like other sources, you select a device to work with it. For example, to configure the content on an iPhone, click the iPhone button on the navigation bar to make its management screens appear in the main part of the window.

Tracks

Although it is easy to think of tracks as the songs on a CD, iTunes considers everything that you listen to or watch to be a track. So, each episode in a season of a

TV series you download from the iTunes Store is a track, as is each section of an audiobook. Each row in the Content pane shows a track.

Tags

To organize the content of your
library, iTunes uses the information
associated with the tracks: artist,
track name, track number, album,
genre, rating, and other information.
Each data element is called a *tag*.
Each tag can appear in a column in
the Content pane, and you can view

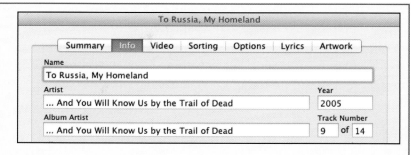

all the tags for a track in the Info window. Tags are important because they enable you to identify and
organize content. Much of the content you add to your library contains some tags — for example, songs you
buy from the iTunes Store contain the most important tags, and iTunes can download tag information for
CDs you import. You can also add or edit tags manually when you need to.

Playlists

One of the best things about iTunes is that you can create custom collections of
content you want to listen to or watch. These collections are called *playlists*.
Playlists can include any combination of content organized in any way. There are
two kinds of playlists: standard playlists and Smart Playlists. A standard playlist is a
playlist to which you add content manually and choose its play order. A Smart
Playlist is a playlist that iTunes builds based on the criteria you specify. After you
have created a playlist, you can listen to it, burn it to disc, or move it to an iPad,
iPhone, or iPod.

The iTunes Way

No matter which kind of
content you are working with
in iTunes, you use the same
techniques for accessing and
manipulating the content.
First, you select the source of
the content you want to work
with; this can be a Library

category, device, or playlist. Second, you browse or search for content you want within the selected source if
the content is not ready for you immediately. Third, you select the specific track you want. And fourth, you use
the iTunes controls to play the content. This process is consistent regardless of the type of content, so once
you get the hang of it, you can quickly enjoy any content you want. The only exception is e-books, for which
you should use the iBooks application instead of iTunes.

Browse or Search for iTunes Content

You can find the audio or video you want by browsing or by searching your library. Browsing is a good way to find something when you have not decided exactly what you want to listen to or watch. Searching is useful when you know exactly what you want but not where it is. You can use several views for browsing and searching. This task shows Songs view, which provides the Column Browser feature for browsing the songs your Library contains, and Albums view, which displays each album as a cover picture you can click to reveal the songs.

Browse or Search for iTunes Content

Browse for iTunes Content

1 Click the **Source** button.

2 Click **Music**.

3 Click **Songs** on the navigation bar.

4 Click **View**.

5 Click or highlight **Column Browser**.

6 Click **Show Column Browser**.

7 In the Genres column, click the genre you want to browse.

8 In the Artists column, click the artist you want to browse.

9 In the Albums column, click the artist you want to browse.

Ⓐ The songs in that album appear.

10 Double-click the song you want to play.

11 Use the playback controls to play the track.

Note: You can change the columns displayed in the Column Browser by clicking **View**, clicking **Column Browser**, and then selecting and deselecting check box options on the submenu.

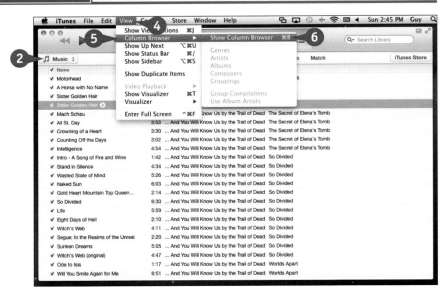

Search for iTunes Content

1 Click the **Source** button.

2 Click the content source you want to search. For example, click **Music**.

3 Click **Albums**.

iTunes displays the list of albums, showing the cover picture or a placeholder for each.

4 Click in the Search bar.

5 Start typing the characters for which you want to search.

B The Search Results panel appears.

6 Click the result you want to see.

iTunes displays the matching items.

7 Double-click an item to start it playing.

Note: When searching, you can refine your search by clicking the **Search** button ( ) and then clicking the tag by which you want to limit the search.

How can I make a column wider to see all of its information?

Point to the line at the right edge of the column. When changes to , drag to the right to make the column wider or to the left to make it narrower.

How can I show the Column Browser when it sometimes disappears?

When you select a source for which the Column Browser is not normally useful, iTunes hides the Column Browser. You can show it again by clicking **View**, clicking **Column Browser**, and then clicking **Show Column Browser**.

Play Music in Albums View

When you want to browse your Library visually for a particular CD cover, switch to Albums view. In this view, iTunes displays a list of the albums in your music library, along with an image of each album's cover. If iTunes has no cover picture for an album, it displays a placeholder instead. iTunes sorts the list alphabetically, first by artist and then by album title, but you can choose another sort order if you want. After you find the album you want, you click it to reveal the songs it contains. You can then play a song.

Play Music in Albums View

1 Click the **Source** button.

2 Click the content source you want to search. For example, click **Music**.

3 Click **Albums**.

iTunes displays the list of albums, showing the cover picture or a placeholder for each.

Note: To change the order in which iTunes sorts the albums, click **View** and then click **View Options**. In the View Options dialog, click the **Sort By** pop-up menu (⬍) and select the first field for sorting. Click the **then** pop-up menu (⬍) and select the second field. Click **Close** (⬛) to close the View Options dialog.

4 Click the album whose contents you want to view.

The album's songs appear.

5 Double-click the song you want to play.

Note: Click the album's cover to hide the songs again. You can also press <kbd>Esc</kbd> or click **Close** (⬛) at the upper-left corner of the songs pane.

Play Music with the MiniPlayer

When you are browsing for music, it is helpful to have the iTunes window at a large size or even full-screen. But once you have found the right music and begun playing it, you may prefer a smaller window that gives you more space to work with other applications. The iTunes MiniPlayer feature reduces the application to a miniature window that shows the playing song. When you move the mouse ▶ over the MiniPlayer, the playback controls appear. You can also switch the MiniPlayer to a square window that shows the album art for the current song.

Play Music with the MiniPlayer

1 Click **Switch to MiniPlayer** (▭).

Note: You can also switch to the MiniPlayer by pressing `Option`+`⌘`+`M` or clicking **Window** and then clicking **Switch to MiniPlayer**.

The iTunes window switches to the MiniPlayer.

2 Move the mouse ▶ over the MiniPlayer.

The playback controls appear.

Ⓐ You can click **Switch from MiniPlayer** (▭) to switch back to the full iTunes window.

3 Click the album art picture.

The MiniPlayer window expands to show the album art.

Note: iTunes hides the controls if you do not use them for a few seconds. To display the controls again, move the mouse ▶ over the MiniPlayer window.

Ⓑ Click the album art thumbnail to return to the small version of the MiniPlayer.

4 Click **Switch from MiniPlayer** (▭).

The full iTunes window appears.

Listen to Audio Content

When you have located an audio track you want to listen to, you can start playing it. You can start and pause playback with either the trackpad or the keyboard, move quickly to any point in a song, or skip forward and backward through the songs in your current selection or playlist. iTunes also provides a graphic equalizer that you can use to fine-tune the audio so it sounds the way you like.

Listen to Audio Content

1 Double-click the song you want to hear.

Note: You can also click the song and then click **Play** (▶).

A A blue speaker icon (◀) indicates the track that is currently playing.

2 Click **Pause** (⏸ changes to ▶) or press Spacebar to pause the audio.

3 Click **Previous** (⏮) to jump back to the previous track.

4 Click **Next** (⏭) to jump ahead to the next track.

5 Set the volume level by dragging the slider.

6 Drag the Playhead (◻) to move to a different position in the song.

7 Click **Window** and then click **Equalizer**, or press Option + ⌘ + 2.

8 Select the **On** check box (☐ changes to ☑).

9 Click the pop-up menu (↕) and select the equalization to apply.

10 Click **Close** (⊗).

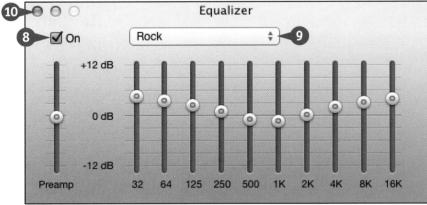

Watch Movies and TV Shows

iTunes works as well for video content as it does for audio content. You can watch movies, TV shows, music videos, and video podcasts within the iTunes window, in the Artwork/Video viewer, or in full-screen mode. You can easily switch between modes to suit your preference.

Watch Movies and TV Shows

1. Click the **Source** button.

   The Source pop-up menu appears.

2. Click the content source you want to search. For example, click **Movies**.

   The movie tracks in your library appear.

3. Click **Unwatched**.

   The list of unwatched movie tracks appears.

4. Click a movie track.

   The information panel opens.

5. Click **Play** (▶) or press Spacebar.

   Ⓐ The video begins to play.

6. Position the pointer over the video image.

   Ⓑ The video controls appear.

7. Use the controls to play the video.

   Ⓒ You can click **Full Screen** (▦) to display the video full screen.

8. To stop the video and return to the list of movies, and then click **Close** (⊗).

Add Audio CD Content to the iTunes Library

If you have audio on CDs, you can add it to your library by importing it into iTunes. Once imported, the tracks become part of your iTunes library and you can listen to them, add them to playlists, put them on custom CDs you burn, and so on. You will need to connect an optical drive to your MacBook Air, either via USB or via the Remote Disc feature. First, you need to do a one-time configuration of iTunes to import audio the way you want. Then you can import CDs to build up your iTunes library.

Add Audio CD Content to the iTunes Library

Prepare to Import CDs

1. Click **iTunes**.
2. Click **Preferences**.
3. Click **General**.
4. Click the **When you insert a CD** pop-up menu (⬍) and select **Show CD**.
5. Select the **Automatically retrieve CD track names from Internet** check box (☐ changes to ☑).
6. Click **OK**.

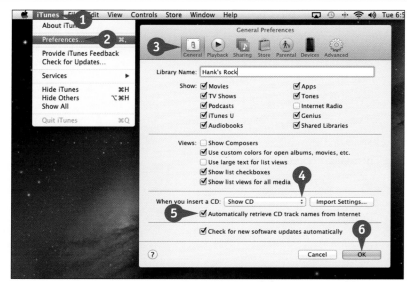

Import an Audio CD

1. Insert an audio CD in an optical drive connected to your MacBook Air.

   Ⓐ iTunes selects the CD's button on the navigation bar.

   Ⓑ The CD's tracks appear.

2. Click **CD Info**.

   The CD Info dialog opens.

3. Make any changes needed. For example, you may want to change the genre.

4. Click **OK**.

   The CD Info dialog closes.

5. Click **Import CD**.

The Import Settings dialog appears.

Note: By default, iTunes encodes all audio content using the Advanced Audio Coding format, AAC for short, and the iTunes Plus setting. These settings are good for general use.

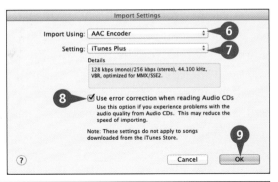

6 Click the **Import Using** pop-up menu (⬍) and select the encoder to use.

7 Click the **Setting** pop-up menu (⬍) and select the setting.

8 Select the **Use error correction when reading Audio CDs** check box (☐ changes to ☑).

9 Click **OK**.

The Import Settings dialog closes.

iTunes starts importing the songs.

C iTunes displays a progress symbol (▨) on the song it is currently importing.

D The Information pane shows details of the import process.

E A green circle with a check mark appears next to songs iTunes has imported.

10 After iTunes finishes importing the songs, click **Eject** (⏏).

Your MacBook ejects the CD.

TIP

How should I encode music from audio CDs?

AAC is the best option for most people because it provides good sound quality in relatively small files. This means you can store more content in your iTunes library and on iPods, iPads, or iPhones. If you need the absolute highest audio quality, use the Apple Lossless format. This produces significantly larger files with slightly better sound quality. If you need MP3 files, use the MP3 format.

Buy Music and More from the iTunes Store

The iTunes Store has a lot of great content that you can easily preview, purchase or acquire for free, and download to your MacBook Air, where it is added to your iTunes library automatically. When you find content you are interested in, you can preview it to decide whether you want it. To buy an item you want, you simply click its **Buy** button. One of the advantages of the iTunes Store is that you usually can buy individual tracks or shows. This way if you just like one or two songs on an album, you can buy just those songs instead of paying for the entire album.

Buy Music and More from the iTunes Store

Display the iTunes Store

1 Click **iTunes Store** at the right end of the navigation bar.

Note: You can also go to the home page of the iTunes Store by clicking **Store,** and then clicking **Home**.

The iTunes window displays the home page of the iTunes Store.

Browse the iTunes Store

1 On the home page of the iTunes Store, click **Browse**.

The Store Browser appears.

2 Click a content category.

Note: This example uses Music. Different types of content have other categories to browse.

3 Click the genre.

4 Click the subgenre.

5 Click the artist.

6 Click the album.

Ⓐ The album's tracks appear in the lower pane of the window. This pane works just like the Content pane when you browse your iTunes library.

You are ready to preview and purchase content.

Search the iTunes Store

1 In the iTunes Store, click the Search box.

2 Type your search terms.

Ⓑ As you type, iTunes presents the matches on a pop-up menu.

3 If a match appears, click it on the pop-up menu to perform the search; if not, continue typing until you have typed all the text you want to search for and press Return.

Ⓒ The results of your search appear.

4 Click **Albums** to display the results by albums; click **Songs** to display the results by songs; or click **All** to see all results.

5 To get more information for a specific album, click its cover.

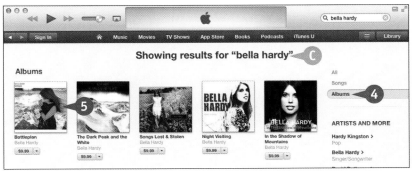

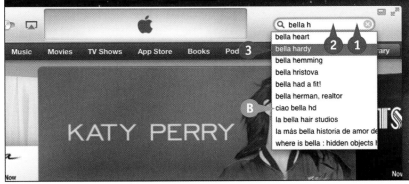

continued ▶

You can move around the iTunes Store in many ways. Just about every object on the screen is linked to more specific information about something, until you get down to the individual items that you purchase, such as songs, movies, or TV shows. Browsing and searching are both useful techniques for finding the content you want. In addition to previewing content, you can read reviews to find out what other people think about the content in which you are interested.

Buy Music and More from the iTunes Store (continued)

D The album's page appears.

6 Click **Songs**.

The Songs pane displays the list of songs on the album.

E You can click **Ratings and Reviews** to see ratings and reviews for the album.

Preview iTunes Store Content

1 Hold the mouse ⬉ over the item you want to preview.

2 Click **Preview** (⊙).

A preview plays. If the content is audio, you hear it. If it includes video, you also see the video.

You can control previews with the same controls you use to play content in your iTunes library.

F Click **Preview All** to play all the previews in sequence. This is the best way to get an overall impression of the album.

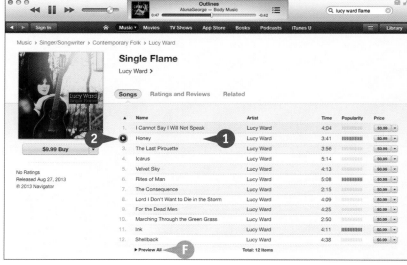

Buy and Download Content from the iTunes Store

1 Locate and preview the content you are interested in.

2 Click the price button for the content you want to purchase.

3 Type your account's password.

4 To have iTunes remember your password for future purchases, select the **Remember password** check box (☐ changes to ☑).

5 Click **Buy**.

iTunes downloads the content to your Library.

6 Click **Library**.

Your Library appears.

How can I use content I purchase from the iTunes Store?

Audio content you purchase from the iTunes Store is not restricted by any limitations. Video content does have some limitations, including the number of computers it can be played on; each computer has to be authorized with your iTunes Store user account to be able to play it. You can play rented video content on only one device at a time. iTunes automatically deletes the rented content after 30 days or after 24 hours from when you first start to play it. Outside the United States, the period is typically 48 hours from when you first start to play the rented content.

continued ▶

You can buy items individually, such as songs or episodes of TV shows, from the iTunes Store. You can also buy collections, including albums or seasons of TV shows. You can even pre-purchase some kinds of content. For example, you can purchase a season pass for a current TV show; when new episodes appear in the iTunes Store, iTunes automatically downloads them to your Library. You can also pre-order music; as soon as it is released, iTunes downloads the music to your MacBook. And you can add items you are interested in to your Wish List and buy them at a later time.

Buy Music and More from the iTunes Store (continued)

7 Click the **Source** button.

8 Click **Music**.

9 Click **Playlists**.

iTunes switches to Playlists view.

The Playlists pane appears on the left of the iTunes window.

10 Click **Purchased**.

The contents of the Purchased playlist appear.

Note: iTunes automatically adds each item you buy — or get for free — from the iTunes Store to the Purchased playlist.

11 Double-click an item.

The item starts playing.

Add Content to Your Wish List

1 Locate some content you want to save in your Wish List.

2 Open the menu at the right end of the Buy button and then click **Add to Wish List**.

iTunes adds the item to your Wish List.

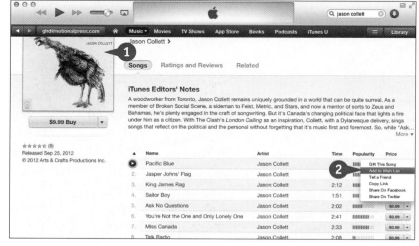

3 Click the button that shows the name of your iTunes account. This button appears toward the left end of the navigation bar.

4 Click **My Wish List**.

G Your Wish List opens. You can browse your list, preview items, and purchase them as you can from other pages in the iTunes Store.

Note: If you set iTunes to remember your password, iTunes purchases the content as soon as you click a **Buy** button. You can use your Wish List to store items you are thinking about buying so you have a buffer between being interested and actually buying.

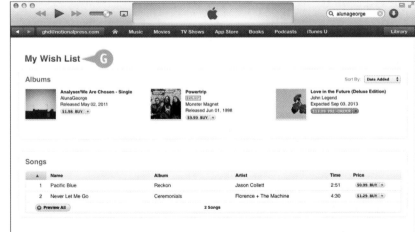

Subscribe and Listen to Podcasts

Podcasts are episodic audio or video programs that you can listen to or watch. You can find podcasts on many different topics. You can subscribe to many different podcasts in the iTunes Store. Once you have subscribed, iTunes automatically downloads episodes for you so that they are available for you to listen to or watch, which you do in the same way as with other content in the Library. You can also download podcasts as MP3 files from other sources, including podcasts for which you must pay, and add them to the iTunes library by dragging them to the main part of the iTunes window.

Subscribe and Listen to Podcasts

Find Podcasts

1. Enter the iTunes Store.

2. Click **Podcasts** on the navigation bar.

3. Browse for a podcast that interests you.

Note: You can also search for podcasts.

4. Click a podcast to get more information.

   The podcast's home page appears.

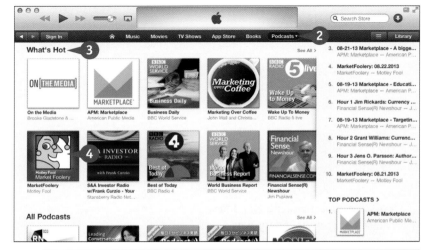

5. To play an episode, double-click it.

Note: Because most podcasts are free, the entire episode plays instead of just a preview.

6. Read about the podcast.

7. To subscribe to a podcast, click its **Subscribe** button.

8. Click **Subscribe**.

   iTunes adds available episodes of the podcast to your Library, and some of the recent episodes download to your computer.

Listen to Podcasts

1. Click the **Source** button.

2. Click **Podcasts**.

3. Click **List**.

4. Click a podcast's disclosure triangle (▶) to expand it.

5. Select and play an episode of a podcast.

Ⓐ iTunes marks unplayed podcasts with a blue dot (●).

6. To download an episode, click **Download** (▣).

Note: Option+click **Download** (▣) to download all episodes.

Configure Podcast Settings

1. On the Podcasts screen, click **Settings**.

2. Click the **Check for new episodes** pop-up menu (⬍) and select **Every hour**, **Every day**, **Every week**, or **Manually**.

3. Click the **Settings for** pop-up menu (⬍) and select **Podcast Defaults** or the podcast you want to configure.

4. Click the **When new episodes are available** pop-up menu (⬍) and select **Download all**, **Download the most recent one**, or **Do nothing**.

5. Click the **Episodes to keep** pop-up menu (⬍) and select the item for the episodes you want to keep.

6. Click **OK**.

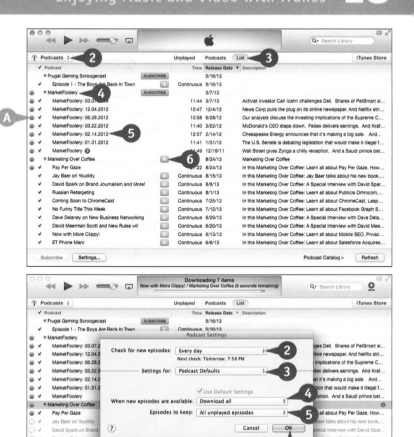

TIP

How do I subscribe to a podcast when it is not available in the iTunes Store?

Some websites provide a URL to a podcast subscription. Copy this URL, click **File**, click **Subscribe to Podcast**, paste the URL in the dialog, and click **OK**. Other sites provide podcasts as MP3 files that you can download and add to the iTunes library; you work with these files just like tracks from a CD.

Copy iTunes Content from Other Computers

If you have another computer with iTunes content on it, you can use the Home Sharing feature to copy content you have purchased from the iTunes Store and any other iTunes content on your MacBook Air to build up your iTunes library. This is a fast and simple way to fill your iTunes library with audio and video content.

First, you set up Home Sharing on the computer from which you will copy content. Second, you access the sharing computer and import its content into the iTunes library on your MacBook Air.

Copy iTunes Content from Other Computers

Turn On Home Sharing

1 In iTunes on the computer receiving content, click **File**.

The File menu opens.

2 Highlight **Home Sharing**.

The Home Sharing submenu opens.

3 Click **Turn On Home Sharing**.

The Home Sharing screen appears.

4 Type your Apple ID if iTunes does not enter it automatically.

5 Type your password.

6 Click **Turn On Home Sharing**.

Another Home Sharing screen appears.

7 Click **Done**.

Note: You can set up shares on multiple computers at the same time.

Home Sharing

Home Sharing makes it easy to play or copy music, movies, and more among computers in your home. Just use the same Apple ID on up to five computers.

Enter the Apple ID used to create your Home Share.

macuser@example.com ── **4**   •••••••••••••••••••••••••••• ── **5**

No Thanks   Turn On Home Sharing ── **6**

Don't have an Apple ID?

Import Shared Content to the iTunes Library

1. Click the **Source** button.

   The Source pop-up menu opens.

2. Click the name of the shared music library.

   The songs in the shared music library appear.

3. Click the **Show** pop-up menu (🔽) and select **Items not in my library**.

Note: In the Show pop-up menu, you can click **All** to display all the songs in the shared music library. Normally, it is more helpful to display only those not in your library. This helps you avoid importing duplicates of songs your library already contains.

4. Select the content you want to add.

5. Click **Import**.

   iTunes copies the content you selected into the iTunes library.

How can I automatically add new content?

To import content automatically into iTunes, click the **Settings** button, select the check box for each type of content you want iTunes to automatically copy, and click **OK**.

How else can I share content?

Open the **Sharing** pane of the iTunes Preferences dialog. Select **Share my library on my local network** (☐ changes to ☑). Select **Share entire library** (☐ changes to ☑). Click **OK**. Other iTunes users on your network will be able to listen to music in your library but will not be able to copy songs unless their computers also use your Apple ID.

Create a Genius Playlist

iTunes Genius is a feature that tries to select music for you based on a specific song. Genius places similar music in a Genius playlist that you can listen to; put on an iPhone, iPad, or iPod; or burn to a disc. Genius picks songs based on the song you select according to sophisticated programs Apple has developed. The programs use standard information, such as the artist, genre, year, and number of beats per minute, as well as proprietary information, such as which related songs, albums, or artists people buying the same song on the iTunes Store have also bought or shown interest in.

Create a Genius Playlist

Start Genius

1 Click **Store**.

   The Store menu opens.

2 Click **Turn On Genius**.

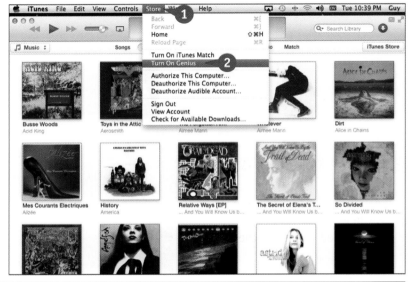

The Playlists screen appears, showing the Genius information.

3 Click **Turn On Genius**.

The Sign In screen appears.

④ Type your Apple ID if iTunes does not enter it automatically.

⑤ Type your password.

⑥ Click **Continue** and follow the on-screen instructions to complete the Genius configuration, which includes agreeing to terms and conditions.

Create a Genius Playlist

① Navigate to the song on which you want Genius to base the playlist.

② Control+click the song.

③ Click **Create Genius Playlist**.

Ⓐ You can click **Genius Suggestions** to have Genius display a list of songs considered related to the song you chose.

The playlist's contents appear. You can play the playlist just like other playlists.

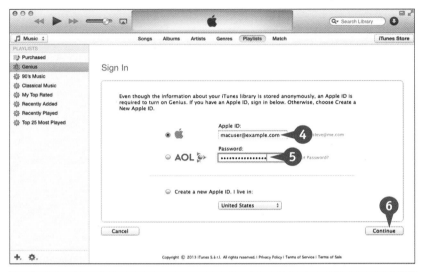

TIPS

How can I save a Genius playlist?
Genius saves each playlist automatically under the name of the song on which you based the playlist. To rename the playlist, click it once, then click it again after a pause, and then type the new name and press Return. To have Genius update the contents of the playlist, click **Refresh**.

How else can I use Genius?
Click **Playlists** to display the list of playlists in the Sidebar on the left side of the iTunes window. In the Sidebar, click **Genius Mixes** to display a list of mixes Genius has created based on the songs in your library. Double-click a mix to start it playing.

Create a Standard Playlist

Playlists enable you to create custom content collections that you can then play, burn to disc, or copy to an iPhone, iPad, or iPod. You can add to each playlist exactly the songs you want it to contain, and you can arrange them in your preferred order. You can even include the same track in a playlist multiple times if you want to hear it over and over again. A standard playlist is one in which you manually place and organize songs. By contrast, a *Smart Playlist* is one that iTunes creates for you automatically based on criteria you specify.

Create a Standard Playlist

1 Click the **Source** button.

The Source pop-up menu opens.

2 Click **Music**.

Your music tracks appear.

3 Click your preferred method of browsing for music. This example uses Albums.

Note: You can also locate songs for a playlist by searching for them.

The list of albums appears.

4 Select one or more songs you want to add to the playlist.

5 Drag the songs toward the right side of the iTunes window.

The Playlists pane appears.

6 Drop the songs in open space in the Playlists pane.

Note: You can add the songs to an existing playlist by dropping them on that playlist in the Playlists pane.

Ⓐ The songs appear in the playlist.

⑦ Type the name for the playlist and press **Return**.

iTunes applies the name to the playlist.

⑧ Add more songs to the playlist by dragging them from other albums or sources.

⑨ Click a song and drag it up or down the playlist to change the play order as needed.

⑩ Click **Done**.

iTunes saves the playlist.

⑪ Click **Playlists**.

The Playlists pane appears.

⑫ Click your new playlist.

You can now start playing the new playlist.

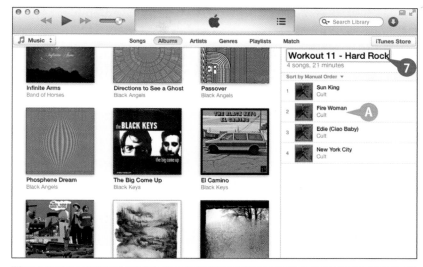

TIPS

Can I sort the contents of a playlist?
You can sort a playlist that you create by clicking the column heading by which you want to sort it. Click the left-most column heading to restore the original order.

Is there another way to create a playlist?
You can quickly create a playlist by selecting songs or other content and then clicking **File**, highlighting **New**, and then clicking **Playlist from Selection**. You can also press **Shift** + **⌘** + **N** to give the New Playlist from Selection command easily.

Create a Smart Playlist

Instead of adding content to a playlist manually, you can define the criteria for a Smart Playlist and have iTunes build and maintain it for you. iTunes identifies matching content in your Library and puts it in the Smart Playlist for you. iTunes can also automatically keep the Smart Playlist updated as your Library changes, which keeps your Smart Playlist fresh and interesting.

Create a Smart Playlist

1. Click the **Source** button.

2. Click **Music**.

3. Click **Playlists**.

4. Click **New** (![+]).

5. Click **New Smart Playlist**.

6. Click the first pop-up menu (![]) and then select the first tag, such as **Genre**.

7. Click the second pop-up menu (![]) and select the operator, such as **contains**.

8. Type the condition to match.

9. To add another condition to the Smart Playlist, click **Add Condition** (![+]).

10. Repeat steps **6** to **8** to set up the condition.

11. Add further conditions as needed.

12. Click the **Match** pop-up menu (![]) and select **all** to narrow down the tracks, or **any** to draw together separate groups of tracks.

Note: Selecting **all** when creating a Smart Playlist narrows down the tracks. Selecting **any** when creating a Smart Playlist draws together several separate groups of tracks.

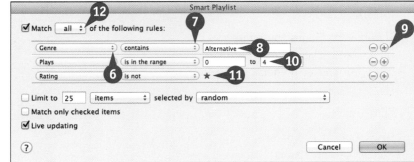

13 Select the **Limit to** check box (☐ changes to ☑) if you want to limit the size of the playlist; if not, skip to step **17**.

14 Click the first pop-up menu (◉) and select the parameter by which you want to limit the playlist, such as **hours**.

15 Type an appropriate amount for the limit you specified in the Limit to field, such as the number of hours.

16 Click the second pop-up menu (◉) and select the way you want iTunes to choose the songs.

17 To include only tracks whose check box is selected in the Content pane, select the **Match only checked items** check box (☐ changes to ☑).

18 If you want iTunes to update its contents over time, select the **Live updating** check box (☐ changes to ☑).

19 Click **OK**.

Ⓐ iTunes adds the Smart Playlist to the Playlists pane.

Ⓑ The tracks in the playlist appear.

20 Type the playlist's name and press (Return).

The Smart Playlist is ready to play.

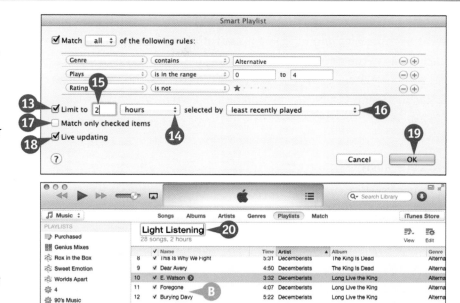

TIP

How do I change the contents of a Smart Playlist?
To change the contents of a Smart Playlist, you edit its criteria. Click **Playlists** to display the Playlists pane, then Control+click the playlist and click **Edit Smart Playlist**. Use the resulting Smart Playlist dialog to change the conditions. iTunes then changes the playlist's content.

Understanding How iOS Devices Work with Macs

Apple iOS devices — iPhones, iPads, and iPod touches — are incredibly popular, and for good reason. They offer amazing functionality in small, extremely mobile devices. An iOS device (or two) makes an ideal companion for your MacBook Air because you can easily share content that is stored on your MacBook Air with an iOS device. For example, you can access the same e-mail messages using the Mail application on a MacBook Air and the Mail app on an iOS device. Your iOS device acts as an extension of your MacBook Air.

iOS

iOS is the name of the software that runs iPads, iPhones, and iPod touches. It was the first major operating system that you could control solely by using finger gestures on the screen. Since Apple released the iPhone, other manufacturers have imitated the iOS software because it has proven to be so well designed. Apple has incorporated a number of iOS features into the OS X system software that runs your MacBook Air, such as the trackpad gestures.

Synchronization

Synchronization keeps information on each device consistent with the most current version of that information. For example, when you add an event to the Calendar application on your MacBook Air, you also want that event to appear in the Calendar app on an iOS device, and vice versa. You can sync a wide variety of data easily using your iCloud account.

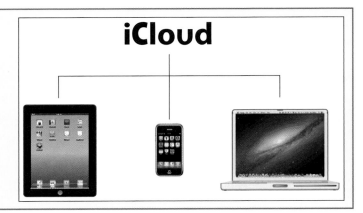

iTunes

In addition to all the great audio and video functionality that iTunes offers, as explained in Chapter 18, iTunes enables you to work with iOS devices. You can use iTunes to sync data between your MacBook Air and iOS devices. You can also use iTunes to maintain an iOS device through updates of the iOS software or to correct problems by restoring that software. Furthermore, connecting an iOS device to your MacBook Air charges the device's battery; make sure the MacBook Air is connected to a power outlet to charge the iOS device quickly without depleting the laptop's battery.

iCloud

iCloud also works with iOS devices. The "cloud" provides online storage of information, documents, photos, and more that you can access with your MacBook Air and iOS devices. This enables you to sync your computer and your iOS devices. The benefit of syncing through iCloud is that it is wireless so that you can use iCloud whenever you have an Internet connection. For more information about iCloud, see Chapter 10.

Other Online Services

iCloud is one of several online services that you can use with your MacBook Air and an iOS device. Other services work similarly. For example, Microsoft Exchange is the most widely used e-mail and calendar system among businesses and large

organizations. You can configure an Exchange account in the Mail application on your MacBook Air and iOS devices so that you can access your Exchange data from each one. Google offers similar features, including e-mail, calendar, and contacts.

Device Management

In addition to keeping information synced on iOS devices, you can use your MacBook Air and the iTunes application to manage your iOS devices. This includes keeping the

operating system software current by updating it, solving problems on the device by restoring the software, and keeping the device's battery charged. You can also use iTunes to configure the Home screens and install and update the apps on your iOS devices.

Using iTunes to Sync Music with Your iOS Device

O ne of the great things about an iOS device and the iPods is that you can carry music with you and enjoy it wherever you go. Chapter 18 explains how to create a music library in iTunes on your MacBook Air. You can copy any music in your library onto an iOS device or iPod. Once there, you can use the device's Music app to listen to it. You can configure the specific music that you move onto an iOS device or iPod by choosing your entire library or by selecting playlists, artists, albums, and genres.

Using iTunes to Sync Music with Your iOS Device

1 Connect your device to your MacBook Air.

If iTunes is not open already, it launches after you connect the device.

2 In iTunes, click the device's button on the navigation bar. For example, click **iPhone**.

The management screens for the iOS device or iPod appear.

3 Click the **Music** tab.

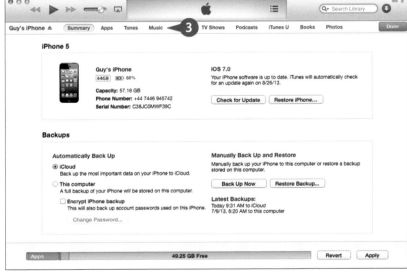

4 Select the **Sync Music** check box
(☐ changes to ☑).

5 Choose whether to sync all your music
library or part of it.

Ⓐ Select **Entire music library** (◯
changes to ◉) to sync all your music,
and then skip to step **11**.

Ⓑ Select **Selected playlists, artists,
albums, and genres** (◯ changes to
◉) to sync a selection.

6 To have iTunes fill up any empty space
on the device with music, select the
**Automatically fill free space with
songs** check box (☐ changes to ☑).
This is not a good idea for an iPhone,
iPad, or iPod touch, but it works well
for other iPods.

7 Select each playlist you want to include
(☐ changes to ☑).

8 Select each artist you want to include
(☐ changes to ☑).

9 Select each genre you want to include
(☐ changes to ☑).

10 Select each album you want to include
(☐ changes to ☑).

11 Click **Apply**.

iTunes copies the music you selected
to the device.

Note: Every time you connect the device
to your MacBook Air, it will sync using the
current settings.

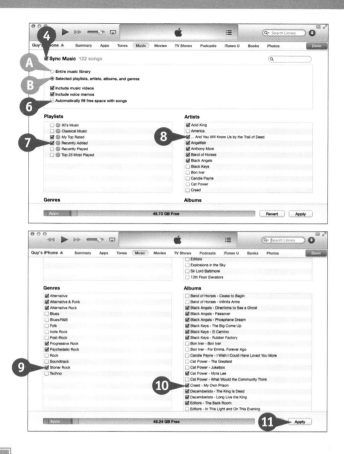

TIP

How can I add music to my device over Wi-Fi?

You can sync an iOS device wirelessly by selecting **Sync
with this device over Wi-Fi** (☐ changes to ☑) on the
Summary tab and then clicking **Apply**. To sync the device,
click its button on the navigation bar, click **Summary**, and
then click **Sync**. You can also open the Settings app on the
device, tap **General**, tap **iTunes Wi-Fi Sync**, and then tap
Sync Now.

Using iTunes to Manage Apps on Your iOS Device

Oone of the reasons iOS devices are so useful is the incredible number and diversity of apps that you can run on them. You can use iTunes to download apps from the iTunes Store similarly to how you download music and other content. After you have downloaded the apps to your MacBook Air, you can copy them onto the device through the sync process. You can also use iTunes to update apps; the next time you sync the device, iTunes copies the updated apps onto the device.

Using iTunes to Manage Apps on Your iOS Device

1 Connect your iOS device to your MacBook Air.

If iTunes is not open already, it launches after you connect the device.

2 In iTunes, click the device's button on the navigation bar. For example, click **iPad**.

The management screens for the iOS device appear.

3 Click **Apps**.

The Apps tab appears.

On the left side of the window, you see the apps in your iTunes library.

A Optionally, click the pop-up menu (⬍) and select how you want iTunes to list the apps from the menu, such as **Sort by Kind** or **Sort by Name**.

4 Click **Install** for each app you want to install. Install changes to Will Install.

Note: To remove an app that is already installed, click **Remove**.

5 Click the thumbnail for the Home screen you want to customize.

B The Home screen appears.

6 To install an app on the Home screen that is displayed, click the app in the Apps list and drag it to where you want it on the screen.

Note: You can also drag the already installed apps to different positions on the Home screen.

7 To reorder the Home screens, click a Home screen and drag it to where you want it to appear.

8 Click **Apply**.

The iOS device arranges the Home screens in the order you chose and containing the apps you specified.

TIPS

How do I create app folders?

To create a folder, drag one app icon on top of another. A new folder appears and opens; edit the default name of the folder if you want. Click outside the folder to close it. Drag more app icons onto the folder to add them to it.

How do I use iTunes to update my apps?

Click the pop-up menu ( ) at the left end of the navigation bar at the top of the iTunes window, and then click **Apps**. Click **Updates** in the navigation bar, and then click **Update All Apps**. iTunes downloads the updates. The next time you sync the device, iTunes installs the updated apps on it.

Using Photo Stream to Sync Photos with iOS

Current iOS devices have cameras, so if you carry your device with you, you can take photos wherever you are. You can use iCloud Photo Stream to automatically upload photos you take on an iOS device to the cloud. From there, they can automatically download to other devices, including your MacBook Air. Chapter 10 provides the steps for setting up your MacBook Air to use Photo Stream.

Using Photo Stream to Sync Photos with iOS

1 Press the **Home** button.

The Home screen appears.

2 Tap **Settings**.

The Settings screen appears.

3 Tap **iCloud**.

The iCloud screen appears.

4 Tap **Photos**.

The Photos screen appears.

5 Set the My Photo Stream switch to On (⬜).

6 To enable photo sharing, set the Photo Sharing switch to On (⬜).

Using iCloud to Sync Documents on iOS Devices

You can use iCloud to synchronize documents and data to the cloud from where other devices can access those documents and data. Using iCloud to synchronize documents is useful because you always have the current versions of your documents available to you on all of your devices. This enables you to work on documents no matter which device you are using.

Using iCloud to Sync Documents on iOS Devices

1 Press the **Home** button.

2 Tap **Settings**.

3 Tap **iCloud**.

4 Tap **Documents & Data**.

The Documents & Data screen appears.

5 Set the Documents & Data switch to On (⬛).

6 In the Allow apps to store documents and data in iCloud list, set the switch for each app to On (⬛) or Off (☐), as needed.

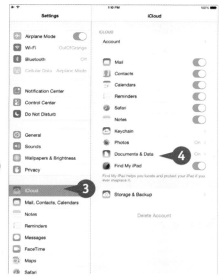

7 If you want to be able to work with iCloud documents and data while the device is connected to a cellular network, set the Use Cellular Data switch to On (⬛).

Note: If your cellular data plan allows only a limited amount of data before you incur additional fees, set the Use Cellular Data switch to Off (☐) so that you can transfer documents and data only when connected to a Wi-Fi network.

Index

A

access point, 120
Account Mailbox Folders (Mail app), 216
Account Mailboxes (Mail app), 216
Action button (iTunes), 321
Action pop-up menu, 36
activity, monitoring, 304–305
Add Button (Messages app), 240
Address bar (Safari), 190
address labels, printing, 283
Advanced button (Security & Privacy preferences pane), 169
Advanced preferences, 215
AirDrop, sharing files with, 134–135
AirPlay, setting up Apple TV for, 150
AirPlay button (iTunes), 320
AirPort
    about, 119
    configuring, 124–125
    enabling NAT on, 128
AirPort Express, 127, 150–161, 155
AirPort Extreme, 124, 127
AirPort Utility, 125, 126–127
Album List (iTunes), 321
Albums view, playing music with, 328
alert notifications, viewing, 52
alerts, 287
All-Day Events (Calendar app), 284
Alternate Function Key, 5
Analog/Digital Audio In/Out, 6, 7
App Exposé, 87
App Store, 72–73, 300–301
appearance, choosing for Finder, 92
Apple ID, 72
Apple menu, 11
Apple support (website), 143
Apple Thunderbolt Display, 149
Apple TV, displaying HDTV on, 150–151
applications (apps)
    about, 70
    accessing in folders, 77
    controlling, 80–81, 354–355
    expanding to Full Screen mode, 86
    folders for, 355
    hiding, 80
    hung, 318–319
    installing from App Store, 72–73
    installing from distribution files, 74–75

    launching from desktop, 78–79
    launching with Launchpad, 76–77
    preferences, 71
    quitting, 81
    removing, 77
    restoring, 77
    showing windows for, 49
    switching, 80, 81
    titles, 25
    updating, 302, 355
    windows, 10, 25, 80, 87
Applications folder, 79
application-specific tools, 25
Artist List (iTunes), 321
Artists button (iTunes), 321
audio, listening to, 330
Audio Chat window (Messages app), 240
audio chats, 246–247
AutoFill, completing web forms with, 208–209
Automatic Login feature, 8, 112

B

Back button (Safari), 190
backgrounds, adding in video chats, 250
backing up, 308–313
banner notifications, viewing, 52
battery, monitoring, 164–165
Birthdays calendar, 293
Bluetooth devices, connecting, 152–153
Bonjour, 263
Bookmark Editor, organizing bookmarks with, 204–205
bookmarks
    creating, 202
    navigating to websites with, 193–194
    organizing in Sidebar, 203
    organizing with Bookmark Editor, 204–205
    reordering, 205
Bookmarks bar (Safari), 190
Bookmarks Editor (Safari), 191
Bookmarks mode (Safari), 191
borders
    document windows, 25
    Finder windows, 24
brightness, screen, 103
Brightness button, 5
broadband wireless modem, 162–163
Browse mode (Safari), 190

There's a Visual book for every learning level...

Simplified®

The place to start if you're new to computers. Full color.

- Computers
- Creating Web Pages
- Digital Photography
- Excel

- Internet
- Laptops
- Mac OS
- Office

- PCs
- Windows
- Word

Teach Yourself VISUALLY™

Get beginning to intermediate-level training in a variety of topics. Full color.

- Access
- Adobe Muse
- Computers
- Digital Photography
- Digital Video
- Dreamweaver
- Excel
- Flash
- HTML5
- iLife

- iPad
- iPhone
- iPod
- Macs
- Mac OS
- Office
- Outlook
- Photoshop
- Photoshop Elements
- Photoshop Lightroom

- PowerPoint
- Salesforce.com
- Search Engine Optimization
- Social Media
- Web Design
- Windows
- Wireless Networking
- Word
- WordPress

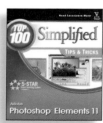

Top 100 Simplified® Tips & Tricks

Tips and techniques to take your skills beyond the basics. Full color.

- Digital Photography
- eBay
- Excel

- Google
- Office
- Photoshop

- Photoshop Elements
- PowerPoint
- Windows

...all designed for visual learners—just like you!

Master VISUALLY®

Your complete visual reference. Two-color interior.

- 3ds Max
- Creating Web Pages
- Dreamweaver and Flash
- Excel
- iPod and iTunes
- Mac OS
- Office
- Optimizing PC Performance
- Windows
- Windows Server

Visual Blueprint™

Where to go for professional-level programming instruction. Two-color interior.

- ActionScript
- Excel Data Analysis
- Excel Pivot Tables
- Excel Programming
- HTML5
- JavaScript
- Mambo
- Mobile App Development
- Perl and Apache
- PHP 5
- SEO
- Ubuntu Linux
- Vista Sidebar
- Visual Basic
- XML

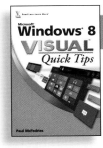

Visual™ Quick Tips

Shortcuts, tricks, and techniques for getting more done in less time. Full color.

- Digital Photography
- Excel
- Internet
- iPhone
- iPod & iTunes
- Mac OS
- Office
- PowerPoint
- Windows

e Available in print and e-book formats.

For a complete listing of Visual books, go to wiley.com/go/visual